DAYS OF FURY

GHOST TROOP AND THE BATTLE OF 73 EASTING

MIKE GUARDIA

Copyright 2021 © Mike Guardia

From *Warrior's Rage: The Great Tank Battle of 73 Easting* by Douglas MacGregor. Used by permission of the Naval Institute Press. Any third-party use of this material, outside of this publication, is prohibited. Interested parties must apply directly to the Naval Institute Press for permission.

From *The Fires of Babylon: Eagle Troop and the Battle of 73 Easting* by Mike Guardia. Used by permission of Casemate Publishers. Any third-party use of this material, outside of this publication, is prohibited. Interested parties must apply directly to the Naval Institute Press for permission.

Published by Magnum Books
PO Box 1661
Maple Grove, MN 55311

www.mikeguardia.com

ISBN-13: 978-0-9996443-6-2

All rights reserved, including the right to reproduce this book or any part of this book in any form by any means including digitized forms that can be encoded, stored, and retrieved from any media including computer disks, CD-ROM, computer databases, and network servers without permission of the publisher except for quotes and small passages included in book reviews. Copies of this book may be purchased for educational, business or promotional use. Contact the author/publisher for pricing.

For Marie and Melanie

Also by Mike Guardia:

American Guerrilla

Shadow Commander

Hal Moore: A Soldier Once…and Always

The Fires of Babylon

Crusader

Hal Moore: A Life in Pictures

Tomcat Fury

Wings of Fire

Foxbat Tales

Co-authored with Lt. General Harold G. Moore:

Hal Moore on Leadership

CONTENTS

Introduction	vii
Chapter 1: From the Ashes of Vietnam	1
Chapter 2: The Dragoons	5
Chapter 3: "DEFORGER-90"	41
Chapter 4: Life in the Desert	61
Chapter 5: Into Iraq	131
Chapter 6: Day of Battle	149
Chapter 7: Cease-Fire	181
Epilogue: After the Storm	197
Appendix A: Paul Hains' Letter of March 3, 1991.	207
Appendix B: Waylan Lundquist's Citation for the Silver Star Medal.	211
Appendix C: Official Rules of Engagement (ROE) for Checkpoint Duty in An Nasiriyah.	213
Bibliography	215

INTRODUCTION

In the summer of 1990, mankind stood on the brink of a new era. Gone were the days of the Cold War—the Iron Curtain had fallen and the once-mighty Soviet Union lay on its deathbed. After nearly fifty years of ideological struggle, the United States stood as the world's lone superpower. But as Communism disappeared from Eastern Europe, and America reaped the benefits of her "peace dividend," a new conflict loomed on the horizon.

On the morning of August 2, 1990, Iraqi forces under the command of Saddam Hussein invaded the tiny emirate of Kuwait. Within hours, the Kuwaiti defenses collapsed under the onslaught of the Iraqi Army. The invasion drew fierce condemnation from the international community and prompted the United Nations to demand Saddam's withdrawal. Undeterred by the rhetoric, the Iraqi dictator massed his forces along the Saudi Arabian border and dared the world to stop him. In response, the US military led a coalition of thirty-four nations in what became Operation Desert Storm—a violent air and ground campaign to eject the Iraqis from Kuwait. At the tip of the spear were the men of Ghost Troop in the US Army's 2d Armored Cavalry Regiment.

Commanded by Captain Joseph Sartiano, Ghost Troop was among the lead elements of the US VII Corps' advance into Iraq. On February 26, 1991, Ghost Troop encountered a brigade-sized element of the Tawakalna Division— the elite frontline forces of Iraq's Republican Guard. Although significantly outnumbered and outgunned, Ghost Troop won a decisive victory with minimal losses to their own ranks. History would call it the Battle of 73 Easting.

Most battles throughout history have taken the name of a nearby town or landmark (Stalingrad, Thermopylae, King's Mountain, etc.). The

Battle of 73 Easting, however, was named for its position on a military map. In military parlance, an "easting" refers to a longitudinal grid line. Since much of the ground war took place in the featureless deserts of Iraq, military commanders often had no other way of identifying their battles. Despite its unusual name, 73 Easting has since been regarded as "the last great tank battle of the twentieth century."

The Armored Cavalry Regiment (ACR) was an organization unique to the United States Army. Independent, heavily-armored, and rapidly deployable, the ACR's purpose was to provide armored reconnaissance, surveillance, and mobile security to heavy forces in the field. Unlike conventional armor and infantry units—which are descendingly organized into brigades, battalions, and companies—cavalry units are respectively organized into *regiments*, *squadrons*, and *troops*. Each ACR contained three armored cavalry squadrons, an aviation squadron, and a support squadron. An armored cavalry squadron normally consisted of a headquarters troop, three armored cavalry troops, a pure tank company, and a self-propelled howitzer battery. The ACR's aviation squadron provided aerial reconnaissance and ground attack capabilities through a combination of Cobra, Blackhawk, and Kiowa helicopters. The support squadron, meanwhile, provided the logistical and maintenance assets for the ACR's combat mission. During the Gulf War, the Army had three active ACRs: the 2d, 3d, and 11th. The 2d and 11th ACRs were forward-stationed in Germany, while the 3d ACR resided at Fort Bliss, Texas. Today, all three cavalry regiments are still active, but none have retained the traditional heavy ACR configuration. The 2d and 3d ACR have since converted to the M1126 Stryker-series vehicle, while the 11th ACR is now a conventional heavy brigade.

The armored cavalry troop (like Ghost) was the centerpiece of the ACR's ground network. A troop consisted of two tank platoons (each equipped with four M1A1 Abrams tanks) and two mechanized scout platoons (mounted atop six M2/M3 Bradley Fighting Vehicles). Two specially-modified M113 Armored Personnel Carriers comprised the mortar section, whose job was to provide indirect fire support. The troop's maintenance section carried the massive M88 Recovery Vehicle, a tracked behemoth that could tow any disabled vehicle in the Army's inventory. As a testament to their elite subculture within the US Army, the ACRs used their own phonetic alphabet to identify their troops. Thus, instead of Alpha Company, Bravo Company, and Charlie

Company, a typical ACR would designate its units as Apache Troop, Bandit Troop, and Crazyhorse Troop.

The idea for *Days of Fury* began in the Summer of 2015, following the release of my previous book, *The Fires of Babylon: Eagle Troop and the Battle of 73 Easting*. Throughout my research, I discovered that Ghost Troop's actions tied in closely with Eagle Troop's during the battle. Moreover, Ghost Troop's actions contributed greatly to the enemy's defeat. I could not, therefore, tell the full story of 73 Easting without including Ghost Troop's combat chronicle—a story of modern warfare told from a "soldier's-eye-view."

The Gulf War remains one of the most defining events of the latter 20th Century. The origins and outcomes of Desert Storm still resonate within the political discourse of the Middle East. Moreover, America's victory in that conflict underscored the remarkable transformation that its Army had undergone during the post-Vietnam era. It was also the first war fought predominantly by a generation of post-Baby Boomers. Indeed, the elder members of Generation X (born between 1964-72) did most of the fighting and dying on the frontlines in Iraq. For the elder Millennials like myself (born after 1980), Desert Storm was the first major conflict that occurred during our lifetime. We were in grade school at the time, but many of us remember watching the nightly news with our parents, listening to the likes of Peter Jennings and Ted Koppel as they narrated the events unfolding halfway around the world. Some of our parents were mobilized reservists and, in our classrooms and churches, we drew pictures of the American flag and sponsored care packages for those serving in the Gulf. The Desert Camouflage pattern became a fashion statement for kids nationwide and "Stormin Norman" became a household name.

Many Ghost Troopers graciously gave their time for interviews—sharing memories, photographs, and war diaries from their time in the Persian Gulf. Some of the men featured in this book (as recounted through the various interviews and diaries) are not portrayed in the most flattering light. Thus, to protect their privacy, I have given them pseudonyms or, wherever possible, avoided using their names entirely. Every pseudonym appearing in this book is followed by the parenthetical notation "(not his real name)."

Interviews and archival material have formed the backbone of this narrative. Interviews, although reliable sources of information, are not without liability. As with any event that happened years ago, memory can (and often does) distort or innocently rearrange the facts of the story. The Ghost Troopers whom I interviewed were all of sound mind and recalled their actions in the Gulf with remarkable consistency. Inevitably, though, there were a few discrepancies. For example, one trooper may recall an event happening on a Friday while another trooper recalls the same event happening on a Wednesday. Furthermore, accounts of the battle often differ between members of the same vehicle. For instance, a tank commander and his gunner may remember an engagement differently. I have made every attempt to reconcile these discrepancies against the archival documentation. Where this was not possible, I simply recorded whatever version was most commonly remembered by the majority of Ghost Troop. The reader must bear in mind, however, that time and monetary constraints prevented me from interviewing every Ghost Trooper. Some troopers never responded to the inquiry, while others simply couldn't be found. My search to locate these missing troopers returned only a handful of dead phone numbers or addresses that had long since changed. Other troopers provided their diaries and photographs but politely declined to be interviewed.

The reader must also bear in mind that this is a book about Ghost Troop. Their experiences are the driving force behind the narrative. Therefore, the reader will not find any detailed discussion about the broader aspects of the Gulf War. While I have included some discussion of these aspects for the sake of context, they are discussed largely inasmuch as they relate to Ghost Troop's deployment. As with *The Fires of Babylon*, my intent is to provide the reader with an earnest, intimate, no-holds-barred account of modern warfare, as told by the brave men who lived it. *Days of Fury* is their story.

FROM THE ASHES OF VIETNAM

Major Douglas Macgregor, the Operations Officer (S-3) of 2d Squadron, 2d Armored Cavalry Regiment, surveyed the damage in front of him. It was unbelievable: in less than 100 hours, American ground forces had destroyed the fourth-largest army in the world. From among the huddle of POWs, one Iraqi officer made an appeal: "Why do you not go to Baghdad? You have the power. Your army rules the heavens and the earth. Do you think we love Saddam? Saddam killed our best generals. He kills everyone. Major, you must go to Baghdad and end this. You must save Iraq."

Macgregor wished he could; but orders were orders. President George Bush had already announced the cease-fire, making it clear that America's mission was to restore the sovereignty of Kuwait, not to conquer Iraq. Still, the Iraqi officer's remark that the US Army commanded "the heavens and the earth" struck a tender nerve with Macgregor. From the appearance of the battlefield, he found no cause to argue. But this victorious army was a far cry from the one Macgregor had joined in 1975. Back then, the US Army ranked just above sanitation workers in a survey of public confidence.

Emerging from Vietnam, the Army found itself crippled by a crisis of confidence and a growing culture of apathy and neglect. Throughout the early seventies, nearly half of the soldiers stationed in Germany admitted to drug use—including heroin, hash, and marijuana. Desertion and violent crime were on the rise and barracks became war zones in their own right as soldier gangs ruled through fear and intimidation. Racial unrest had also found its way into the Army. On a few occasions, on-post race riots between black and white soldiers spread into the streets of nearby towns. In garrison communities across the country, officers, noncommissioned officers, and even their families, were frequently attacked by renegade soldiers.

Amidst this public backlash from Vietnam, the Army routinely lowered its recruiting standards just to maintain its end-strength. But even with these lower entry standards, and the transition to an all-volunteer force, the Army still fell 20,000 men below its quota. By 1975, nearly forty percent of new recruits had no high school diploma and many more had criminal records. Meanwhile, young officers and non-commissioned officers found themselves "trying to lead an Army stuck in Purgatory." Faced with the prospect of a thankless job, a hostile American public, and increasingly undisciplined soldiers, these young leaders began leaving the Army by the thousands.

The first attempt to revive this shattered Army began in 1973. Both at home and overseas, the Army adopted a "zero tolerance" policy for drugs and began enforcing new standards of discipline. In Europe alone, the Army discharged more than 1,300 soldiers who were known to be drug addicts, gang members, and other small-time criminals. By removing these criminals from their ranks, the Army could once again focus on training and rebuilding soldier discipline.

During the latter years of Vietnam, unit training and readiness had sunk to an all-time low. The single-minded focus on counterinsurgency had eroded many of the Army's core competencies and ignored the more immediate threat from the Communist Bloc in Eastern Europe. Furthermore, "training" had been reduced to classroom instruction—where soldiers and officers learned the theory of warfare instead of practicing their craft in the field. According to Brigadier General Robert Scales, "the most realistic peacetime battlefield for infantrymen and tankers was still the firing range."

Determine to reverse these trends, senior Army leaders established the Training and Doctrine Command (TRADOC) in 1973. TRADOC emphasized a return to realistic field-based training which focused on small unit tactics and basic combat skills. To this end, TRADOC created the Army Training and Evaluation Program (ARTEP) in 1975. As a gauge for measuring combat readiness at the company, battalion, and brigade-level, ARTEP exposed units that "looked good in garrison, but failed to meet the standard in the field."

Alongside ARTEP, Army officials began to push for more modernized equipment. By 1975, many of the Army's combat vehicles had fallen a generation behind their Soviet counterparts. While Americans continued training on their 1950s-era equipment, the Soviets fielded the T-72 Main Battle Tank and the BMP—the first true "infantry fighting vehicle." To keep pace with the Warsaw Pact (and make up for time lost during Vietnam), Army Chief of Staff General Creighton Abrams put forth a new weapon systems plan known as "The Big Five." These included a new main battle tank, an infantry fighting vehicle, two helicopters—an attack aircraft and a troop transport—and a missile defense platform. Respectively, these weapons became the M1 Abrams, the M2 Bradley, the Apache and Black Hawk helicopters, and the Patriot missile.

But even with new training methods and the promise of new equipment, the Army still had difficulty attracting and retaining quality recruits. Although the Army was steadily dragging itself out of the post-Vietnam malaise, the American public (and potential recruits) remained skeptical of the Army's vitality. Straddled by massive budget cuts and a lukewarm Congress, a soldier's quality of life steadily declined throughout the 1970s. Because military pay and allowances had failed to keep pace with inflation, many soldiers found themselves living off food stamps.

Beginning in 1980, however, Congress approved more money for military spending. Over the next two years, soldier salaries increased by twenty-five percent and the Army launched its "Be All You Can Be" campaign. Realizing that the existence of an all-volunteer force wasn't enough to attract quality recruits, the Army aimed to convince America's youth that military service was a marketable skill. "Thanks to the positive image-making and improving quality of life within the Army, the 'Willie and Joe' image from the drafted Army gave way to the Army's new image as a caring, challenging, high-tech outfit." By the end of the 1980s, nearly 100 percent of new recruits were high school graduates. As the Army attracted higher-quality recruits, the incidents of AWOL, desertion, and drug abuse fell dramatically.

The push for more money and better recruits went hand-in-hand with a revitalization of the Army's tactical doctrine. As the focus returned to the defense of Western Europe, General Donn Starry, commander of the Army's V Corps, realized that the current doctrine of "Active Defense" couldn't defeat the Warsaw Pact in a conventional showdown. The concept of Active Defense stipulated that NATO ground forces could fix and destroy the first wave of the Soviet invasion at key points along the Inner-German border. After the first wave of Soviets were destroyed (or at least neutralized), the NATO defenders could then regroup and engage the following echelons. However, Starry noticed that V Corps had neither the time nor resources to "reset the defense" before being overwhelmed by the second echelon.

Starry's solution, therefore, was to attack the enemy's rear echelons before they had a chance to mobilize them. This required integrating Air Force assets at the Corps-level, something which had never been done in the Cold War-era Army. Utilizing strike and reconnaissance aircraft, NATO could severely disrupt the enemy's rear echelons before they could engage the West German defenses. Simultaneously, NATO artillery fire and electronic warfare would disrupt the enemy's frontline battle rhythm. Starry's principles became known as "AirLand Battle," codified in the 1982 edition of FM 100-5 *Operations*. AirLand Battle served as the blueprint for the ground attack phase during Desert Storm and remained the backbone of Army tactical doctrine well into the twenty-first century.

Little by little, these trends lifted the Army out of its post-Vietnam malaise. However, the most glaring testament to the Army's revival was the conduct of its soldiers in the field. During the 1970s, West German and other NATO forces often commented on the lethargy of American tank crews. During joint maneuvers, American tankers frequently caused collateral damage to German homes, businesses, and farms. Whenever an American tank broke down or became immobile during maneuvers, the crew would often sit atop their vehicle, light a few cigarettes, and wait for their vehicle to be recovered. By 1985, however, American tankers had earned a much better reputation. Tank crewmen now sprang into action fixing and troubleshooting their vehicles. Two years later, an American tank crew won the Canadian Army Trophy Gunnery Competition for the first time in nearly a quarter-century. Meanwhile, at the National Training Center at Fort Irwin, California, rotating units were continuously defeating their mock-aggressor forces in staged battles across the Mojave Desert.

In less than two decades, the Army had transformed itself from a decrepit, post-Vietnam rabble into the most professional, high-tech fighting force the world had ever known. This was the Army of 1990, the revitalized Army that had defeated Saddam Hussein in less than 100 hours—the Army that ruled "the heavens and the earth."

THE DRAGOONS

John Mecca, Ghost Troop's Executive Officer during the 2d ACR's annual Regimental Ball. The son of an Air Force officer, Mecca was a product of the Army ROTC program at Rutgers University.
Photo courtesy of Andy Kilgore

MECCA

Lieutenant John Mecca, Ghost Troop's Executive Officer, was the proud son of an Air Force veteran. Born in New Jersey, he hailed from an Italian-American family who took pride in their lineage of military service. John's father had earned his commission via Air Force ROTC at Rutgers University during the 1950s; John's paternal grandfather was a World War I veteran—an Italian immigrant who earned his US citizenship by fighting in the trenches. While fighting the Germans, John's grandfather had been wounded during a chemical attack—the poisonous gas rendering him partially blind for nearly a year. Regaining his eyesight, however, the elder Mecca made a good living running a kiosk on the streets of New York City. His maternal grandfather, meanwhile, had been a proud sailor—a veteran of America's Great White Fleet.

"Having all those great examples," he said, "of people who were in the military, it was just natural for me to want to join." Graduating from high school in 1983, the young Mecca decided to follow in his father's footsteps to Rutgers University. Unlike his father, however, Mecca was attracted to the culture and lifestyle of the United States Army. Enrolling in the Army ROTC program, John Mecca knew he had found his calling.

His first exposure to the world of tank warfare came in the summer of 1986, while attending the ROTC Summer Advanced Camp. A four-week training course held at various Army posts including Fort Riley, Kansas and Fort Bragg, North Carolina, Advanced Camp was the culminating event for an ROTC cadet's career. Typically, cadets attended the camp during the summer before their senior year of college. Evaluated on their leadership skills throughout a variety of tactical scenarios, a cadet's Advanced Camp score largely determined his or her ranking on the national Order of Merit List (OML) by which Army planners would assign new lieutenants to their career fields. A high rank on the OML virtually guaranteed a cadet his or her top choice of career field and duty station.

During Advanced Camp, representatives from each of the Army's branches gave presentations to the cadets—"dog and pony shows," as Mecca recalled, highlighting the more glamourous aspects of the various Army career fields. The presentation that truly captured his attention, however, was the Armor branch—"tanks and mechanized warfare." Indeed, the Armor branch representatives brought their latest and greatest equipment for sampling, including the M1 Abrams tank. "They had us driving around in the tanks!" Following that brief introduction to the power of armored warfare, Mecca was sold on becoming an Armor officer.

Returning to Rutgers for his senior year, Mecca began pondering where he wanted to go for his first assignment. "I had heard about Germany," he said, "and I thought it would be amazing." In 1986, the Cold War was at its height, and an assignment along the Inner German border was considered prime posting for young officers who sought to make the Army their career. Approaching his ROTC instructors, Mecca was pleased to hear that his chances of being assigned to Germany would increase if he selected Armor as his branch. During the Cold War, the US Army designated its Armor officers as "critical personnel" for assignments along the Iron Curtain. Because the Soviet Army had a massive tank footprint in Eastern Europe, NATO needed a tank force of comparable strength to deter any aggression from the Warsaw Pact.

"When it came time for us [cadets] to get our Branch selections," he recalled, "and find out who was going Active Duty or Reserves, I got exactly what I wanted"—a commission as an Armor Officer with an assignment to Germany. Mecca recalled that everyone in his family was elated by the news…except his mother. "My mom was crying," he said. "We were at the height of the Cold War, and the 'Red Horde' was on the other side of the border in Germany, and she was worried."

Trying to assuage her, John simply said: "Don't worry mom, it'll be fun."

As far as he knew, the likelihood of going to war was slim.

Graduating from Rutgers in the fall of 1987, Mecca reported to the Armor Officer Basic Course at Fort Knox, Kentucky in January 1988. Like most lieutenants who were headed to cavalry units, Mecca attended the Armor Officer Basic Course and the Scout Platoon Leader Course. He knew he was going to Germany, and that he'd likely be assigned to an armored cavalry unit, but he didn't know which one. "I remember showing up in Frankfurt," he said, "at the Replacement Center, and I saw my name under the '2d Armored Cavalry Regiment.' I'm like: 'All right, whatever.'" But Mecca had not yet been introduced to the culture of the cavalry regiment.

Speaking to the reception staff in Frankfurt, they told him: "I hope you're not married."

"What do you mean?"

"You're going to be in the field constantly."

"Great!"

After all, Mecca hadn't become an Armor Officer to spend his days behind a desk. "When I got to Germany in September of 1988, I went to Eagle Troop as the 4th Platoon Leader (tanks), and a week later, we went to REFORGER [Return of Forces to Germany]." Throughout the Cold War, the US Army conducted annual REFORGER exercises with its NATO allies in preparation against a possible attack from the Soviet Union. During REFORGER, stateside units deployed to West Germany to reinforce the forward-stationed American units and conduct large-scale defensive maneuvers across the German countryside—"and I basically learned how to be a platoon leader during all of this, which was an amazing opportunity."

Coming back from REFORGER, Mecca and his platoon had less than two weeks of recovery time before they headed to Grafenwoehr for tank gunnery. Short of combat, gunnery was the critical event for Army tank crewmen. Working as a highly-synchronized team, the driver, loader, gunner, and tank commander would maneuver the tank, engaging a series of pop-up targets that resembled enemy vehicles. The sequential levels of tank gunnery were designated by "Tables." For instance, "Table XII Gunnery" referred to all four tanks within a platoon conducting gunnery while maneuvering against day and night targets. Each level of gunnery was scored out of a possible 1,000 points, with a minimum of 700 points needed for a passing score.

And the pressure was high for these young crewmen to perform.

Indeed, any tank crew that failed to achieve the minimum score at gunnery was subject to formal humiliation: they had to point the main gun tube over the rear deck of the tank and leave the gun in that position until the unit returned to its motor pool. It was a universal sign of disgrace among tankers. For John Mecca, however, his tank crew earned a top score of 950—an accomplishment that earned him the Army Commendation Medal. "I had a fantastic crew," he said. "We came home from Grafenwoehr, got cleaned up, and went out for a border tour."

Although Gorbachev had come to power, and had promised reforms throughout the Soviet Union, the Cold War was still at the forefront of American defense policy. As such, the 2d ACR was still intently focused on its Cold War mission of guarding the Inner-German Border. All border operations were governed by a field manual known as the *Border Standing Operating Procedure*, or BOSOP—covering topics such as how to process Soviet defectors and what to do if engaged by hostile fire from an enemy border guard. "We spent Thanksgiving and Christmas on the border," he said—a testament to the priority that the Army gave to its border mission. According to Mecca, it was an incredible learning experience, "working on our general deployment and defense plans, making sure that we were ready for the Russian horde."

By the spring of 1989, Mecca's performance as a tank platoon leader was such to earn him a promotion to scout platoon leader. Commanding a scout platoon was considered the pinnacle of an Armor lieutenant's career. Only the best young officers from the line companies were considered for the position, and the scout platoon leader typically bore twice as much responsibility as his fellow lieutenants. A mechanized scout platoon consisted of thirty soldiers and six M2/M3 Bradley Fighting Vehicles. The platoon's mission was to perform reconnaissance ahead of the battalion's main force—acting as an early warning system and the proverbial "eyes and ears" of the battalion commander.

"I took over 3d Platoon, Eagle Troop," he said, "and I was actually on the border when the Berlin Wall came down in November 1989." He and his scout platoon were manning their positions along the Inner-

German Border at Camp Harris. At the time, Mecca was the acting camp commander, and was both elated and dumbfounded to hear the news that the Berlin Wall had opened. To be sure, East and West Germany were still separate countries, but the die had been cast for reunification. It was only a matter of time before these border missions would become a thing of the past.

Standing down from their post along the border, Mecca wondered: "What are we going to do now?" For years, the 2d ACR had protected the Frontier of Democracy, focused on defeating the "Red Menace" if and when the Cold War became "hot." But as the 2d ACR struggled to find its mission in a time of geopolitical uncertainty, John Mecca received the unexpected good news that he would become the Executive Officer (XO) of Ghost Troop. "In early 1990, I became the XO for Ghost Troop under Captain Eric Tamke." All told, Mecca was surprised by the sudden reassignment. Being the XO put him second-in-command to the Ghost Troop commander. But as the squadron commander explained: "John, you're a doer, and we need you to go do it!"

Deskevich

Lieutenant Joe Deskevich, Ghost Troop's Fire Support Officer, was the quintessential All-American boy. Born in Rockville, Maryland, and raised in a God-fearing household, he was a "Son of the American Revolution"—meaning that he had ancestors who fought in the Revolutionary War. In Joe's family, military service had become somewhat of a tradition, as he could trace at least one person in his lineage to every major American conflict.

"It's just what my family does," he said.

"I went to St. John's Catholic Military High School in DC, so I was wearing that uniform since I was fourteen." Attracted to the rough-and-tumble aura of military life, Deskevich received an Army ROTC scholarship to the University of North Georgia (UNG). Renowned as the "Military College of Georgia," UNG was famous for its highly-regimented Corps of Cadets, similar to Texas A&M University and Virginia Tech.

"I had always wanted to be a tanker," he said—fascinated by the rich history of armored warfare and the panache of being a tank commander. These ambitions soon changed, however, when he arrived at the ROTC Summer Advanced Camp. At camp, Deskevich and his campmates went

Joe Deskevich, Ghost Troop's Fire Support Officer. Deskevich came from a long lineage of military service; members of his family had served in every major American conflict since the Revolutionary War.
Photo courtesy of Joe Deskevich

through the mandatory "Call for Fire" class—a module that familiarized cadets with the equipment and procedures of the Field Artillery. To this point, the young Deskevich had only a passing familiarity with the concepts of cannon fire.

Today's demonstration, however, would permanently change his outlook.

"I *loved* Call for Fire," he said.

While most of his campmates were unimpressed by the Field Artillery demonstration, Joe Deskevich was enthralled. When he returned to UNG that fall, he knew he was going to be a Field Artillery officer.

Graduating from UNG in the spring of 1989, Deskevich reported to the Field Artillery Officer Basic Course (FAOBC) at Fort Sill, Oklahoma—learning the fundamentals of gunnery and delivering fire support. "When I went through FAOBC in 1989," he said, "it was very fire support centric. We learned how to support the different maneuver formations—infantry, armor, and learn how they move. The AirLand Battle doctrine was still hot and heavy, and FAOBC wanted to make sure that we [artillerymen] could be part of that combined arms team." At the time, AirLand Battle was the governing tactical doctrine for the US Army. Designed to counter the Soviet threat in Eastern Europe, AirLand Battle stressed synchronization of air and artillery assets to strike at the enemy's rear echelons before he had a chance to mobilize them.

But, as Deskevich noted, the political climate of 1989 was remarkably different than what it had been in 1982—the inaugural year of the AirLand Battle doctrine. In fact, the frost of the Cold War had begun to thaw, and the first round of defense budget cuts had already taken effect. Because he wanted to serve along the Frontier of Democracy, and see the Iron Curtain before it disappeared, Joe Deskevich requested an assignment to Germany.

Receiving orders to the 2d ACR, Joe was excited about the prospect of joining an elite armored unit. As an artilleryman, being assigned to a cavalry unit would be radically different from serving in a regular formation. Within the ranks of the cavalry, artillerymen were expected to do everything that a scout platoon leader could do. There was no stovepiping of occupational specialties; indeed, *every* trooper in the cavalry (whether a cook, supply clerk, or intelligence analyst) was expected to fight and communicate as if he were a bona fide cavalryman. Moreover, providing fire support to cavalry units involved much more planning than in regular maneuver units. Cavalry-based artillerymen had to diversify their fire support schemes to include mounted *and* dismounted elements, close air support, mortars, air assault teams, and even naval gunfire. "You have so many more opportunities than you would in a divisional-type unit," said Joe. Luckily, one of his FAOBC instructors had been a veteran of the 11th ACR, and spent extra hours preparing him for the dynamics of cavalry-based fire support.

When Joe reported to the 2d ACR Headquarters in December 1989, the Berlin Wall had already fallen, but the US Army continued manning its posts along the Inner-German Border until the country reunified in October 1990. "That Christmas [1989]," said Joe, "the squadron's howitzer battery was on the border," conducting surveillance along one of the largest swaths of the Iron Curtain—the tri-zonal area where the borders of East Germany, West Germany, and Czechoslovakia converged. "The howitzer battery did regular border rotations just like the cavalry troops did." Seeing just how fast the 2d ACR's operational tempo could be, Deskevich realized that his FAOBC instructor had been correct when he said: "Cavalry isn't a branch, it's an attitude."

When Deskevich reported to Ghost Troop, he was struck by how often 2d Squadron conducted its maneuvers and border missions. By virtue of being a Field Artillery officer, he technically belonged to 2d Squadron's howitzer battery, but was "on loan" to Ghost Troop as its Fire Support Officer—responsible for coordinating the battery's artillery fire in support of Ghost Troop's field maneuvers. In May 1990, Deskevich did his first rotation to the Combat Maneuver Training Center (CMTC) in Hohenfels. Squaring off against mock aggressors in the German countryside, these training maneuvers replicated "World War III" scenarios based upon the anticipated actions of the Warsaw Pact. "But we didn't have a very long life expectancy if the Russians were to come racing across the border," he said wryly. For even at maximum firepower, NATO's frontline forces would be little more than a "speedbump" for the Red Army—hopefully buying enough time for friendly reinforcements to arrive in theater. During that first rotation to the Inner-German Border, Deskevich recalled looking at a map of NATO's defensive positions.

But one particular map symbol had caught his attention.

"Three letters—DIP"

Asking a fellow officer what that symbol meant, Joe was shocked to learn that "DIP" stood for "Die in Place"—meaning that the unit could retreat no farther than the DIP symbol, and was expected to fight to the last surviving man. "We were expected to hold the Soviets at the border until the 1st Armored Division could get there," he said. This scenario forecasted a near-90% casualty rate for the 2d ACR. "It was no joke," he recalled, "and that's why we took the training so seriously."

On other occasions, Ghost Troop would do a training exercise with one of its NATO partners—typically a British or West German reconnaissance unit. The training tempo was such that Ghost Troop spent most of its time in the field. "For my first two years in the 2d ACR," he said, "I don't think I ever spent more than a month at home. Right after coming back from the field we would go straight to gunnery."

On August 2, 1990, Joe Deskevich was preparing for Operation Dragoon Saber, one of many Tactical Operation Center Exercises (TOCEX)* that the squadron conducted throughout the fiscal year. While considering the fire support integration for the TOCEX, Deskevich was suddenly interrupted by the news that Iraq had invaded Kuwait.

At first, Joe didn't know what to make of it.

Yet, somehow, he was *convinced* that he would deploy to the Middle East.

"We all had a feeling that we were going," he said. "I don't know how we knew…but we knew."

GARWICK AND HAINS

Ghost Troop's scout platoon leaders, Keith Garwick and Paul Hains, had been destined for military service. Both men were the sons of West Point graduates, and both had come from a well-established military pedigree.

---

* Pronounced "tock-ex"

Commanding a scout platoon was the dream of every career-minded armor lieutenant; and Hains and Garwick had certainly earned their due. Garwick was a 1988 West Point graduate; while Hains had commissioned via the ROTC program at Texas Christian University.

Said Keith Garwick: "My dad was a West Point graduate, Class of 1962, but he took a commission in the Marine Corps." Indeed, every year, West Point and Annapolis allowed a small percentage of each graduating class to accept commissions in another branch of the Armed Services. Of the nearly 600 graduates in the Class of 1962, Garwick's father was one of 11 who accepted commissions into the Marine Corps. "I grew up in Hawaii, Camp Pendleton, Quantico, Camp Lejeune…and I ended up at a high school in London," said Garwick. "While I was looking at my career options, West Point was the most viable educational opportunity that I had."

Keith Garwick, Scout Platoon Leader. A 1988 West Point graduate, Garwick grew up around the world as the son of a career Marine officer. *Photo courtesy of Keith Garwick*

While at the Academy, Garwick's first qualitative exposure to the Armor Branch occurred during the summer before his junior year. That summer, he participated in a 60-day training deployment with the 2d Infantry Division, forward-stationed in South Korea. Although Garwick was training with a straight-leg infantry unit, he noticed a nearby tank unit on the local firing range. Impressed by their firepower and rapid mobility, Garwick recalled that this real-time demonstration was what "really sparked my interest in Armor."

Returning to the Academy that fall, he registered for elective courses in the history of armored warfare—and took a keen interest in the Arab-Israeli tank battles of Yom Kippur. Graduating with the Class of 1988, Garwick selected Armor as his branch of choice and requested an assignment in Germany. Although the frost of the Cold War had begun to thaw, he was eager to serve along the Frontier of Democracy. After attending AOBC and the Scout Platoon Leaders Course, Garwick arrived in West Germany in the summer of 1989.

Reporting to the 2d ACR, Garwick distinctly remembered: "I was wearing a pair of flip-flops, some board shorts and a colored t-shirt. The airline lost all my luggage. I landed with nothing except what I was wearing and what was in my pockets! I had to scramble to get some clothing together." Understandably, reporting to his unit while dressed like an adolescent beachcomber was among the most memorable days of his life.

During his time in the 2d ACR, Garwick held a variety of jobs beyond the purview of a normal armor lieutenant. "The first job I had was an artillery coordinator," he said, "even though I wasn't artillery." Still, the job gave him an intimate knowledge of artillery fire that most maneuver officers never got—and it was knowledge that would serve him well during Desert Storm. "Then I went to Ghost Troop, where I had 4th Platoon, but I had very little time as a tank platoon leader before I got promoted to scout platoon leader"—a position that put him charge of 1st Platoon and their six Bradley Fighting Vehicles.

During his time with the scouts, Garwick did several rotations to the major training centers throughout Germany—including Hohenfels, Grafenwoehr, and Wildflecken (which the troops often called "Wild Chicken"). Of the three, he recalled Hohenfels as the "muddiest, foggiest place on Earth." Getting lost in the forests of Hohenfels was almost a rite of passage for young maneuver leaders—"there's no way you *can't* get lost in those woods," he said.

Paul Hains was a fifth-generation military man. "I was born to an active duty US Army officer serving in the Berlin Brigade," he said, "defending West Berlin from the Communist threat." Like most military sons of the era, Paul remembered that his father was either "fighting wars or training to fight the next war." Paul's father did two tours in Vietnam—one of which culminated in the command of an armored cavalry squadron. "I was the youngest of three," he said, "so I pretty much caught the tail end of his career."

By the time Paul began grade school, his father had become the Senior Advisor to the Texas Army National Guard (49th Armored Division)—an assignment which precipitated a move to Austin, where Hains's family ultimately set their roots. But whereas his grandfather, father, and brother had all attended West Point (Classes of 1924, 1952, and 1983, respectively)

Paul Hains, Scout Platoon Leader. The son and grandson of West Point graduates, Paul Hains had come from a well-established Army pedigree. His grandfather had also been a member of the 1926 Olympic Pentathlon Team and commanded an armored regiment in the North African campaigns of World War II.
Photo courtesy of Paul Hains

Paul Hains chose the ROTC route, enrolling at Texas Christian University in Fort Worth.

Arriving on campus in the fall of 1983, Hains enrolled in the college of business. "I was going to set the world on fire," he chuckled, "and make my first million by the age of 35; you know, all that stuff." Throughout his days as an ROTC cadet, Hains was impressed by the caliber of his Military Science instructors. Many of them were Vietnam veterans. Of particular note was the Professor of Military Science—an infantry colonel who had earned the Silver Star Medal in Vietnam, along with a glass eye for wounds he had suffered in combat. "He always tried to make the training as exciting as possible."

Being the son of a career-minded cavalryman, it came as little surprise when Paul Hains commissioned as an Armor Officer in the spring of 1987. "It was during the height of the Reagan buildup," he said—and active duty billets were plentiful for those who wanted them. The priorities of the training pipeline, however, meant that the West Point graduates attended their respective Officer Basic Courses before the ROTC and OCS graduates could likewise attend. Thus, Paul Hains's AOBC class wouldn't start until January 1988. Not wanting to stay idle for the next seven months, Hains went to the Professor of Military Science.

"What am I going to do until January, sir?"

"You're going to be my Gold Bar Recruiter!"

It was the job that *no* second lieutenant wanted. The Gold Bar Recruiter was a "make-work" position at various ROTC schools, designed to keep second lieutenants gainfully employed until they reported to their Officer Basic Courses. In theory, the Gold Bar Recruiter generated prospects for ROTC enrollment, often conducting presentations at local high schools and regional JROTC events. In practice, however, the Gold Bar Recruiter was more often an "errand boy," for the senior cadre. "But I had nothing better to do," said Hains, "and I was broke."

After Christmas 1987, Hains loaded his vehicle and drove from Texas to Fort Knox. "Good God Almighty, I had never seen so much snow!" he said. "Growing up in central Texas, you never saw that." Like most of his fellow lieutenants, Paul Hains enjoyed the 1980s-era AOBC. Back then, it was considered the most "gentlemanly" of the combat arms courses, while still teaching its graduates to "shoot, move, and communicate." Although most of the armored force had transitioned to the M1 Abrams, much of AOBC was still being taught with the older M60. The M60 was the last in the so-called "Patton" series of tanks, which had been in US service for more than 25 years. Despite its longevity, crews often complained about the M60's high silhouette and poor gas mileage. According to one AOBC instructor, students trained on the M60 because: "The M1 Abrams can travel faster than a lieutenant's brain. So, we have to train these kids on the slower tanks."

As AOBC drew to a close, Hains prepared himself for an assignment to Germany. On the one hand, he was excited to see the Frontier of Democracy. On the other hand, he took heed of his friends' warnings. "You're in for a real hardship," they said. The frontline units in Europe habitually patrolled the East German border, and had little downtime between training events. After the Scout Platoon Leaders Course, Hains landed in Frankfurt, Germany at the VII Corps Reception Center. Alongside the rest of the incoming GIs, Paul remembered that: "We got on this bus…maybe like 18 passengers, and we proceed to drive all around the kasernes* and finally got to Bamberg"—home of the 2d Squadron, 2d ACR.

He reported to the squadron commander, then-Lieutenant Colonel Hurd. "He was a large, imposing fellow, with a big meaty handshake," said Paul.

Hurd wasted no time.

"Welcome to the 2d Squadron, 2d Armored Cavalry Regiment!" he boomed.

"Tell me about yourself, Paul!"—he continued. But Hains had barely mentioned a few particulars before Hurd stopped him and said: "Okay,

---

*Pronounced "kay-sern;" the German word for "barracks." It became a loanword used by American forces in Germany, who began referring to their own posts as "kasernes."

that's good! Hey listen, grab your hat. We're going to go to the railhead."

Hains didn't know whether to be excited or apprehensive.

"Okay, I'll play along," he thought to himself.

Paul then jumped into the commander's Humvee and headed to the Bamberg railhead. He soon discovered that this "railhead" was a loading platform where the regiment loaded its tanks and Bradleys onto flathead railcars for movement into the various training centers throughout Germany.

As Hurd and Hains arrived, Hawk Company (the pure tank company within the squadron) was unloading its tanks from their recent rotation to Grafenwoehr. "Listen," said Hurd, "you're going to be the first platoon leader. See that guy over there?"—pointing to a group of soldiers gathered at the railhead—"That's your platoon sergeant. Go meet him. Good luck!" With that, Hurd departed, leaving Hains to take charge of his new soldiers. Undaunted, Paul went right up to the senior sergeant and stuck out his hand:

"Hi. Are you Sergeant Sumner?"

"Yes sir. Are you Lieutenant Hains?"

"Yes, I am."

"Great! I've been waiting for you."

Thus began Paul Hains' 13-month tour as a platoon leader in Hawk Company.

Taking helm of his platoon's four tanks and their crewmen, Haines quickly discovered the high training tempo of the unit. "You were patrolling the border," he said. "And if you weren't patrolling the border, you were at gunnery. And if you weren't at gunnery, you were doing some kind of maneuver training, usually at Hohenfels." Hains also recalled the number of alert drills—most of which occurred during the pre-dawn hours. "When we'd get these alerts," he said, "they'd call you in the middle of the night…like three in the morning, and you'd jump in your tank, line up your platoon, and bust the gate, going to your first rally point." These alert drills tested how quickly NATO's frontline forces could respond to a hypothetical Soviet invasion.

After thirteen months in command of Hawk Company's 1st Platoon, Hains was unexpectedly promoted to Scout Platoon Leader—a promotion that reassigned him to Ghost Troop, wherein he took command of the six Bradley Fighting Vehicles in 3d Platoon.

Kilgore

Of the officers in Ghost Troop, Lieutenant Andy Kilgore's path to commissioning had been the most unorthodox. He began his career as an enlisted soldier with the Mississippi Army National Guard in 1985, "when I was still in high school," he added. Shortly after signing his name, however, someone recommended that he pursue college ROTC—the Simultaneous Membership Program (SMP) allowed National Guardsmen to enroll in an ROTC program while still serving their weekend duty obligations. Intrigued by the notion of being a citizen-soldier and an ROTC cadet, Kilgore enrolled at Mississippi State University and attended Basic Training at Fort Dix, New Jersey. "I went to Basic with 62 members of the Mississippi National Guard," he said, "about seven from my hometown."

As an SMP cadet, Kilgore attended Airborne School and discovered that he could receive constructive ROTC credit for his National Guard service. Thus, he commissioned as a National Guard officer after only *two* years in the ROTC program. At the time, the Army National Guard required only two years of college to commission as a lieutenant.

Andy Kilgore, Tank Platoon Leader. Initially assigned to the 1st Infantry Division (Forward) in Stuttgart, Germany, Kilgore transferred to the 2d ACR after his former unit was selected for deactivation. *Photo courtesy of Andy Kilgore*

Although National Guardsmen were citizen-soldiers who served part-time in their local communities, they went through the same training as their active duty counterparts. Moreover, during a time of war, they could be "federalized" by the President, and sent to fight overseas.

In the summer of 1988, Andy Kilgore, while still a college student, reported to Fort Knox, Kentucky for AOBC. Becoming an armor officer seemed like the natural choice for him—the Mississippi National Guard's home unit was the 155th Armored Brigade, and many of its prime postings were tank/cavalry billets. After graduating from AOBC, Kilgore returned to Mississippi State while continuing to serve as a part-time armor officer. "That's how I paid for the rest of school," he said. For the remaining two years of college, Andy served as a National Guard tank platoon leader and held a variety of other junior officer billets.

During this time, he deployed twice to the National Training Center (NTC) at Fort Irwin, California. NTC was in its infancy but, for the past few years, it had steadily become the Army's premier training center. As part of the post-Vietnam revitalization, the Army had established the Fort Irwin complex to train and evaluate maneuver units on a rotational basis. These maneuver exercises pitted the rotating units against mock aggressors who employed the same enemy tactics likely to be seen on the plains of Europe or other "hot spots" around the world.

Graduating from Mississippi State, Kilgore applied for active duty in the summer of 1990 and once again reported to Fort Knox. "They tried to make me go through AOBC again," he said—and he had to produce documentation confirming he had already attended the course. "So after about two weeks of doing nothing but running and working out, I finally got orders to Stuttgart, Germany," where he would be joining the forward-stationed elements of the 1st Infantry Division.

His first few days in Germany, however, were tinged by disheartening news. Kilgore arrived at 3d Battalion, 34th Armor Regiment (3-34 Armor) just in time to hear that the unit had been selected for deactivation. Indeed, now that Germany had been reunified (and the Cold War was effectively over) the US had begun drawing down its forces in Europe.

Because 3-34 Armor was now disbanding, Kilgore had little choice but to solicit other nearby units for a potential vacancy. Otherwise, he would spend the next several months idling at the VII Corps headquarters until the "powers that be" figured out where to send him. It was September 1990 and, with war on the horizon, he did not want to be at the mercy of a bureaucratic machine that would likely send him away from the conflict. Luckily, Andy and one of his fellow lieutenants landed a new assignment by knocking on doors and making calls to the 2d Armored Cavalry Regiment.

As a brand-new platoon leader in 2d Squadron, Kilgore was the most experienced lieutenant among his peers. He had been a tank platoon leader in the National Guard for two years and had shot more gunneries than any other junior officer in the squadron. Unfortunately, Kilgore arrived in 2d Squadron just as the unit was getting ready to deploy. Thus, he would have little time to bond with his troops before arriving in Saudi Arabia. Yet the bonds they would forge in the fires of combat would be the strongest bonds any of them would ever make.

GEOFFROY

Like Keith Garwick, Jeff Geoffroy was also a West Pointer—Class of 1989. Like every West Point class, the 1989 graduates had an unofficial graduation motto. For the Class of 1989, theirs was "No War Until '94"—a tongue-in-cheek reference to their five-year active duty commitment. The motto was both ironic and unprophetic, however, as more 1989 graduates served in Desert Storm than any other West Point class.

Geoffroy hailed from north-central Massachusetts, near the New Hampshire border. Like many of the officers in Ghost Troop, Geoffroy had come from a military family. His grandfather, a mechanical engineer by trade, had been a lieutenant colonel in the US Army during World War II. The younger Geoffroy knew he wanted to follow in his

Jeff Geoffroy, Tank Platoon Leader. A 1989 West Point graduate, Jeff Geoffroy selected his assignment to the 2d ACR because he wanted to serve along the Frontier of Democracy, and because he wanted to hit the slopes of the Bavarian Alps. *Photo courtesy of Andy Kilgore*

family's tradition—and had applied simultaneously to West Point and various ROTC programs. "But West Point was always my first choice," said Jeff. He received his acceptance letter just after Thanksgiving 1984.

At the Academy, Cadet Geoffroy excelled in the classroom—landing high enough in his class rank to earn a commission as an Armor officer with a prime posting to the 2d ACR in Germany. He had chosen the Armor branch due to its heavy firepower and rapid mobility. As the Cold War was still ongoing, it seemed that armored forces would play a decisive role in any future conflict against the latter-day Soviets.

Like many of his comrades in the 2d ACR, he had chosen Germany because it offered the best training opportunities for a young Armor officer. As a cadet, he had done CTLT with the 11th ACR in Fulda, Germany. Seeing the dynamics of their border mission, Geoffroy was determined to be assigned to a frontline ACR. "I picked the 2d ACR," he said, "because the Berlin Wall was still up, and 2d ACR had the latest equipment." But because the 2d ACR was headquartered in Bavaria, Jeff also realized that this posting offered numerous recreational opportunities. "I heard that Bavaria was closer to the Alps, and I liked to ski," he said with a chuckle.

Before arriving in Germany, however, Jeff reported to Fort Knox to complete AOBC. Among the highlights of AOBC were the tank battle simulations conducted in the Simulator Network (SIMNET). SIMNET was a vast complex that housed several tank simulators hooked into a computer network where students could engage one another in video game tank battles. Adding to the realism, each simulator contained a full-scale mockup of the tank's turret where students could assume the roles of loader, gunner, and tank commander. Even with its 8-bit graphics display, SIMNET was among the best virtual training tools in the Army.

Upon completing AOBC, Jeff reported to the 2d ACR's Regimental Headquarters in Nuremberg. "Paul Hains was my sponsor," he said. "He brought me out to a guest house for dinner"—a family of local Germans whom Paul had befriended. When the meal was served, however, Jeff was shocked to see that it was a delicately-cooked fish *with its eyeballs still intact*. "That was my first impression of Germany," he snickered.

Settling into his role as the 4th Platoon Leader (tanks), Geoffroy realized that he had an outstanding group of soldiers. Aboard his own tank, he had one of the top-rated gunners in the squadron. Still, like most young officers, Geoffroy spent his first few months in Germany coming to grips with the end of the Cold War mission. Throughout his military education, Jeff had been taught to fight and fear the Communists. For years, the Army's tactical doctrine had focused exclusively on defeating the Soviets and their Eastern Bloc counterparts in a protracted war on the European mainland. Now, in 1990, the Cold War was over and US Army Europe (USAEUR) struggled to find its mission in a time of geopolitical uncertainty.

"Ghost Troop was actually on the border," he said, "when the Wall came down." A few months later, the Inner-German Border was declared "open," and East German refugees poured into the countryside by the thousands. For Jeff Geoffroy, the end of the border mission was almost surreal. After nearly two generations of enduring the East-West divide, Germany was now on the path to reunification. But now that Communism had faded from Eastern Europe, Jeff wondered, as did many of his comrades, what the 2d ACR's new mission would become.

Lundquist

Waylan Lundquist, Andy Kilgore's platoon sergeant, had a much different path to the military than his young platoon leader. Prior to joining the Army in 1979, Lundquist had never ventured much farther than his hometown of Palo, Minnesota. "We grew up poor," he said, "and there

Waylan Lundquist, Tank Platoon Sergeant. Joining the Army in 1979, Waylan served in one of the first armored units to receive the new M1 Abrams Main Battle Tank.
Photo courtesy of Waylan Lundquist

was a lot of us [in the family] growing up in a pretty small space." Growing up in the rural townships of northern Minnesota, his interest in the Army was born of necessity—"I needed something to do after high school, and college seemed out of reach." His intent was to join the Army and earn enough money for college.

"When I went to the recruiter's office in Minneapolis," he said, "he showed me a picture of a tank with a *plow* on it"—an apparatus used to clear landmines. Prior to seeing that photograph, Waylan admitted that: "I didn't know the front end of a tank from the back end." But he was intrigued to the point where he enlisted as an armored crewman. When he flew to Fort Knox that summer, it was the first time he had ever been on an airplane.

When Lundquist arrived at the Fort Knox reception unit, he had shoulder-length hair, which earned him the nickname "Jesus" from the reception staff. "This was the late 70s," he added, "so a lot of guys were showing up with long hair, afros, and dark sunglasses." This was also a time when it wasn't popular to be a soldier. Indeed, neither the US Army nor the American public had fully recovered from the Vietnam Syndrome.

Despite the leftover animosity from Vietnam, however, he found the Basic Training unit to be an intense, fast-paced, and highly-professional outfit. "It was a challenge, to say the least," he recalled, "definitely not the kinder, gentler military of today." Indeed, by most accounts, it was still the rough-and-tumble Army of the mid-twentieth century. The enlistees wore Olive Drab fatigues and conducted physical training while wearing combat boots—"the Army didn't have tennis shoes back then."

While adjusting to the rigors of Basic Training, and avoiding the wrath of his battle-hardened drill sergeants, Waylan Lundquist had a chance encounter with Hollywood actor Bill Murray. In preparation for the upcoming film, *Stripes*, Murray had come to Fort Knox seeking to interview select trainees about their experiences. "There were six or seven of us that were selected," said Waylan, "and Bill Murray's asking us these pretty random questions." At one point, Murray asked Lundquist and his fellow trainees:

"What's the wildest thing you've ever done?"

While most of the trainees recounted their youthful pranks, Waylan Lundquist told a story of a friend who had attempted lascivious acts upon a stolen cow, to which Bill Murray replied: "I wanna party with you, cowboy!" The conversation left Murray so inspired that he added it to the script for the Basic Training scenes in *Stripes*.

Lundquist graduated from Basic Training that fall with an assignment to the 1st Cavalry Division at Fort Hood, Texas. But, as he recalled: "Fort Hood was pretty understrength in 1979." Indeed, the 1st Cavalry Division had recently converted from an airmobile unit to an armored division—a monumental reorganization. And considering the draconian defense budgets of the 1970s, it was a process that would take years to complete.

"We had five tank platoons in those days," Waylan recalled—each equipped with M60A1 Patton tanks. However, at the time of his arrival, Lundquist's company had barely enough resources to man and equip *two* platoons and the Company Headquarters. In fact, the company was so understaffed that the Executive Officer had to double as the 1st Platoon Leader. To make matters worse, the company leadership was still reeling from the bitterness of Vietnam. "The First Sergeant kept a bottle of whiskey in his drawer," said Waylan. Every day, most of the noncommissioned officers (NCOs) would file into the First Sergeant's office, where they would spend the afternoon drinking. "They were all drunks coming out of Vietnam," he said, "so we didn't have a lot of supervision."

The culture of the unit began to change, however, when they received the XM1 Abrams—the Army's newest tank. It was being fielded to stateside units on an experimental basis, hence the "XM1" designation. The M1 Abrams was a marked improvement over the M60-series. With improved armor, a lower silhouette, and a 105mm cannon, the M1 could presumably stand toe-to-toe against any tank in the Soviet arsenal.

"These were the first production-line M1 tanks rolling out of Detroit," said Waylan. As it turned out, this new equipment revitalized the unit's sense of professionalism. Alongside delivery of the new XM1, Lundquist also earned a promotion to Specialist (E-4), and an appointment as a tank gunner—a role typically reserved for a junior sergeant. Hence, aboard the Army's newest tank, he was now punching above his weight class.

After two years in the 1st Cavalry Division, Waylan unexpectedly received orders to the 2d Armored Division, at the opposite end of Fort Hood. Nicknamed "Hell on Wheels," the 2d Armored Division had likewise received its first contingent of M1 Abrams tanks, and Lundquist was among the many qualified crewmen sent to the newly-minted M1 units. The new assignment also earned him a temporary stint to Fort Greely, Alaska where he served on the delegation to test-fire the M1E1—an experimental, upgraded version of the M1 Abrams featuring a 120mm smoothbore cannon. Following its test trials, the M1E1 officially entered production as the M1A1.

Returning to Fort Hood from Alaska, Lundquist began to ponder his next assignment. It was now the winter of 1984, and he had been on the cutting edge of the M1 Abrams for nearly five years. Following the advice of a senior NCO, Lundquist requested an assignment to Germany. Some of the European-based units had already received the M1, and they needed experienced crewmen to man the frontline units along the Iron Curtain. Moreover, West Germany was considered prime posting for an NCO who wished to hone his craft as a young leader. Thus, in the spring of 1985, Waylan Lundquist arrived in Bamberg with orders to the 2d Squadron, 2d Armored Cavalry.

Initially, Lundquist was assigned to Hawk Company, the squadron's pure tank company. "I liked serving in the tank company," he said, "we had a different mission from the cavalry troops." Lundquist remembered that the tank company would act as a "mobile reserve," ready to provide an "armored punch" for any cavalry troop in contact. During his time in Hawk Company, Lundquist was promoted to tank commander and graduated from the prestigious Master Gunner School—a course that turned young NCOs into experts on all technical matters related to tank gunnery. Becoming a "Master Gunner" was considered the hallmark achievement for an armored crewman.

Waylan's most memorable moments in Hawk Company, however, revolved around border duty. During one border rotation, Waylan and one of his comrades witnessed an illegal border crossing near the town of Mödlareuth—a town that was split, literally, by the Inner German Border. In fact, the Americans often referred to it as "Little Berlin," because the border wall separating East Germany from West Germany ran directly through the middle of town. On this night, Waylan Lundquist saw an East German soldier cross the border into western Mödlareuth. Giving chase aboard his Jeep, Lundquist was determined to wrangle the fleeing Communist. The elusive guard, however, disappeared back into the darkness. "We spent a good part of the night trying to find that guy," he said.

Days later, however, Waylan discovered that this East German soldier had crossed the western border hoping to find the local speakeasy. "All the border guards used to jump the fence," he said, "and go into town to this little guest house and drink." It was a regular occurrence, and the local barkeeps usually winked at these illegal border crossings because the Communists were, after all, paying customers.

The irony, however, was not lost on the young Sergeant Lundquist.

Even the East German border guards were willing to risk life and limb to enjoy Western goods.

Waylan remained in Hawk Company for three years until his Master Gunner rating earned him a planning position with the squadron's Headquarters Troop. Now as a young staff sergeant, he wanted to become a platoon sergeant. Normally, it was a billet awarded to a sergeant first class, but given his border experience and Master Gunner certification, Waylan Lundquist had more technical knowledge and leadership experience than many senior sergeants in the squadron. When the squadron's command sergeant major, Freddie Chapman, announced the vacancy for a platoon sergeant in Ghost Troop, Waylan jumped at the opportunity. Five times, Waylan asked Sergeant Major Chapman to consider him for the job.

He asked Chapman first on a Monday.

"No," said Chapman. "And don't come back."

Waylan asked again on Tuesday.

"No!" yelled Chapman. There were more senior sergeants who had to be considered.

He asked again on Wednesday and Thursday.

"NOOOO!!" bellowed Chapman.

When Waylan asked *again* on Friday, Sergeant Major Chapman erupted into a furious tirade—ordering Waylan never to return to his office. Yet, surprisingly, Chapman called him on Monday morning, saying simply:

"Report to Ghost Troop."

Indeed, Lundquist had been the only staff sergeant in the squadron who was actively seeking the job. The Sergeant Major, although annoyed by his repetitive inquiries, admired Waylan's tenacity and assertiveness—qualities that would serve the young staff sergeant well in the deserts of Arabia.

THE GRATEFUL DEAD

The crewmen of Ghost 16★ (the sixth Bradley of 1st Platoon) were among the most colorful members in Ghost Troop. Consisting of Staff Sergeant Don Chafee (vehicle commander), Sergeant Andrew Moeller (gunner), Private First Class Patrick Bledsoe (driver), and Private Terry

---

★Pronounced "one-six".

The crew of Ghost 16—"The Grateful Dead." From left to right: Don Chafee, Patrick Bledsoe, and Andrew Moller. *Photo courtesy of Don Chafee*

Lorson (dismount), the crew had nicknamed their Bradley Fighting Vehicle "The Grateful Dead"—a nod to the psychedelic rock band fronted by Jerry Garcia.

At 38 years old, Don Chafee was the eldest member of Ghost Troop. He had initially joined the Army Reserve in 1977 as a supply specialist. Not satisfied with serving only "one weekend a month; two weeks a year," he soon applied for active duty and entered Fort Knox as a cavalry scout. Because he had already gone through Basic Training as a reservist, however, Chafee was permitted to enter the scout training during "mid-cycle."

During his time at Fort Knox, Don received training on the M113-series of cavalry vehicles. The M113 Armored Personnel Carrier was, by design, little more than a "battlefield taxi" intended to deliver infantrymen to the frontline. Since its debut in 1960, however, the Army had gradually adapted it to other roles: ambulance, fire support vehicle, mortar carrier, air defense platform, and, as of 1979, a surface-to-surface missile launcher. Dubbed the M901, this missile launcher variant was hailed as the next great step in mechanized cavalry before the M2/M3 Bradley could come online.

As a newly-minted cavalry scout, Chafee's first duty station was Fort

Lewis, Washington—not far from his hometown in Spokane. Fourteen months later, however, he received unexpected orders to Germany. Assigned to the 1st Armored Division, Chafee noted that many of his senior NCOs were Vietnam veterans—men with great tactical expertise, but who were now looking forward to their retirement.

Chafee served in the 1st Armored Division from 1979 to 1981—a time when the European contingent was still recovering from the post-Vietnam malaise. Gang violence, drug abuse, and other disciplinary problems were still prevalent—but not to the scale that they had been during the early 1970s.

Slowly but surely, the US Army in Europe was getting better.

Returning stateside, Chafee served at Fort Carson, Colorado, before returning to Germany in 1984. This time, however, he was assigned to Heilbronn, where he served on the task force guarding NATO's Pershing II nuclear missiles. Soon thereafter, he received orders back to Fort Knox for the new Bradley Leaders Course.

By the mid-1980s, the Army was fully integrating the Bradley into its frontline formations—a replacement for the aging fleet of M113-based cavalry vehicles. Although the Bradley carried more firepower, it had a higher silhouette and a smaller crew capacity. The Bradley's 25mm main gun automatically loaded its rounds through a chain-link feeder. However, operating the gun required strict synchronicity between the gunner and Bradley commander—the only two crewmen in the turret. For larger targets, the Bradley carried the dual-mounted, Tube-Launched, Optically-Guided, Wire-Controlled (TOW) missile launcher. While the TOW packed enough firepower to destroy an enemy tank, it was a troublesome weapon because: (a) it could not be fired on the move, and (b) the crew had to guide the missile onto its target. This increased the vehicle's exposure time and made it more vulnerable to enemy fire. Taken together, the Bradley's light armor, high silhouette, and low-caliber main gun put it at a disadvantage on the modern battlefield.

Don Chafee remained stateside until January 1988 when he received orders to the 2d ACR in Germany. Ghost Troop would be his home until January 1992. Although by now an experienced gunner and Bradley commander, Chafee spent much of his time in the arms room. Owing to his prior service as an Army Reserve supply technician, Chafee had been given the additional duty of managing the arms room, maintaining and inventorying smaller-caliber weapons such as the Colt 45 and the M240 machine gun. It was within the confines of Ghost Troop's armory that

Chafee learned of the Iraqi invasion on August 2, 1990.

Patrick Bledsoe, the driver aboard Ghost 16, grew up on the beaches of Oxnard, California. The son of a Navy family, he shocked his relatives when he announced his decision to join the Army. In February 1988, he enlisted under the Delayed Entry Program—a recruiting system that gave enlistees one calendar year to settle their academic and/or personal affairs before entering Basic Training.

Reporting to Fort Knox in the spring of 1989, he endured the normal variety of tribulations meted out by the drill sergeants. While taking their verbal abuse in stride, however, he admittedly enjoyed the tactical training. Land navigation, reconnaissance tactics, scout gunnery, and demolition were among his favorite subjects. "I was a Boy Scout, but I had never done *anything* like this," he chuckled.

Like many of his comrades, Bledsoe wanted an assignment in Europe. The Cold War had begun to thaw, but he wanted to experience life along the Inner German Border. His orders initially assigned him to the 8th Infantry Division in Baumholder. But, for reasons unknown, those orders were amended at the eleventh hour. His new destination was now the 2d Armored Cavalry Regiment.

Settling into 1st Platoon, Ghost Troop, Bledsoe realized just how intense the unit's training tempo could be. On the day of his arrival, the troop was coming back from another rotation along the East German border. Within days, they would redeploy to Grafenwoehr for gunnery. "I was assigned to Ghost 15 for the first few months I was there," he recalled. "We qualified gunnery and then went right back to the border." Following another rotation to Hohenfels, Bledsoe and his crew went to REFORGER 90. "So, it was pretty busy the first few months I was there," he said.

Throughout most of his time aboard Ghost 15, Bledsoe served as the proverbial "JAFO" (Just Another F★cking Observer)—the colloquial name for the dismounted scout who sat in the back of the Bradley. Although the dismounted scout was typically the lowest ranking member of the Bradley crew, there was no shortage of work for him to do. Bledsoe had to load the ammunition for the 25mm main gun and load the TOW missiles into their launcher. Reloading the TOW in combat, however, could be a perilous task—the dismounted scout had to exit the Bradley, manually insert the missiles into their respective tubes from the rear hatch of the vehicle, and hope that he didn't get shot in the process. And when he wasn't performing his regular duties aboard the vehicle, the JAFO was prime fodder for guard duty in the field. Returning from REFORGER, however, Bledsoe was made the driver aboard Ghost 16, joining Chafee and the rest of the "Grateful Dead."

The youngest member of Ghost Troop, seventeen-year-old Terry Lorson, entered Basic Training on July 25, 1990—just eight days before the Iraqi invasion. Prior to reporting to Fort Knox, one of his friends had asked him:

"Hey man, aren't you worried about going to war?"

But Terry shrugged it off.

After all, it was the summer of 1990. The Cold War was over and the Soviet Union was now an ally. Yet, on the morning of August 2, Lorson and his fellow recruits awoke to the news that Iraq had invaded Kuwait. "It was a *big* surprise to us," he said.

Although the recruits were not allowed to watch news programs, Lorson and his comrades would often catch glimpses of the television in the company's day room. News broadcasts ran recurring footage of the coalition's buildup in Saudi Arabia. "We'd see pictures of guys wearing gas

Private Terry Lorson, the dismounted "JAFO" aboard Ghost 16. At seventeen years old, he entered Basic Training on July 25, 1990—eight days before Iraq invaded Kuwait. *Photo courtesy of Terry Lorson*

masks, and we were wondering what the heck was going on over there."

Like many of his fellow Ghost Troopers, Terry Lorson was the product of a military family. His mother was an Air Force veteran who settled her children in northeastern Pennsylvania following her enlistment. Growing up in that Air Force family, Lorson credited his mother with inspiring him in the ways of military service. But, for reasons he never fully understood, he gravitated more towards the *Army* than the Air Force. And like many of his fellow cavalrymen, Lorson received his initial training on the M901 missile-launching variant of the M113. He never saw a Bradley until he deployed to the Persian Gulf.

Upon completing Basic Training, Terry learned that he had been posted to West Germany. Although the Cold War had ended, and the Inner German Border had collapsed, he was still happy to receive an overseas assignment. When he arrived at the Welcome Center in Frankfurt, however, a senior sergeant nonchalantly greeted him with the news:

"Your unit's going to the desert."

Indeed, he had been assigned to the 2d ACR.

"By the time I got to Ghost Troop," he said, "they had already shipped their vehicles and equipment out." Barely four weeks after his arrival, Terry Lorson was on a plane to Saudi Arabia as the dismounted JAFO aboard Ghost 16.

Michalec

Rick Michalec, the commander of Ghost 36 (sixth Bradley of 3d Platoon), hailed from the working-class suburbs of St. Paul, Minnesota. He enlisted in the Army straight from high school in the summer of 1984. Attracted to the high-tech, revitalized Army of the 1980s, Michalec chose the path of a cavalry scout. Rick had planned to serve only his initial term of service, then parlay his GI Bill benefits into a civilian career. But it wasn't long before he discovered how much he enjoyed the life of a cavalryman.

He reported for Basic Training in August 1984. Following graduation, however, his first duty assignment was, coincidentally, still at Fort Knox. Indeed, for the next eighteen months, he served in the 194th Armored Brigade as an M901-based scout. However, as part of the ongoing effort to build up NATO's footprint along the Iron Curtain, Michalec received orders to Germany in the spring of 1986.

All told, Michalec didn't know what to expect in his new assignment. "I was intimidated," he said, "because at Fort Knox, I was on 113s and it was pretty laid back." The frontline cavalry units in Germany, however, were renowned for their high operational tempo and uncompromising standards of tactical fieldwork.

Michalec arrived in 2d Squadron just as the unit was converting to the M2/M3 Bradley Fighting Vehicle. Most of his comrades were happy to be shedding the M113-series, but few regarded the Bradley as a qualitative "improvement" over its predecessor. According to one famous quip, as heard in the film *Pentagon Wars*, the Bradley Fighting Vehicle was:

"a troop transport that can't carry troops; a reconnaissance vehicle that's too conspicuous to do reconnaissance...and a quasi-tank that has less armor than a snowblower, but carries enough ammo to take out half of DC."

Rick Michalec takes a moment to relax at the Squadron Barracks in Bamberg, Germany. He was one of the youngest Bradley commanders in 2d Squadron, and among the youngest certified "Master Gunners" in the regiment.
Photo courtesy of Rick Michalec

Still, Rick Michalec was proud to be part of an elite unit along the Frontier of Democracy. "They put you to work right away," he said. "The things that they expected you to know in a very short period of time was pretty intimidating for me." Border operations, tactical surveillance, REFORGER plans, and cyclic gunneries were among the many topics that Michalec had to master within his first few months in the 2d ACR.

After four years in Ghost Troop, Rick had distinguished himself as a dismounted scout, driver, and Bradley gunner. His performance in the latter billet was such to earn him a seat at the Bradley Master Gunner Course in Fort Benning, Georgia. "The school was about four months long," he said. But for many of his classmates, the Iraqi invasion shortened their stay at the Master Gunner Course. Indeed, Michalec was in class on the morning of August 2, 1990. Within weeks, many of his classmates were being recalled to their home stations as their units deployed. "The guys from Fort Bliss,"—then home to the 3d Armored Cavalry Regiment and several Patriot missile batteries—"got pulled right out of school." The students from Fort Hood, Texas (1st Cavalry Division) were the next to be recalled.

Luckily, Rick was able to complete the Master Gunner Course. But he returned to Germany just in time to receive the news that 2d ACR had been alerted to deploy as well.

CARDOSA

When Ruben Cardosa joined the Army in 1982, the era of "Be All You Can Be," was in full swing. Born and raised in San Antonio, Ruben's interest in the military was piqued when he saw the 1981 comedy, *Stripes*. In many ways, the Bill Murray film capitalized on (and perhaps accelerated) the thawing of America's resentment towards its military. The film highlighted two misfits who unwittingly found their calling in the Army. Then, through a combination of irreverence and ingenuity, these misfits saved their friends from the clutches of the Red Menace.

Inspired by the film, Ruben and his best friend joined the Army, although each man chose a different specialty. His score on the Armed

Ruben Cardosa, stands proudly atop the rear deck of his tank. Initially assigned as the gunner aboard Ghost 43, Cardosa later became the vehicle's commander.
Photo courtesy of Ruben Cardosa

Services Vocational Aptitude Battery (ASVAB) was such that it qualified him for armored cavalry. He initially joined the Army as a cavalry scout, assigned to the 3d ACR at Fort Bliss, Texas. Serving in 2d Squadron, 3d ACR, his squadron commander was, coincidentally, Lieutenant Colonel Don Holder, who later commanded the 2d ACR during Desert Storm.

Settling into his new role as an M113 scout, however, Ruben was shocked when he was suddenly re-classified as a tank crewman. As it turned out, by the mid-1980s, the Army was understaffed on tankers, and overstrength on cavalry scouts. Thus, to normalize its ranks, the Army began converting its excess cavalrymen into armored crewmen. He then reported back to Fort Knox in 1986 for familiarization on the M60-series tank.

This crash course on tank operations came with a follow-on assignment to Fort Carson, Colorado with 2-34 Armor, then part of the 4th Infantry Division. During this year-and-a-half tour, Ruben had the chance to see the burgeoning National Training Center (NTC) at Fort Irwin, California. At the time, the training center still had little in the way of infrastructure. That Fort Irwin was located in the middle of the Mojave Desert (forty miles from the nearest town) added to the desolation. Still, it gave Ruben the opportunity to work alongside Fort Irwin's "Visually Modified Vehicles," or VISMODs as they were known. VISMODs were typically older vehicles (like the M551 Sheridan) that were used by the mock aggressor units, and were modified to resemble a Soviet T-72 or BMP.

The following year, Ruben received unexpected orders to Germany—assigning him to the 2d ACR. Having served in the 3d ACR, Ruben was pleased to be going back to a cavalry unit. Unlike conventional armor units, the cavalry units had a culture all their own—the "best of the best" in the US Army's mounted force. When he arrived in Ghost Troop, however, he was shocked to learn that the unit was equipped with M1 Abrams tanks. To this point, he had only served on M60s and had zero knowledge of the M1's operating systems. Apparently, the Army had neglected to send him to an M1 familiarization course prior to his arrival in Germany, a place where the M60 was a dying breed.

Undaunted, Ghost Troop's leadership sent him down the road to the VII Corps' M1 familiarization school at Grafenwoehr. Upon his return, he would join 4th Platoon (tanks) as the gunner of Ghost 43. The timing was fortuitous, as he graduated the M1 course just in time to accompany Ghost Troop on another border guard mission, where he became the gunner aboard Ghost 43. "Every three months, we rotated onto the border for 30 days," he said. "Then, we'd come back and shoot gunnery." Taken together, these operational requirements left the unit with little time in garrison.

Although Ruben enjoyed gunnery and maneuver, he was less enthusiastic about the border mission. Indeed, border operations were more constabulary in nature. One trooper described it as a combination of police work, surveillance, and intelligence-gathering. Units that rotated along the border had to be briefed (and subsequently debriefed) by local CIA operatives. They also had to coordinate their daily operations with the *Bundesgrenzschutz*—the West German Border Police.

In fact, Ruben was standing along East Germany's border on the day it officially ceased to exist. Watching the East German refugees flow unrestricted into the countryside, he wondered if 2d ACR would still have a mission.

Four months later, he would have his answer.

CARPENTER

John Carpenter, the driver of Ghost 34, grew up with a deep-seated fascination for the military—inspired by his grandfather's service in World War II. Hailing from the rural townships of Colorado, John enlisted in the Army directly from high school in 1988. Within a few weeks of taking his oath, he was on a plane to Fort Knox.

Although his rural upbringing had prepared him well for the rigors of Army life, he still remembered Basic Training as a "mind bender" and a "culture shock." Early on during his training, he admitted to his drill sergeants that he could play the trumpet—a confession that unwittingly landed him as the

John Carpenter, the driver of Ghost 34. Joining the Army in 1988, Carpenter distinguished himself in Basic Training as an excellent runner and a self-admitted horrible bugler. *Photo courtesy of John Carpenter*

company bugler. But, as he remembered: "I butchered every one of those bugle calls," as some of the notes and tempos were beyond the range of what he could comfortably play. Indeed, "Taps;" "Reveille;" and "Call to Mess" all sounded like garbled, off-key versions of their true form.

He partially redeemed himself, however, through his abilities as a runner. For better or worse, the US Army was a "runner's culture"—and fewer things would earn a soldier more respect than a fast run time. At various points throughout Basic Training, soldiers were required to pass the Army Physical Fitness Test (APFT)—a three-event test consisting of push-ups, sit-ups, and a two-mile run. In many ways, the APFT was considered a benchmark for soldier success. For even if a soldier wasn't tactically strong, he could still buoy some respect if he had a high APFT score. John Carpenter—already a gifted trooper (minus his bugle calls)—earned a solid reputation in Basic Training for his exemplary run times.

As his time at Fort Knox came to a close, he discovered that he had unexpectedly been assigned to Germany. "I did not request it by any means," he said. "But I was on active duty, and I wasn't married. So, why not?" Like many of his comrades, when John arrived in Bamberg, his gaining unit was in the field.

"They were shooting gunnery," he recalled.

Such was the tempo in 2d ACR. Whether firing gunnery, conducting maneuvers at Hohenfels, or guarding the East German border, these ACRs trained so frequently that the incoming personnel rarely had a chance to meet their comrades while in garrison.

Assigned to Ghost Troop's 3d Platoon, Carpenter became the driver for Sergeant First Class Joseph Woytko—the platoon sergeant. Woytko, like his contemporaries, was a tough-as-nails NCO who demanded excellence, and got results. Gunnery was a top priority for Woytko's men. Indeed, they had fired several 1,000-point engagements over the past year—a perfect score on the US Army's Bradley Gunnery Tables.

Aside from gunnery, Carpenter also recalled the surrealism of his first tour along the border. Back home, news outlets had boasted about the impending "thaw" between East and West. But from what he could see along the Inner German Border, the Cold War was still very much a reality. "It was like something out of a movie," he said—guard towers, border markers, roving patrols—all the popular images of life along the Frontier of Democracy. The surrealism intensified after the border fell in 1990. East German refugees poured into the countryside—many of them driving their two-cylinder, state-built Trabant automobiles. "It was pretty overwhelming," he said. But these geopolitical dynamics would pale in comparison to the storm brewing in the Persian Gulf.

On August 2, 1990, John Carpenter and several of his friends were in the Rec Room at Camp Coburg—one of many guard stations along the now-disintegrating Inner German Border. "I remember seeing it on TV," he said. But he never anticipated that, within a mere four months, he would be on a plane to Saudi Arabia—part of a growing coalition to roll back the tide of Iraqi aggression.

HARRISON AND FOLEY

Tony Harrison and Brian Foley were cut from the same cloth. Both were proud sons of the South, and both had been inspired by their family lineage of military service. Tony had grown up in Fort Walton Beach, Florida, while Brian hailed from the rural suburbs of Orange, Texas. Both men took readily to the military lifestyle and both were assigned as tank crewmen in Ghost Troop's 2d Platoon.

Tony Harrison joined the military at age 26. He had been a successful plumber, but suddenly decided that "I wanted to try something different."

Tony Harrison, the driver aboard Ghost 22. Prior to joining the Army, Harrison had been a successful plumber. Wanting to try something new, he enlisted as an armor crewman at the age of 26. *Photo courtesy of Tony Harrison*

Thus, in March 1988, he sauntered into the local recruiter's office, asking about career options in the United States Army. His subsequent score on the ASVAB was such that the recruiter suggested Tony pursue a technical career. His response was swift:

"No! I want to be where the action is!"

When the recruiter offered him a slot as an armored crewman, Harrison signed his name on the dotted line.

Although still relatively young, Tony Harrison was older than most of his fellow recruits. Most of his contemporaries were between the ages of 17-21. Despite the age difference, however, he had no problems keeping up with the younger ilk. But regardless of age, every recruit met their match on the slopes of "Agony," "Misery," and "Heartbreak"—the three steepest hills at Fort Knox. Every Basic Training post had its landmark for physical exhaustion. Whether a hill, tower, or obstacle course, every recruit recalled their encounter with said landmark as a rite of passage. The so-called Agony, Misery, and Heartbreak hills were popular among drill sergeants who wanted to take their recruits on endurance runs.

Throughout Basic Training, Harrison knew that there was a *possibility* of going to war. But in 1988, the thought of imminent hostilities seemed laughable. The Soviet Union was no longer the "menace" it had once been, and the first round of US military cutbacks were on the horizon. Like his comrade John Carpenter, there was nothing calculated about Tony Harrison's assignment to Germany. It was simply where the Army had placed him. Although the Cold War was winding down, the defense posture in Western Europe was such that it gave American soldiers access to the best equipment. Indeed, while many stateside units still operated the M60 tank, nearly all the European-based units had converted to M1s.

Arriving at the VII Corps Welcome Center in Frankfurt, Harrison learned that he had been assigned to 2d Squadron, 2d ACR. "They picked me up in a Humvee," he said, "and drove me through the 1st Armored Division compound," en route to the regiment's gated complex. As the Humvee rolled up to the 2d ACR's main gate, Harrison saw the entryway sign emblazoned with:

"If You Ain't Cav; You Ain't Sh★t!"

That's when being a cavalryman suddenly became real. "It was a different world," he said, "and I liked it!" The armored cavalry regiments trained at a higher intensity and tempo than any other mechanized units in Europe. "You were always on the go," he remembered. Assigned to 2d Platoon, he found his home as the driver of Ghost 22.

Brian Foley (bottom left) and the crew of Ghost 24. Hailing from the Gulf Coast of Texas, Foley served as the loader aboard Waylan Lundquist's tank.
Photo courtesy of Brian Foley

Brian Foley, the loader aboard Ghost 24 (Waylan Lundquist's tank) had taken a slightly different path to Germany than his friend Harrison. Foley was another young trooper who had joined the Army while still in high school—a product of the Delayed Entry Program. He had debated whether to join the Army or the Air Force, but ultimately selected the Army because he liked the "big guns" of the M1 Abrams tank.

Reporting to Fort Knox in June 1989, Foley admittedly enjoyed Basic Training. He found that his rough-and-tumble, East Texas upbringing had prepared him well for the challenges at Knox. "I didn't have a problem keeping my mouth shut around the drill sergeants," he said, "but I did have a problem keeping my mouth shut around other soldiers," he added with a chuckle. Foley, not one to suffer fools gladly, would push back against fellow recruits who would try to throw their weight around, or those who refused to be team players.

Like Harrison, Foley likewise had his encounters with Agony, Misery, and Heartbreak—one of which gave him his first blister as a recruit. Still, he remembered the tank crew training as the thrill of a lifetime. During the trainees' first gunnery, for example, they would rotate through three of the four crew positions—driver, loader, and gunner. Firing the tank's main gun, and feeling the thrust of its recoil was a sensation like none other. The main gun breech had a massive recoil that could reach the back of the turret's wall. Tank crewmen had to stay clear of the breech as the recoil was strong enough to sever a human hand.

After graduating in September 1989, Foley found himself thrust into the frontline formations along the Iron Curtain. Like Tony Harrison, Foley was another unwitting selectee for posting to Germany. "I got there [to Ghost Troop] on a Friday after everything had closed," he remembered. "So, my platoon took me out and introduced me to German alcohol!" German society had a more liberal view towards alcohol, and its consumption was never discouraged at social gatherings. In fact, many Germans considered it rude not to share a drink with friends. Beer and liqueurs, after all, were among Germany's top exports.

As it turned out, Foley had arrived in Ghost Troop just as they were transitioning from base-model M1s to the upgraded M1A1s—"so we went from having a 105mm gun to 120mm." The higher-caliber main gun and improved fire controls made the new M1A1 even deadlier than its groundbreaking predecessor. And when Ghost Troop went to its first qualifying gunnery in the new M1A1s, Foley remembered that: "It was the first time I had ever seen heavy snow!"—an unseen novelty in the humid flatlands of East Texas.

By the summer of 1990, Harrison and Foley had earned their due as armored crewmen. On the afternoon of August 2, both men were at Grafenwoehr, intently focused on completing the current round of tank gunnery. Second Platoon had shot several 1,000-point engagements and they were intent on maintaining their reputation as the strongest tank crews in the squadron. When news of the Iraqi invasion broke, neither Harrison nor Foley knew what to make of it. "I knew where Iraq was," said Foley, "but I knew nothing about Kuwait." At first, both men thought that the conflict would simply pass them by. After all, the 2d Armored Cavalry wasn't an "expeditionary" force.

Its sole purpose was to defend Western Europe.

"DEFORGER 90"

As news of the Iraqi invasion spread, many didn't know what to make of Saddam's aggression. Younger troops like John Carpenter and Brian Foley expected the conflict to run its course without their involvement. Others were excited by the prospect of going to war. After years of squaring off against mock aggressors along the Inner-German Border, they would finally have the chance to prove themselves in combat. Others had cause for concern. Aside from the brief interludes in Panama and Grenada, the US had not seen a full-scale ground war in nearly twenty years. With memories of Vietnam still fresh in their collective minds, many older troops wondered if the US had the political fortitude to withstand another high-intensity conflict. Others were simply dumbfounded. Still, the same question lingered on every trooper's mind:

"What was Saddam thinking?"

As it turned out, Saddam Hussein had carefully calculated the risks and determined that the odds were in his favor. He was certain that his army—the fourth-largest in the world and equipped with the latest in Soviet armor—would make short work of any rescue force that came to liberate Kuwait. He wagered that the Americans would lead a military response against Iraq but, as he famously quipped, America was "a society that cannot accept 10,000 dead in one battle." Indeed, the memories of Vietnam were as galvanizing to Saddam Hussein as they were disheartening to the American public. He was confident that after the Americans had suffered a few thousand casualties, they would sue for peace on Iraq's terms.

Saddam Hussein rose to power in 1968 following the Ba'ath Party revolution. As vice-president under Ahmed Hassan Al-Bakr, Saddam introduced a number of popular reforms—including the nationalization of Iraqi oil and promoting free education. As Al-Bakr's health declined during the 1970s, Saddam gradually became the *de facto* ruler of Iraq. However, as he ascended to the presidency, Saddam ruled Iraq with a brand of brutality reminiscent of Hitler and Stalin. He nevertheless seemed poised for a long and prosperous rule of Iraq until his fortunes changed in the wake of the Iranian Revolution.

Fearful that the Ayatollah's rhetoric would galvanize Iraq's Shiite majority, Saddam preemptively invaded Iran on September 22, 1980. The ensuing Iran-Iraq War would last eight years and ended in a bloody stalemate that claimed more than 300,000 Iraqi dead. Aside from the untold cost in human suffering, the conflict left Saddam straddled with a multi-billion-dollar war debt, most of which had been financed by Kuwait. But rather than pay his debt to the Kuwaiti government, the "Butcher of Baghdad" simply invaded his neighbor to the south. To justify the invasion, Saddam reignited the long-standing border dispute between the two countries. He also made false allegations that the Kuwaitis had been slant-drilling Iraqi oil and that they were deliberately trying to keep the price of oil low by producing more than OPEC's set quotas. Kuwait held ten percent of the world's oil reserves and generated 97 billion barrels of crude each year. Thus, Saddam reasoned that if he could not repay his debt, he would simply annex the tiny emirate and take over its petroleum industry.

In the days leading up to the invasion, satellite imagery revealed several thousand Iraqi troops massed near the Kuwaiti border. On July 25, 1990, US Ambassador April Glaspie met with Saddam Hussein to discuss the sudden mobilization. Aware of his increasingly hostile rhetoric in the border dispute with Kuwait, Glaspie stated:

> "We can see that you have deployed massive numbers of troops in the south. Normally that would be none of our business, but when this happens in the context of your threats against Kuwait, then it would be reasonable for us to be concerned. For this reason, I have received an instruction to ask you, in the spirit of friendship—not confrontation—regarding your intentions: Why are your troops massed so very close to Kuwait's borders?"

Saddam assured the ambassador that he was committed to finding a diplomatic solution. In his conversation with Glaspie, Saddam informed her that Egyptian leader Hosni Mubarak had arranged for Kuwaiti and Iraqi delegations to meet in Riyadh and that more negotiations were scheduled in Baghdad. Moreover, he relayed to Mubarak that "nothing serious will happen" with Kuwait before the negotiations began.

Glaspie concluded her meeting with Saddam by stating that the US had "no opinion" of Arab-Arab conflicts such as the border dispute with Kuwait. "All that we hope," she said, "is that these issues are solved quickly." But for Saddam Hussein, the only quick solution was to destroy the emirate of Kuwait.* Thus, on the morning of August 2, 1990, more than 100,000 Iraqi troops and several hundred Iraqi tanks stormed across the border, the spearhead of an eighty-mile blitzkrieg into Kuwait City. Encountering only piecemeal resistance, Iraqi tanks thundered into the heart of the Kuwaiti capital, assaulting the city's central bank and carrying off with its wealth. A coordinated air-ground attack decimated the Dasman Palace, home to Kuwait's ruler Emir Jabel al-Amhad al-Sabar. The emir himself and a few members of his staff barely escaped with their lives as they fled Kuwait by helicopter. The last transmission made over the state-run radio network was an appeal for help.

What truly shocked the international community, however, was the sheer barbarity of Iraq's Army. At times, it seemed that Iraqi soldiers were torturing Kuwaitis simply for their own amusement. Tank crews randomly fired their guns into places of commerce while other soldiers loaded their cargo trucks with various items of loot, laughing and shouting "Ali Baba! Ali Baba!" According to Middle East Watch, a New York-based human rights group,

> "Summary executions of scores of people have been carried out in detention centers and in public, in front of their families. Families are being terrorized by midnight searchers and there have been arbitrary arrests of close to 5,000 people—including children. Detainees are subject to torture…and kept in crowded and unsanitary conditions. Collective punishments are meted out for acts of armed resistance: houses are burned, buildings demolished, curfews imposed and families of suspects detained. Occupation authorities interfere with food distribution, warehouses are seized, food cooperatives

---

* Following the invasion, Glaspie drew fierce criticism for her remarks, with many accusing her of giving Saddam tacit permission to invade Kuwait. However, she acted entirely within State Department protocol. American diplomats do not have license to make threats or implications of military force. Also, per State Department policy, the US does not take sides in border disputes between two of its allies.

plundered, and food distribution volunteers detained, terrorized and in some cases executed."

The United Nations responded by issuing their normal variety of condemnations. Economic and military sanctions soon followed while President Bush authorized the first US deployments to the region. On August 6, 1990, elements of the US XVIII Airborne Corps received their orders to the Persian Gulf. These forces included the 82d Airborne Division, 101st Airborne Division (Air Assault), and the 24th Infantry Division (Mechanized). Within days, the aircraft carriers *Saratoga* and *Eisenhower* were steaming towards the Persian Gulf while coalition air squadrons began pouring into Saudi Arabia by the hundreds. This first wave of deployments became known as "Operation Desert Shield"—a deterrent against Saddam Hussein lest he try to invade the Kingdom of Saud.

Watching the crisis unfold from their dayrooms in Western Europe, the men of Ghost Troop wondered if they would be the next to deploy.

As it turned out, that call came on November 9, 1990.

In a televised address, President Bush announced that the US VII Corps in Europe would deploy to Saudi Arabia. By now, it had become increasingly clear that the Iraqis would not respond to a diplomatic solution. These additional forces demonstrated the President's resolve that the occupation of Kuwait would be reversed by force if necessary. Aside from the 2d Armored Cavalry, the units identified by President Bush included the 1st Armored Division; the forward-deployed 3d Brigade of the 2d Armored Division★; the 3d Armored Division; and the 11th Support Command. This deployment would raise the number of US ground forces in the Persian Gulf to more than 400,000 by the end of December.

Every man in Ghost Troop remembered where he was when he heard the announcement. Most were at their homes or in the dayrooms of their barracks, huddled around the TV anticipating the President's address. Joe Deskevich had just returned from dinner when he heard the announcement over the Armed Forces Network radio. He promptly called the Howitzer Battery commander.

"Hey sir, I heard on the radio that we're going to war."

★ The 2d Armored Division was headquartered at Fort Hood, Texas. Two brigades resided at Fort Hood, while the third brigade was forward-stationed in Garlstedt, Germany.

"Yep. No PT in the morning," replied the commander.

Jeff Geoffroy heard the announcement, ironically, via the local German news station. "I had taken two semesters of German at West Point, so my German was pretty basic. But I could hear the German announcer say: 'Saudi Arabia,' 'Bamberg,' and *Zweites Aufklärungsregiment*—German for 'Second Reconnaissance Regiment.'" The next morning, Jeff jumped onto his Kawasaki Ninja motorcycle and sped towards the Bamberg barracks. Meeting his platoon sergeant near the entryway, their exchange was brief and matter-of-fact:

"Sir, did you hear the news?

"I think so," Jeff replied.

"Yeah, we're going to Saudi Arabia."

Pat Bledsoe and his roommates had had a premonition that they would deploy. They knew that if additional forces were called into the Persian Gulf, the coalition would need armored assets to counter Iraq's tank-heavy force. The two forward-stationed armored corps in Germany were the closest assets to the Saudi theater. So, as far as Bledsoe was concerned, it was only a matter of time before President Bush decided which of the two corps he would send to the Middle East. It thus came as little surprise to him when the president announced that VII Corps would deploy. "I remember I ran to the payphone outside of our barracks with a handful of change and called home. I talked to my mom and told her I was going. I wanted her to hear it from me."

Some Ghost Troopers learned of the deployment while participating in the squadron's promotion board—an oral exam that evaluated young soldiers for promotion to their next rank. Without warning, the new squadron commander, Lieutenant Colonel Matthew Sullivan (not his real name), barged in and said, with his usual deadpan delivery:

"Gentlemen, we have been alerted to deploy."

Sergeant Major Freddie Chapman, took pause from his duties as the board president and replied, "Ok sir, we'll get to it. We've got a board to finish."

Without another word, Sullivan departed, closing the door behind him.

Most of the officers in 2d Squadron were well-liked and well-respected by their soldiers. Lieutenant Colonel Sullivan, however, was neither liked nor particularly respected. A diminutive figure with a prominent nose and a high-pitched, nasally voice, Sullivan had recently been awarded command of the squadron by stroke of luck—"after a popular and widely respected lieutenant colonel had been removed from the command list," thereby catapulting Sullivan from the alternate to the primary list. A 1972 West Point graduate, Sullivan had come of age during the post-Vietnam years and his leadership style reflected the bitterness of the era. To boot, he was sarcastic, condescending, and at times belittling. He also didn't seem to trust his subordinate officers. During one of their pre-deployment seminars, for example, Major Macgregor, the squadron operations officer, was conducting a map exercise with the troop commanders, discussing "various missions and potential schemes of maneuver for the squadron." The first mission they discussed was a "movement-to-contact." Hearing Macgregor's brief, however, Sullivan interrupted with a question about "actions on the objective."

"The question took me by surprise," Macgregor said, because it showed that Sullivan didn't truly understand the nature of a movement-to-contact drill. "Movement-to-contact operations," Macgregor recalled, "are conducted when the enemy's exact location and disposition in the zone of attack are unknown. In other words, finding and ultimately destroying the enemy are the true purposes of the maneuver. An objective in the form of a large circle is usually placed on the map for such operations, to generally orient the movement of the attacking force."

Macgregor hesitated to answer Sullivan's question because "I had no desire to make the squadron commander feel foolish in front of the troop commanders." Still, Sullivan persisted until Macgregor finally corrected him, telling the commander that their objective was simply a map control point upon which they orient the squadron's movement.

Upon hearing this, Sullivan blew up.

"He told me I was completely wrong and insisted that my response to him bordered on disrespect." The troop commanders winced as Sullivan's tirade grew stronger and louder. Macgregor could hardly fathom it; after producing nothing but good results for his commander, Sullivan was accusing him of incompetence *and* disrespect. "Furious, he announced a break in the discussion until after lunch and stormed out of the room."

After Sullivan left the room, Macgregor said nonchalantly, "Well, I guess I will start planning to seize the objective," and dismissed the troop commanders for lunch. Shortly thereafter, however, Sullivan returned to the room with a copy of the field manual *Cavalry Operations*, FM 17-95, in his hand.

"Doug, you were right. I looked it up in the manual. I f*cked up."

As the squadron commander turned to leave, Macgregor thought to himself, "I can only guess what would have happened if there had been no 'book answer' to turn to, as is so often the case in the real world of combat." Still, he admired that Sullivan "had the humility to admit he was wrong. I respected him for it then, and I still do." Nevertheless, it underscored Sullivan's brusque and temperamental way of handling things. Many of the troops were thrilled by the prospect of going to war, but none were excited at the thought of riding into battle under Sullivan's leadership.

While tempering their anticipation for the upcoming deployment, Ghost Troop received an unexpected change to its leadership. The current troop commander, Captain Eric Tamke, had completed his tenure of command and was being promoted to the squadron maintenance staff. Now taking the reins of Ghost Troop was Captain Joseph Sartiano, a 1984 West Point graduate who had been a starting member of the Army Football Team. As Major Macgregor described him: "Sartiano looked like a combination of Dean Martin and Andy Garcia, with a deceptively relaxed manner." Macgregor recalled that the young captain's demeanor was refreshing—especially in an Army where uncaring martinets seemed to be the norm.

At the time, Joe Sartiano was working at the Seventh Army Training Center, and he desperately wanted troop command. Approaching Macgregor, Sartiano wasted no time: "I really want to get out of the Seventh Army Training Center," he said, "and command a cavalry troop in the 2d Cavalry." He added that HR McMaster—one of his West Point classmates, and currently commanding Eagle Troop—had told him great things about 2d Squadron. Macgregor abruptly stopped him:

"If you want to command a cavalry troop, that's fine."

Macgregor asked Sartiano how his family would feel about relocating from Grafenwoehr to Bamberg—a move of more than 70 miles. "Joe said he was divorced," Macgregor recalled, "and that moving across Germany was not an issue. We talked for approximately ten minutes. I liked what I saw and heard."

So, too, did the men of Ghost Troop.

By the time Sartiano arrived to take command, John Mecca had been working feverishly with Captain Tamke, developing troop-level tactics and procedures for desert warfare. Drawing lessons from the North Africa campaign during World War II, it was clear that tanks were the weapon of choice. Aside from anti-tank mines and long-range artillery, few weapons posed a serious threat to the tank. The deserts of Iraq would be ideal terrain for armored warfare, but the enemy had no shortage of mines or artillery.

In many ways, the tactics and concepts for desert warfare closely resembled those of naval warfare. Like the carrier groups and dreadnought battleships, tanks in the desert kept tight formations and engaged one another from standoff distances. Their maneuvers were also relatively slow—not prone to sudden bursts of acceleration and/or hopping between points of defilade, as was common during the annual REFORGER exercises.

Joe Deskevich, meanwhile, continued to refine Ghost Troop's fire support operations. As the field artillery liaison to Ghost Troop, Deskevich brought to bear the full range of indirect fires. "We already had a pretty robust training schedule," he said, "and every Tuesday we would go out to the local training area behind the kaserne and practice fire support procedures." Deskevich and his men would drill the scouts and tankers on calling for fire and "figuring out different ways to employ the mortar section," he added. "I learned a couple of things they don't teach you in FAOBC. The mortars are very similar to artillery, but they can do things that artillery can't." In close contact, mortars could provide immediate suppressive fires to troops in contact, with minimal collateral damage, and with a smaller margin of error than cannon artillery. Plus, there was no "wait time" for priority of fires.

Historically, field commanders relied too much on artillery and neglected their own mortar teams. Because mortars were closer to the frontlines, commanders had a tendency to keep them silent so as not to draw enemy fire. This would cost the frontline troops precious time in combat because close-range targets were difficult to engage with long-range artillery. In Ghost Troop, however, Deskevich ensured that his mortar teams were fully integrated into the unit's planning process.

Within a few days of receiving their alert, Ghost Troop had all their tanks and fighting vehicles loaded onto flatbed railcars, ready to ship to the port of Bremerhaven. Because the vehicles had to get into theater quickly, the tanks and Bradleys were shipped to Saudi Arabia in their woodland camouflage paint scheme. They would be repainted "desert tan" once they arrived at the Saudi port of Al-Jubail. All throughout the night, Ghost Troop worked tirelessly to ensure that their vehicles were properly loaded onto the railheads. It was a painstaking process, and one that required the utmost precision from the drivers and their ground guides. Indeed, one false move could flip a tank upside down.

Elsewhere in Europe, the 1st and 3d Armored Divisions loaded their vehicles as well. Tanks, Humvees, and various howitzers sat silently aboard the midnight trains as they meandered through the countryside. This mass movement reminded many of the annual REFORGER exercises, only now the equipment was leaving Germany. In fact, their motor pools depopulated so quickly that the troops began calling it "DEFORGER 90"—a name that would forever become synonymous with their deployment to Saudi Arabia.

"Those first few days were insane," said Joe Deskevich, "but everyone was pretty excited." Surprisingly, there were no outward feelings of dread or apprehension. "It was like we had just made it to the Super Bowl; now let's go kick some ass!" As the men of Ghost Troop began stowing their sidearms and personal gear, there was a collective sense that this upcoming deployment would be the adventure of a lifetime.

Some, however, anticipated fighting a horrendous battle in the deserts of Iraq. Defense analysts and other "experts" anticipated as many as 20,000 casualties on the first day of the ground war. And this estimate didn't take into account what would happen after coalition forces met the Republican Guard. "I probably should have been more scared than I was," said Waylan Lundquist. After all, the Iraqi Army had strength in numbers, and they had recent combat experience on familiar terrain. The Americans, on the other hand, would be riding into battle on equipment that was untested in combat. "But I remember thinking to myself," Waylan continued, "these guys [the Iraqis] don't stand a chance." Indeed, Ghost Troop had unshakable confidence in their equipment and in their fellow soldiers.

As fall turned to winter, Captain Sartiano and Major Macgregor began teaching classes on desert survival. In the sands of Arabia, temperatures could reach in excess of 100 degrees during the day but then fall below freezing at night. Theoretically, a soldier could survive in the desert for six days without food, but would perish after only a day without water. A good rule of thumb, therefore, was to make every soldier drink six quarts of water daily. Soldiers were also advised to wear as few layers as possible during the day and, with steadily increasing workloads, they could fully acclimatize to the desert within two weeks.

Adjusting to the climate, however, was only part of the equation. The desert winds could reach hurricane-force velocities and the resulting sandstorms often lasted for days. The sand also made it harder to maintain one's equipment. Without twice-daily cleaning, even the finest grains of sand could render a tank engine inoperable. Troopers also had to be mindful of their hygiene. During the North African campaign, for example, Rommel lost more than 28,000 soldiers in the Afrika Korps from disease. Thus, to ensure a trooper's longevity in the desert, a "field-expedient shower" had to be taken at least every other day. If no water was available, then talcum or foot powder could be used to dry bathe. Troopers were also encouraged to change their undergarments daily (including skivvies, shirts, and socks) and keep them as dry as possible.

While learning the fundamentals of surviving in the desert, Ghost Troop also received intelligence briefings on the Iraqi Army. Following the invasion, every news outlet had reported *ad nauseam* that Iraq had the world's fourth-largest army, but little had been said about their disposition or their fighting tactics. These intelligence briefs, however, indicated that Iraqi forces had much in common with the latter-day Soviet Army. But for as tough as the Iraqi Army sounded, their air force was primitive by NATO's standards and Saddam lacked a viable air defense network. The war against Iraq, if and when it came, would not be won through air power alone, but an aerial campaign could make short work of Saddam's air assets and soften up his ground forces.

The biggest threat, however, were Saddam's chemical weapons—especially Sarin and Mustard Gas. Saddam had used both chemical agents against the Kurds and the Iranians, the effects of which were seen by Ghost Troop through raw documentary footage. Thus, the men received extensive training on how to prepare for a chemical/biological attack. A soldier's first line of defense against a chemical agent was his M17 protective mask. In the event of a chemical attack, the soldier had nine seconds to properly don and seal his mask, else he would succumb to the surrounding gas. The M17 would filter out any harmful air, and retain the soldier's vital functions, but would do nothing to save his exposed skin from harm. Thus, if time permitted, the soldier could also don his chemical protective suit, a rubber outer garment lined with charcoal to neutralize any chemical agents on the soldiers' skin or uniform. Although US intelligence had estimated that the likelihood of a chemical attack was small, the men of Ghost Troop were well-prepared to fight against it.

For the rest of November, Ghost Troop set to work doing practice maneuvers in the squadron's local training area. Since their vehicles had already been loaded onto ships, the troopers did everything on foot. Nonetheless, these foot-based battle drills built their confidence for maneuvering in the desert. To that point, Ghost Troop had maneuvered only within the valleys and forests of the German countryside. Meanwhile, Joe Deskevich's comrades in the Howitzer Battery had loaded up their M109 Paladins, but were keeping busy with their own abbreviated gunnery drills. "They drew howitzers from the rental stockyard at Grafenwoehr," he said—and were firing rounds to keep their crews proficient in the days leading up to their departure.

As Thanksgiving approached, the soldiers wrote their last wills and testaments and had their pre-deployment photos taken. It was a somber but necessary part of the deployment process; if a soldier didn't return from battle, his portrait would be ready to display at the memorial service. Following their month-long marathon of survival classes, mock maneuvers, and pre-deployment metrics, Ghost Troop earned a 3-day pass for the weekend of December 1. However, the respite was abruptly cancelled when Regimental Headquarters announced on Sunday that 2d Squadron would board its flight to Saudi Arabia the following Tuesday, December 4.

From there, the men of Ghost Troop scrambled to the various local shops—gathering as many personal and sundry items as they could. Batteries, Walkmans, Gameboys, and electric razors were among the various consumer goods plundered by the young troops. "We were buying cigarettes, Ramen Noodles, jars of peanut butter, Spam, Vienna Sausages—whatever we could stuff into the corners of our bags," said John Carpenter. In fact, the onslaught of rabid shoppers was so sudden that the Post Exchange (PX) couldn't keep up with the demand. "Those shelves were *empty* by the end of the weekend," one trooper recalled. As it turned out, the Army's supply system was in no better shape—each trooper received only one set of the Desert Battle Dress Uniform and no desert boots.★ The Army's uniform manufacturer simply couldn't keep pace with the oncoming deployment.

As Paul Hains remembered, every man in Ghost Troop received their set of desert fatigues along with one "floppy hat"—the iconic, fully-brimmed headgear reminiscent of the jungle patrols during Vietnam. The lack of desert boots, however, meant that every trooper would have to wear his black leather boots into Saudi Arabia. This was unfortunate because none of the black boots had breathable pores…and the black

---

★ The Desert Battle Dress Uniform was a six-color arid camouflage pattern with black-on-white spots. Many soldiers affectionately called it the "chocolate chip cookie dough" pattern. After the Gulf War, the Desert Battle Dress Uniform was replaced by the three-color Desert Combat Uniform.

leather would only amplify the desert's heat. To make matters worse for Hains, none of his new uniforms fit him properly. "I'm five-foot-six, and maybe 140 pounds soaking wet, but they gave me Extra-Long pants and a shirt that swallowed me whole," he said. "I looked like a six-year-old wearing my Dad's clothes!" Protest as he may, the supply depots simply had no more sizes to accommodate his small stature. Not satisfied with the ill-fitting uniform, however, Paul traded his shirt with another Ghost Trooper. "I got a slightly better top," he said, "which was still too big, but not as big as the first one I got. As for my pants, I ended up taking a pair of scissors and I cut eight inches off the bottom. I looked like a clown. And I ended up going through all of Desert Storm with that stupid uniform!"

By 7:00 AM on the morning of December 3, every trooper had his M-16 rifle, Colt 45 sidearm, and his duffle bags outside the Bamberg barracks. Military buses were scheduled to pick them up within the hour and take them to the Nuremberg airport, where a group of chartered Pan Am flights were waiting on the tarmac.

After a heart-rending round of goodbyes, the troopers of 2d Squadron lined up according to their assigned travel numbers and boarded the buses for their dreary ride into Nuremberg. "It was very, very sad," said Rick Michalec. "As the buses were pulling away, you're looking at your family, and if you had kids, it was just brutal. There were a lot of teary-eyed guys on the bus who wouldn't look at each other. Everybody was looking straight ahead because they didn't want their buddies to see them getting emotional."

Once at the airport, the military and municipal authorities slowly herded the troopers away from the main concourse. Because the troops were carrying weapons, the airport staff didn't want to frighten any civilian travelers. After the officers and NCOs performed one more "head count," Ghost Troop climbed aboard the massive Boeing 747s. Meanwhile, Joe Sartiano and Ghost Troop's First Sergeant, Dwight Roark, boarded separate planes so that one of them may live if the other's plane crashed on the way to Saudi Arabia.

Brian Foley recalled that the flight to Saudi Arabia was eerily silent. Aside from a few token conversations with the flight attendants, most of the troopers kept to themselves. The shock of leaving their families hadn't quite worn off—and they still didn't know what to expect in the Gulf. Five days earlier, the UN Security Council had passed Resolution 678. The resolution, for what it was worth, gave Saddam Hussein a deadline of January 15 to withdraw his forces, or face military action. Still, the Iraqi dictator showed no signs of backing down.

While tempering their thoughts on the Persian Gulf crisis, Ghost Troop enjoyed Pan Am's selection of in-flight movies: *Dick Tracy*, a film adaptation of the popular comic book, starring Warren Beatty; *Narrow Margin*, an action film with Gene Hackman; and *Cadillac Man*, a light-hearted comedy starring Robin Williams.

After a brief layover in Rome, the squadron was airborne once again but, as the 747 vectored over the Mediterranean, its cabin suddenly depressurized. "So we had to fly back to Rome," said Joe Deskevich. "And the Italian Army surrounded our plane!" Indeed, because the Pan Am flight had been designated a "military transport," carrying armed soldiers, it had to be guarded accordingly. "We sat on the tarmac in Rome for eight hours," said Joe, while Pan Am's ground crews tried to fix the plane. "I had never been on a plane that had depressurized," he added. "It felt like someone had taken hot nails and jammed them into your ears; it hurt so freakin' bad!" Deskevich also noted that the plane's poor condition was likely due to Pan Am's deteriorating finances. Despite its long-standing reputation as the unofficial "flag carrier" of the United States, Pan American World Airways had been teetering on the brink of collapse. In a last-ditch effort to keep the airline solvent, the US military awarded Pan Am the contract to fly troops from Germany into the Persian Gulf. However, on December 4, 1991—precisely one year after delivering Ghost Troop into Saudi Arabia—Pan American World Airways ceased operations.

Touching down at the Dhahran Airport, Ghost Troop met the full fury of the desert climate. "We opened that door," said Waylan Lundquist, "and this god-awful heat comes rolling in." It had been barely 31 degrees when the squadron left Germany. Now they were feeling the full blast of a triple-digit heat index. To make matters worse, the morning fog had not yet subsided. In fact, Waylan recalled the fog being so heavy that he could not see the bottom step of the mobile stairway leading them onto the tarmac. "When we walked off that thing," he continued, "you were literally supposed to grab the person in front of you"—so dense was the fog that Ghost Troop had to make a "human chain" simply to keep accountability of their personnel. As every trooper sallied off the plane, a group of VII Corps supply soldiers stood nearby, handing out liter-sized water bottles for immediate consumption. "I remember looking at this thing," said Keith Garwick, "and I was thinking this is an odd way to go to war: carrying a liter-size bottle of Arrowhead water."

Many Ghost Troopers recalled their first moments in Saudi Arabia as a blur of mass confusion. "It was chaotic getting off that plane," said Jeff

Geoffroy, and the troopers marveled at the puffs of white sand that kicked up from under their feet as they meandered around the tarmac.

Suddenly, a caravan of 1970s-era buses rumbled into sight.

"It was like something you'd see on TV," said Rick Michalec; "these raggedy old buses that looked like they had been *taped* together—funny colors, tassels on the windows, various crap stacked onto the roof." The drivers were Arab nationals commissioned by the Saudi government to drive the troops to the port of Al-Jubail. Practically none of them spoke English and they all drove like madmen—speeding, slamming their brakes, drifting between lanes, and even going off-road to navigate shortcuts.

Fitting nearly twenty-five soldiers onto each bus, Ghost Troop suffered the first leg of its white-knuckle drive from the airport onto the Trans-Arabian Pipeline (Tapline) Road. Tapline was one of the few paved roads in the Saudi wilderness and it ran parallel to its namesake pipeline over the length of the Arabian Peninsula. Because the bus caravan stretched for miles back to Dhahran, there was frequent "stop-and-go" traffic along the first leg of the trip. "It took us a long time to get to Al-Jubail," said Tony Harrison, "because each one of the bus drivers got lost." Aside from their reckless driving and poor navigation skills, Don Chafee was even more perplexed when he discovered that "some of these drivers were drag-racing each other!"—clustering their vehicles three-abreast as they sped down the highway.

As the morning sun rose over the dunes, Ghost Troop got its first sustained look at the Saudi desert. "In the American deserts," said Keith Garwick, "you had mountains, cactus groves, and coyotes. But in Saudi Arabia, it was a *pancake*...flat as far as the eye could see." Terry Lorson agreed. "It felt like you were in the middle of nowhere...looking around 360 degrees and not seeing a damn thing." Aside from the occasional oil rig seen in the distance, and the streetlights along Tapline Road, the Saudi desert was indeed flat and featureless.

At four o'clock in the afternoon, the Troop arrived at the VII Corps' Initial Staging Area, a small cantonment known as the "Dew Drop Inn." It was a bustling camp just outside the port of Al-Jubail, where the incoming units anxiously awaited the delivery of their vehicles. "It was a tent city," Lorson recalled, "with new tents being added every day." These tents were standard-issue GP Mediums—each capable of housing approximately 20-25 soldiers—arranged on a grid system comparable to a modern-day suburb. By Army standards, the Dew Drop Inn was a plush arrangement, but the camp was only half-completed by the time Ghost Troop arrived. As it turned out, the National Guard construction battalion hadn't finished building it yet. But after suffering their white-knuckle drive down Tapline Road, the troopers were happy just to be off the buses.

When Keith Garwick saw the National Guard engineers pouring their concrete foundations for the VII Corps tents, he suddenly realized that Desert Shield was not going to be a simple "show of force" mission—the US was serious about its buildup in the Middle East. "You can't pour this much concrete," he said, "if you don't intend on being here for a significant amount of time. That's a pretty heavy investment."

The following day, December 6, Squadron began sending troops to the loading dock at Al-Jubail to meet their incoming vehicles. Ironically, when Andy Kilgore arrived at the port to retrieve 2d Squadron's vehicles, he found his old battalion from the 1st Infantry Division (Forward). Although they had been tapped for deactivation, they had somehow made it onto the deployment roster to Saudi Arabia. "They were the ones downloading our squadron's tanks off the ship," he recalled. "It was nice to see familiar faces handing off our vehicles."

For Ghost Troop, life at the Dew Drop Inn revolved around three tenets: maintenance, hygiene, and trying to stay busy. After they returned from the dock at Al-Jubail, the troopers began taking their vehicles to the VII Corps "paint tents"—where each M1 Abrams and M2 Bradley received its conversion to desert tan. Jeff Geoffroy noted that the paint they used was a meticulously-engineered Chemical Agent Resistant Coating (CARC) paint. "So, if you had chemical weapons fired at your vehicle, you could hose off the chemical agents and it wouldn't peel the paint."

After the paint had dried on every vehicle, one trooper devised a plan to make a unique Ghost Troop "emblem" that could be painted onto each tank and Bradley. "I don't remember who came up with this," said Geoffroy, "but we took some cardboard and made stencils of a palm tree with crossed sabers underneath. It was that palm tree symbol from Rommel's Afrika Korps during World War II—and we painted that on our vehicles."

Ghost Troop then lined up each of their vehicles into picture-perfect rows, just as they had done at the squadron motor pool in Bamberg. Even in the desert, Joe Sartiano wanted his troops to retain the normal discipline of garrison life. As the last vehicle sallied onto the line, each of the crews began loading their ammunition for battle. Each M2 Bradley received 1,500 Armor Piercing rounds each; 480 High Explosive rounds, and 10 TOW missiles. The tanks, meanwhile, received forty main gun rounds each—enough for Ghost Troop to kill 300 enemy tanks.

Aside from the copious stores of ammunition, Paul Hains marveled at the extra weapons they had received—including AT-4s★ and hand grenades. "Better to have it and not need it," he said, "than need it and not have it." In fact, each of his Bradleys was carrying so much lethality that their dismounts hardly had any space to sit, let alone store their personal gear. Thus, for the Bradley crewmen in 1st and 3d Platoons, they stowed their personal bags on the side of the Bradley, tying the straps into whatever apertures they could find.

Despite the influx of AT-4s and main gun rounds, however, Hains was surprised that VII Corps had allocated them barely enough ammunition for their Colt 45s. "We were one of the last units in the Army to carry the Colt 45"—before the M9 Beretta became the standard-issue sidearm. Thinking that he would receive at least a dozen rounds per soldier, he was shocked when First Sergeant Roark delivered him only 100 rounds for the entire platoon. This averaged only three rounds per soldier. "I guess they didn't count on us using our sidearms."

For personal hygiene, Ghost Troop had crudely-fashioned, hastily-built, wooden latrines and gravity-fed showers. At the end of each day, human excrement from the latrines would be mixed with diesel fuel and set on fire. Squadron encouraged everyone to shower at least three times a week. But getting the troopers to adhere to that schedule was another matter; most preferred to clean themselves with baby wipes. Then, too, some troopers avoided taking showers because they didn't want to bathe in the frigid water given to them by VII Corps. For even in the desert, it seemed impossible to heat water without the assistance of a nearby flame. Waylan Lundquist recalled his own experience with the gravity-fed showers: "The water was so cold it literally took my breath away!" His solution, however, was to boil the water in an ammo cannister suspended from the back deck of his tank. The M1's turbine engine produced enough heat to boil water or cook food within minutes. Although the practice was usually discouraged, most unit commanders passively allowed the impromptu heating so long as no one got injured.

Still, the troops placed a higher priority on cleaning their uniforms and equipment rather than their own bodies. Given the harsh conditions

---

★ The AT-4 is a shoulder-fired, anti-tank weapon, more commonly referred to as a "bazooka."

of the desert, one could hardly blame them. "We found out that the desert wasn't really 'sand'," said Pat Bledsoe, "it was dirt and fine dust that stuck to *everything*. But we were good at keeping our weapons clean." Trying to keep their uniforms clean, however, was more of a challenge. "We had a five-gallon pail where everyone washed their clothes," recalled Don Chafee. But by the time five or six troopers had washed their clothes, the pail would have more mud than water. "You were washing your clothes in mud," said Chafee. "You'd get the sand out. But it didn't actually clean your clothes."

Regular applications of foot powder and a change of socks were typically enough to ensure that a soldier's feet stayed healthy. But even the most disciplined powder applications couldn't prevent the occasional bout of athlete's foot. "And I had the worst case of athlete's foot that you could imagine," said Brian Foley. "It was to the point where my toes were swelling up." To make matters worse, the desert sand was highly abrasive to his black leather boots. In fact, many troopers had gone to wrapping their boots in duct tape simply to keep the soles intact.

"At the Dew Drop Inn," said Ruben Cardosa, "the main focus was: Water, Water, Water." Indeed, hydration was key to survival in the desert. Crates of bottled water became skyscrapers in their own right, as every day the Army shipped them into Saudi Arabia by the thousands. Every soldier received three bottles of water daily, and was literally forced to drink each one. Aside from the forced hydration, Ghost Troop also had to endure the forced consumption of nerve agent pills. Considering that Saddam had used chemical agents during the Iran-Iraq War, US forces administered these experimental pills as a potential safeguard against the more deadly aspects of Sarin and Mustard Gas.

The latter of the three tenets (trying to stay busy) was always the most difficult. There was only so much that a soldier could do throughout the day; and idle time often led to mischief or having one's thoughts run away with him. "Everyone was writing letters or playing spades," Michalec recalled. But as the days passed, men like Don Chafee began to wonder if this deployment would amount to anything more than desert guard duty. "I thought this would be a 'show of force' along the Saudi Arabian border," he said. Many in Ghost Troop wondered if an American presence would pressure Saddam into complying with the UN's demands. "We were prepared to fight," Chafee continued, "but we were hoping we wouldn't have to." His biggest concern, however, was ensuring that Terry Lorson, barely one month out of Basic Training, became proficient in his tasks aboard the M2 Bradley. As Lorson admitted: "I had never touched or even seen a Bradley until I got to the desert." But while Chafee pondered the fate of his crew, his comrades in 1st Platoon found more juvenile ways to pass the time: many of them took turns killing ants with a magnifying glass or chasing the local lizards.

Other troopers stayed busy by organizing their own sports teams. For their first few days at the Dew Drop Inn, the troops turned their desert cantonment into a gridiron, playing tackle football in between their daily duties. Their game schedule was cut short, however, when one of the regimental pilots broke his leg during a forward pass. Thereafter, the regimental commander, Colonel Don Holder, put a stop to the football games—only allowing non-contact sports.

For Brian Foley, however, his stay at the Dew Drop Inn was far from pleasant, as both his camera and his film were stolen by marauding comrades. He never learned the identity of the thief, but sufficed to say that he was irate over the loss of his photographic keepsakes. "If someone's going to steal my camera, fine, but leave the film because that's something I can't replace!" Foley had already taken dozens of photographs and now he would never have the chance to get them developed.

For some troopers, however, the most disheartening aspect of life at the Dew Drop Inn was the order to throw away their personal stashes of *Penthouse* and *Playboy*. In war, soldiers often pursue lustful passions simply to maintain their sanity. And the men of Ghost Troop were no different. But 2d Squadron, in its moralistic fervor, demanded that every trooper burn his peepshow magazines. Some troopers complied with the order, but others simply hid their magazines into whatever empty spaces they could find aboard their vehicles.

The following day, Ghost Troop left the primitive comforts of the Dew Drop Inn to the regiment's tactical assembly area (TAA), 180 miles northwest of Al-Jubail. Code-named TAA Seminole, Ghost Troop's sector lay due east of the Wadi al-Batin valley and just north of Tapline Road—the flat, barren, and largely uninhabited portion of the Saudi desert. Because TAA Seminole was so far away, 2d Squadron loaded their tanks and Bradleys onto "low-boy" trailers for the drive along Tapline Road.

But for Ghost Troop, simply getting their tanks and Bradleys onto the trailers seemed like a monumental task. For although these trailers were rated to handle "heavy equipment," it was clear that they had never handled any vehicles as heavy as an M1 Abrams or M2 Bradley. For example, when Paul Hains drove his Bradley onto his assigned trailer, the trailer's rear tires blew out, causing the Bradley to teeter onto its side.

While most of the Troop loaded onto buses (driven once again by reckless Arabs), every tank and Bradley driver had to travel in the cab of whichever tractor-trailer was carrying his vehicle. For most of the tank and Bradley drivers, the trip with their loaded vehicle was uneventful. Pat Bledsoe, for example, recalled that his driver let him take a nap in the sleeper cab as they drove down Tapline Road. For the bus-riding troops, however, it was a repeat of the heart-pounding, white-knuckle drive that they had endured from the airport at Dharan. Aboard Waylan Lundquist's bus, his driver abruptly decided to stop the vehicle along the side of the road and go to sleep. Mark Hayes, one of Ghost Troop's mechanics who was seated alongside Waylan, immediately sprung to his feet, shaking the driver and shouting:

"No, dude! You can't go to sleep!"

Not heeding the young mechanic, the Arab driver simply grumbled, rolled over, and continued his nap. Exasperated, Hayes hopped into the driver's seat and began driving the bus himself. "We had no idea where we were going," said Lundquist, "but there was only one road—Tapline Road." Hayes stayed on the concrete thoroughfare until he saw the cluster of "low-boy" trailers on the horizon—indicating that he had found TAA Seminole. With that, he pulled over the bus and horded his comrades off the vehicle, leaving their sleepy-eyed driver to his blissful slumber.

Within the confines of TAA Seminole, Ghost Troop began building its desert cantonment. Each tank and Bradley were set up along a perimeter that stretched nearly 300 yards in diameter, oriented north facing the Iraqi border. "When we got to TAA Seminole," said Waylan Lundquist, "there were dead sheep and [feces] everywhere." In fact, the TAA was so cluttered with feces and animal carcasses that the M88 had to drive its plow blade into the ground and, literally, clear the area of biohazardous material. To ensure tight communication among the vehicles, Captain Sartiano had the soldiers run a copper landline between each one. Every piece of the wire network was then buried firmly underneath the sand.

By the end of their first week at TAA Seminole, the troopers had made their cantonment livable—complete with tents, wooden latrines, and shower stalls. Most of these early days passed without incident—often described as "another day; another sunburn"—but on the morning of December 16, Ghost Troop experienced its first Scud missile alert. Squadron Intelligence had reported that the Iraqis were planning a test-fire of their Scud-B missile—the same variant used to deliver chemical weapons. Thus, every Ghost Trooper donned his chemical protective suit and gas mask, waiting for the purported 7:00 AM launch. Luckily, the strike never came, but the scare had been enough to put the men on edge for the rest of the day. They still had no idea whether Saddam would unleash his chemical weapons against Allied forces; and every trooper hoped he would never have to find out.

Meals typically consisted of T-Rations, commercially-supplied "Top Shelf" entrees, or the ubiquitous Meals Ready to Eat (MRE). The MRE was a self-contained field ration sealed in a lightweight slip package. Delivering more than 1,000 calories per meal, the MRE featured sealed entrees such as spaghetti, beef stew, and normally had three side courses, including a dessert. Though not a fancy or even fulfilling meal, it was a step up from the canned rations of the Vietnam era. Still, the MRE was a frequent target of ridicule among American soldiers—often referred to as "Meals Rejected from Ethiopia" or "Multiple Rectal Explosions."

As Ghost Troop settled further into its daily rhythm at TAA Seminole, the troopers began to ponder what they'd be facing in the upcoming months. Indeed, by the middle of December it had been four and a half months since Iraq invaded Kuwait. No progress had been made on the diplomatic front and the Butcher of Baghdad was now less than one month away from his January 15 deadline.

LIFE IN THE DESERT

At the Regimental TOC*, Major MacGregor listened intently as Colonel Don Holder, the Regimental Commander, and his staff gave the first operations brief since arriving in Saudi Arabia. Their mission was clear: the 2d ACR was to find the Republican Guard. Major Doug Lute, Macgregor's S-3 counterpart at the regiment, began the brief with his usual round of introductions. Each of the staff officers were presented according to their function—Personnel (S-1), Intelligence (S-2), Operations/Plans (S-3), Logistics (S-4), and Civil Affairs (S-5). Each of them explained that "the regiment's task would be to find and fix the Republican Guard so that it could be destroyed by the main body of VII Corps' divisions. Lute's initial presentation was consistent with what an armored cavalry regiment would do in Central Europe, deploying forward of, or along the flanks of, an armored corps. Only the geographical setting was different."

According to Lute, the 2d ACR was to set the terms and tempo of the battle. Upon first contact, the regiment would establish a base of fire, allowing freedom of maneuver for the VII Corps divisions to destroy the Republican Guard's main forces. "If the enemy is moving," Lute said, "the regiment destroys the advance guard battalions and develops the situation. If the enemy is stationary, the regiment fixes the enemy, finds his flanks, and assists in getting the divisions into the fight." Macgregor recalled that Lute's briefing could have been written for a movement-to-contact operation against the Soviet's Third Army in the Fulda Gap.

Next in line was Major Campbell, the Regimental S-2. He described the Iraqi Army as a Soviet-like enemy with an order of battle reminiscent

---

*Tactical Operations Center; pronounced "tock."

of the Great Patriotic War. He described the Iraqis' disposition as a three-tiered defense around Kuwait. The first tier consisted of twenty-six infantry divisions, "totaling nearly 310,000 men," forward-deployed along Kuwait's border with Saudi Arabia. "Behind them were another eighty to ninety thousand troops in nine Iraqi Army mechanized divisions of higher quality, including eight Republican Guard divisions. These were located well to the rear of the main Iraqi defense." The final tier was the main body of the Republican Guard. From the daily intelligence briefings, however, one thing was certain: these forces along the Kuwaiti border were growing at an ever-increasing rate. By the US Army's estimate, many of these frontline units were battle-hardened cadres of the Iran-Iraq War.

Finally, Colonel Holder said his piece, "noting that the details concerning the exact deployment of the divisions behind the 2d Cavalry had yet to be worked out." Holder favored attacking the enemy on a narrow front, with the 2d Cavalry leading the Corps' tactical formations. "When the main body of the Republican Guard was detected, Holder said, we would hand off the battle to the divisions, moving to the flank or striking northeast to Basra, depending on circumstances at the time."

"No surprises here," Macgregor later said.

But Macgregor doubted that their movements in the open desert would reflect the traditional maneuvers in Central Europe.

In fact, since their arrival in Saudi Arabia, Macgregor had taken great strides to break free from the static defense mentality of the Fulda Gap. For example, when the combat engineers arrived in their bulldozers to dig fighting positions, Macgregor declined. The notion of digging their combat vehicles into static positions, where they would be immobilized against an enemy attack, made no sense.

Meanwhile, the men of Ghost Troop gradually adjusted to life in the desert. When living outdoors, a trooper was often told: "If you don't mess with the wildlife, it won't mess with you." Nevertheless, every man in Ghost Troop had run-ins with the local desert fauna—snakes and scorpions being among the worst offenders. "We caught a couple of snakes inside the perimeter," said Pat Bledsoe—including desert vipers and Arabian cobras. A few of the scouts had even gone to wrangling scorpions and pitting them against each other to see if they would fight to the death. "We put the scorpions in a box, but they never attacked each other," said Rick Michalec. "I never did see a good scorpion fight," he lamented.

According to Ruben Cardosa, however, the worst company at TAA Seminole were the flies. "They got into *everything*," he recalled—including their food and water. Cardosa was perplexed by how these flies could even survive in the desert. But he devised a clever way to trap and kill the pesky vermin. Using an empty water bottle, Cardosa would stuff it with dehydrated food. He then waited for the flies to populate along the bottom of the plastic bottle, and killed them while they gorged themselves on the dehydrated MRE contents.

Some of the biggest offenders among the local wildlife, however, were the goat and camel herds belonging to the local Bedouin tribes. As Bedouin families roamed the Saudi desert, they often let their livestock roam free. The problem, however, was that these animals often vectored into 2d Squadron's training area—leaving a trail of feces and other excrement in their wake. This quickly got the attention of the Regimental health officers, who noted that free-ranging fecal matter posed a serious risk for cholera, dysentery, and typhoid fever. Their solution, recalled Jeff Geoffroy, was simply to dissolve the fecal matter using the same chemical decontaminants reserved for the aftermath of a chemical attack. "They sprayed that stuff to kill all the potential microbes," said Geoffroy.

Other wildlife encounters were quite humorous. "I remember seeing a lot of camels," said Brian Foley. "But what cracked me up was how they ran. They looked like they were running in formation. Four camels running in a column, with one running alongside them, as if they were calling cadence. And they were always in step, too! It was the neatest thing to watch because they were wild animals, yet they were running in formation."

Realizing that inactivity was poisonous for morale, Joe Sartiano devised a daily "battle rhythm" to keep his troops occupied. This included a host of tactical exercises and daily crew drills to maintain their proficiency. Performing these drills during the day, Ghost Troop would post soldiers on guard duty at night. Manning their vehicles, these rotating guards would scan the horizon through the eerie glow of their night vision devices, searching for any activity on the Iraqi side of the border. Most of the guard shifts passed without incident, but late one night, a young private from Ghost Troop got lost while trying to find his way to the latrine. "When the stars were out, you had this incredible illumination because there was no atmospheric clutter," said Waylan Lundquist. "But when there's no moon and its overcast, you can't see a thing."

And tonight was one of those nights.

The wayward private had wandered some 800 meters beyond the squadron perimeter before he started screaming for help. Luckily, a few tankers from Eagle Troop had heard his cries, and used their vehicle lights to guide him back into the perimeter. After that, every vehicle had to be adorned with glowsticks at night, and strings were tied from the vehicles to the latrines.

In the morning, after guard duty had ended, the troopers would then conduct "Stand To"—a tradition reaching back to the French and Indian Wars. "Stand To" meant that every soldier on the line would awaken and man his weapon, ready to fight. This became a standing tradition in the Anglophone armies because the Native Americans were notorious for attacking at dawn. Once Stand To had been completed (normally one hour after sunrise), the troop would begin conducting their personal hygiene.

After Stand To, the troopers would move into their various crew drills. The tanks in Ghost Troop, with their four-man crews, would practice target acquisition and "fire command" drills. During these drills, the gunner would scan the horizon within a set range determined by the platoon leader. Once the gunner identified an enemy target, he would alert the crew by shouting the target description ("tank!" or "BMP!") while simultaneously shooting the Laser Range Finder to the target. Within milliseconds, the laser beam would detect the range to target and send the information to the tank's ballistic computer, which would then compute a firing solution and adjust the tank's main gun accordingly. The main gun fired two types of rounds: SABOT (pronounced "say-bo"; an inert, kinetic energy round) and HEAT (High-Explosive Anti-Tank). The tank commander selected the type of round based on the target description. As a rule of thumb, American tank crews generally used SABOT rounds against enemy tanks; HEAT rounds against tanks and light-armored vehicles.

After the tank commander selected the type of round, the loader would begin his complex choreography of loading that round into the main gun. The loader, although the most junior soldier on the tank, had a vitally important job. The main gun rounds were dreadfully heavy and, under the time constraints, the loader had mere seconds to load and arm the gun before the gunner pulled the trigger. The main gun rounds were stored in an ammunition compartment in the rear of the turret, covered by a sliding door that the loader operated via hydraulic knee-switch. Once the appropriate round was selected, he would load it into the gun breech and push the arming lever up, enabling the main gun to be fired. The best loaders could perform the entire process in less than four seconds.

After the main gun had been fully armed and loaded (confirmed by the loader yelling "Up!") the tank commander gave the command "Fire!" to which the gunner replied "On the way!" as he pulled the trigger. Of course, since the squadron was conserving its ammunition, no live rounds were fired during these desert crew drills.

For the Bradley crewmen, combat drills required some extra legwork because the vehicle carried both mounted *and* dismounted soldiers. However, the Bradley crewmen in Ghost Troop were elated to receive the brand new M2A2 Bradley, shipped into Saudi Arabia that December and delivered to the forward elements of the VII Corps' line. These upgraded vehicles had better armor, higher top speeds, and improved armaments. As it turned out, these Bradleys were, in fact, *brand new*—shipped directly into theater from the factory. Keith Garwick marveled at the prospect of using brand new vehicles. "Cosmoline on the barrels, shrink wrap on the gun controls, and sealed crates of new equipment," he said. "Then there were letters, presents, and even cans of food from the guys at the factory." Their gifts included shaving razors, packages of M&Ms, and notes saying "Be safe!" and "Come home quick!"—thoughtful gestures and words of appreciation from factory workers who knew that these Bradleys were going into battle.

Because the new M2A2s had been designed to accommodate a mechanized infantry squad, each vehicle arrived with six seats in the rear. "We took out all the extra chairs and dumped them in the desert," said Rick Michalec. After all, the scout-based Bradley only needed two dismounts, and Ghost Troop had to make room for all the additional ammo they were carrying.

Paul Hains' scout platoon also received the new TRIMPACK Global Positioning System (GPS), as did Sartiano's command tank and Joe Deskevich's fire support vehicle. The GPS, "though primitive by today's standards," said Major Macgregor, "was marvelous." Except between the hours of 5:00 AM and 7:00 AM, "when the required number of satellites were not in position over the Middle East, the GPS equipment gave our scouts, artillerymen, and Air Force liaison section, the confidence to plan and direct operations and attacks with speed and precision." The GPS calculations were based on the Military Grid Reference System (divided into denominations of one square kilometer) and gave accurate readings within a few meters of ground truth.

Aside from the crew drills, Ghost Troop conducted several practice maneuvers at the squadron level. Out of necessity, Major Macgregor had to devise a training regimen to get the squadron acclimated to maneuvering in the desert. As early as September 1990, Macgregor had been teaching classes on the desert campaigns of World War II. He had seen the parallels between the North African campaign and the current situation in the Gulf. But rather than focus on the campaign from the Americans' perspective, Macgregor took stock in the battles between Rommel's *Afrika Korps* and the British Eighth Army. During the Battle of Gazala and the attack on Tobruk, Rommel's *Panzerarmee*—sometimes outnumbered three to one—defeated the Eighth Army in convincing fashion. Macgregor had told the squadron's officers that, when fighting outnumbered, *quality of leadership* was the overriding factor. "Rommel led from the front," Macgregor told them, "our men deserve nothing less. There is no substitute for leading from the front. I will be up front and I expect you to be there as well!" Still, after decades of working within the confines of the German borderlands, the transition to desert warfare was sure to have its growing pains.

"The problem," said Joe Deskevich, "was that we had to build an *offensive* mindset"—not the defensive mindset that had dominated their tactics in West Germany. Joe Deskevich and Jeff Geoffroy both commented on the similarities between desert warfare and naval warfare. "It's like we're all naval officers now," Geoffroy told his friends. "There's no terrain that we can hide behind, no terrain to follow, and whoever can shoot the farthest is going to win." To that end, though, it seemed that the Americans had the upper hand. Although outnumbered, and untested in combat, their M1 Abrams had a superior fire control system that allowed it to shoot on the move. And its maximum effective range far exceeded that of a T-55 or T-72.

Although the wide-open terrain was favorable for weapons like the tank, Joe Deskevich found it troublesome for planning artillery fire. Indeed, the featureless desert gave him virtually no options for coordinating Final Protective Fires (FPF). FPF referred to an artillery barrage directed onto a particular piece of terrain, acting as a "last line of defense" for a unit that was about to be overrun. In Germany, Joe would template his FPF at 1,000 meters forward of the frontline, and along restrictive pieces of terrain. In the desert, however, there was no terrain wherein he could canalize or disrupt the enemy's movement.

"A thousand meters in the desert is nothing," he said.

"How can I plan FPF? The enemy can just drive around it."

Thus, for any decisive engagement, Joe would have to disrupt the enemy's frontline elements with mortar fire and close air support, while calling artillery fire onto the secondary echelons.

Land navigation was even more problematic as there were no identifiable landmarks or reference points. Thus, any soldier without a GPS had to rely on dead reckoning. This necessitated a vehicle crewman to dismount his track, walk several paces in front of the vehicle, and use his magnetic compass to find an azimuth upon which he could orient his movement. The crewman had to walk far ahead of his tank or Bradley to get an accurate compass reading, else the vehicle's metallic body would skew the azimuth.

Navigation at night brought even more challenges. Even with the tanks' and Bradleys' thermal sights, a soldier could easily get disoriented in the nighttime desert. For instance, Joe Sartiano (prior to receiving his GPS), was coming back from a nighttime briefing at the Squadron TOC, and had to steer his tank back to Ghost Troop's area in the dead of the night. It was pitch black and Squadron had mandated that there was to be maximum "noise and light discipline" when travelling—meaning that no vehicle could travel with its headlights illuminated, lest it draw attention from a lingering enemy. Since the squadron had yet to receive its GPS devices, Sartiano had the unenviable task of navigating the tank via dead reckoning with his compass. After a long haul across the squadron's footprint, and using nothing more than his compass, Sartiano was certain that he was lost. His anger turned to relief, however, as the sun rose, revealing that he was only 100 meters from Ghost Troop's cantonment. Although his dead reckoning had been within 100 meters of ground truth, it underscored how problematic and painstaking the process of night navigation could be.

On another occasion, Joe Deskevich was participating as a "casualty" for a nighttime medical evacuation (MEDEVAC) drill. Upon his exfil, however, Joe remembered that the MEDEVAC vehicle got lost, "and we drove around for 14 hours trying to find the Squadron." He thought to himself: "Dear God, I hope we don't fight like this. Because if I was really injured, I'd be dead by now!"

The encounter prompted Deskevich to practice crew evacuations with his fire support team. His own tracked vehicle was an M113 variant known as the FIST-V (Fire Support Vehicle). "If the FIST-V got hit in combat, we had to figure out how to evacuate casualties." Because their mission in Germany had been to "Die in Place" in the event of a Soviet invasion, MEDEVAC procedures had become little more than an afterthought. But now that their mentality had shifted from *defensive* operations to *offensive* operations, the crews needed to know how to treat casualties while sustaining the forward momentum of the offense. "And these were things that we didn't pay as close attention to in Germany as we did in the Saudi desert," he added.

Navigational hiccups and botched MEDEVACs notwithstanding, many of Ghost Troop's maneuvers passed without incident. While developing the squadron's strategy for the ground offensive, Major Macgregor pondered what tactical formation to use. His operations staff recommended moving with all three cavalry troops—Fox, Eagle, and Ghost—abreast in a linear formation. But Macgregor wasn't convinced. Weighing his options, Macgregor determined that the squadron's attack zone into Iraq measured nearly twenty kilometers across. Having three troops abreast would cover fifteen kilometers—"too much to present to the enemy at one time," he thought.

Eventually, Macgregor opted for the "diamond" formation—consisting of one cavalry troop in the lead, two other cavalry troops on either flank a few hundred meters behind, Hawk Company (tanks) in the middle, and the Squadron TOC at the diamond's southern apex. The diamond formation would allow for a smaller frontage and five kilometers of observation on either flank. Macgregor then directed the operations staff to devise "a series of scenarios, with enemy forces constituted from our combat trains." These "combat trains" were the squadron's support personnel: fuel handlers, ammunition specialists, and logisticians of every stripe.

After several days of practice, Ghost Troop had grown accustomed to maneuvering in the diamond. "Sartiano decided that the best use of the scouts' superior gunsights required the integration of the Abrams tanks with the Bradleys into teams." Indeed, every tank platoon was paired with a scout platoon, turning them into "hunter-killer" teams. Under this construct, the Bradleys would spot targets for the Abrams, allowing the tanks to destroy said targets with their far-reaching 120mm main guns. During these maneuvers, Ghost Troop's fire support team traveled in a wedge formation behind Joe Sartiano's tank. "In drills," said Major Macgregor, "once contact was made with the enemy, it was [Joe Deskevich's] responsibility to watch over and conduct mortar fire in support of the scouts in contact. It was another version of the tactic of holding the enemy's nose with scouts and mortars as the tanks moved to punch him. As the initial round was fired, the fire support team leader [Deskevich] would move to the scout platoon in contact to observe the engagement area. This gave the fire support team leader the ability to observe and report to the attacking tank platoon leaders 'Rounds Complete,' so they wouldn't get caught by any shots still in the air."

Along the way, they discovered a number of techniques to improve their fighting efficiency. As predicted, the tank's engine took in a lot of sand, which necessitated more cleaning and maintenance of the air filters than normal. Therefore, the squadron decided to carry three times the normal number of filters into battle. Ghost Troopers also found that turning off the tanks' engines at every halt saved an enormous amount of fuel. In fact, according to Macgregor, this technique could get the squadron "all the way to Basra in six hours on one tank of fuel, even if we drove at forty miles per hour!"

While conducting these mock maneuvers in the desert, Ghost Troop tested the limits of their vehicles in other ways. Jeff Geoffroy's 4th Platoon, for instance, wanted to test the maximum speed of the M1 Abrams. Most of the technical literature stated that the vehicle's top speed was 45 miles per hour. However, within the confines of the German countryside, no Ghost Trooper had ever driven the M1 to full gallop. In the wide-open deserts of Saudi Arabia, however, 4th Platoon marveled at the sight of an M1 Abrams accelerating to its maximum speed across the dusty terrain, creating their own sandstorms as they sped down TAA Seminole. During these impromptu rally races, Geoffroy learned to regulate the tank's speed depending on the condition of the topsoil—"hard-packed sand versus soft sand"—because the relative density affected how fast the tank could travel.

As Ghost Troop and the rest of the squadron prepared for their first maneuver against the combat trains, Macgregor said, "I put Eagle Troop in the lead, with instructions to make contact, compel the enemy force to halt, and recommend a course of action." Accordingly, Eagle Troop could tell Ghost, Fox, and the tank company to move left or right around either flank and encircle the enemy.

Barely ten minutes after Macgregor commenced the exercise, Eagle Troop identified the column of trucks from the combat trains moving from right to left several hundred meters to their front. Almost immediately, Eagle began attacking the column with simulated direct and indirect fires. However, the combat trains' commander, Captain Rudd, nonchalantly deployed his trucks into the direction of Eagle Troop's attack.

Meanwhile, Eagle told Ghost Troop to maneuver around the right flank, and for Fox Troop to maneuver left, thereby enveloping the enemy in a pincer-like movement. Hawk Company would then move farther around Ghost Troop to deliver the fatal blow to the enemy.

At that moment, however, the exercise devolved into a comedy of errors.

When Hawk Company was called upon to "punch right," they were nowhere to be found. Frustrated, Macgregor called out to the Hawk Company commander: "Hawk 6, Cougar 3★, punch right, acknowledge, over?" Hawk 6 responded that he could not see Eagle Troop through the growing clouds of dust and sand. To make matters worse, Sartiano radioed that his movement had been halted by local wildlife.

Incredulous, Macgregor replied, "Explain wildlife, over?"

"This is Ghost 6, we are surrounded by sheep…I mean, we can blast through them but the local nationals might not like that, over." Meanwhile, Sartiano's driver was pleading with a Bedouin herder to move the sheep out of their way so Ghost Troop could resume its attack. In a tone of unmistakable disappointment, Macgregor replied, "This is Cougar 3, roger. Don't kill the sheep. Catch up when you can. Cougar 3, out."

By this time, Rudd's combat trains were overrunning the squadron, driving right past Eagle Troop. "They had outmaneuvered our combat elements, and they knew it," Macgregor said. "I have to admit that I was truly depressed. Moving a squadron decisively in any direction was something like turning a battleship at sea…all we could do on this last day of our three-day maneuver was hold an after-action review [abbreviated: AAR]."

After the dust settled, Macgregor opened the AAR by restating the mission and having each of the commanders explain their actions and proffer any ways to improve. Sartiano re-iterated his close encounter with the Saudi wildlife, which drew long peals of laughter from the troops. Eagle Troop's commander, HR McMaster, began his portion of the AAR by conceding that the combat trains had held their own throughout the fight. He then drew the squadron diamond on a nearby

---

★ "Cougar 3" was Major Macgregor's call sign. Each squadron officer had a "Cougar" prefix for his call sign, followed by his corresponding staff section number.

whiteboard, identifying the location where the play-enemy had been spotted, and made "a number of comments on how the scouts would liaise with Hawk Company in the future."

During these simulated engagements, Ghost Troop's performance underscored Sartiano's emphasis on teamwork, training, and crew-level initiative. "Before leaving Bamberg," said Macgregor, "Sartiano knew that he had taken command of officers and noncommissioned officers who had great enthusiasm, but less experience. Sartiano's top priority was to forge a close-knit, tightly-integrated unit as quickly as possible. [He] strove both to refine Ghost Troop's maneuver skills and build up the troop's confidence in its leaders."

But the bigger problem, it seemed, was simply maintaining cohesion among the vehicle crews. For instance, aboard Ruben Cardosa's tank (Ghost 43), he had lost his tank commander, Sergeant Richardson, to the Master Gunner Course just weeks before they deployed to Saudi Arabia. Surprisingly, Richardson was one of the few men not to be recalled from the Master Gunner Course when his home unit deployed. Another NCO in Ghost Troop, Sergeant Calvert, had been tapped to replace Richardson. However, a few weeks after arriving in Saudi Arabia, Calvert had to return to Germany due to a family situation.

Thus, Ruben Cardosa was suddenly promoted from gunner to tank commander.

As the new commander of Ghost 43, Cardosa received an in-theater replacement to act as his gunner. However, this "replacement" was a young Specialist (E-4) from the 1st Infantry Division who had zero experience as a tank gunner. To make matters worse for Cardosa, his loader wasn't even a tank crewman, but a scout who had been placed as a loader due to the scout platoons having excess personnel.

Reluctant to send Cardosa into combat with an inexperienced gunner, Jeff Geoffroy offered to transfer his own gunner, Sergeant Adams, to Ghost 43. "We presented the idea to Joe Sartiano about a week before the ground war," said Geoffroy. Sartiano considered it for a moment, but said: "No, because then you're going to have two vehicles that haven't trained together: your tank and his tank."

Crew cohesion was paramount. Gunners and vehicle commanders worked as a highly-synchronized team to engage targets; and spent countless hours training together to ensure quick fire commands and rapid target destruction. Breaking up crews would necessitate rebuilding those metaphysical bonds—something for which they had precious little time to accomplish now that hostilities were imminent.

Andy Kilgore felt the same pressure. As a recent arrival to the 2d ACR, he spent his first few weeks in the desert simply getting to know the men of 2d Platoon. "So, I probably did a lot more crew training and platoon-level training than some of the others who had been there for a while."

Terry Lorson felt likewise.

Reflecting on his time in the Persian Gulf, Lorson recalled that: "I spent most of the deployment being that 'new guy' in the back [of the Bradley], just in the dark, wondering what the hell was going on." During their practice maneuvers, Lorson would be bouncing around inside the rear of Ghost 16, linking together the chains of 25mm ammunition while brushing sand off his uniform. "All this sand would come in through the cracks of the Bradley hatches," he said. For even though they were closed, the Bradley hatches were not airtight.

When they weren't training, the men of Ghost Troop found a number of ways to keep themselves entertained. Early on, one of the greatest forms of entertainment was listening to Baghdad Betty. Saddam's own version of Tokyo Rose, "Baghdad Betty" broadcasted anti-American propaganda to discourage US servicemen stationed in the Gulf. However, her broadcasts were so outlandish and humorously implausible that no one outside of Iraq ever took them seriously. According to one urban legend, Betty once claimed that the wives and girlfriends of American soldiers were sleeping with Bart Simpson. "We thought she was a trip," said Foley. "We called her a 'goofy bitch' because her broadcasts made no sense."

Several troopers also kept themselves entertained by listening to their Sony Walkmans (after cleaning the sand from their cassette tapes), playing Nintendo Gameboy, and writing letters to their families. Aboard their respective tracks, Rick Michalec and Don Chafee figured out how to wire their Walkmans into the vehicle's intercom system so their crews could listen to music while on maneuver. While Chafee's crew enjoyed a variety of music, Rick Michalec had only one cassette tape—*The Doobie Brothers Greatest Hits*. "We listened to the Doobie Brothers for that entire deployment," he laughed. Aboard Ghost 16, however, Andy Moller enjoyed his music in a most unorthodox fashion. "He was smart," Chafee recalled. "He bought a Playskool tape recorder. It looked silly but it was designed to take abuse." Indeed, these Playskool products were designed to withstand the rough-and-tumble nature of a toddler's playtime. Thus, Moller reasoned that if his tape player could endure the

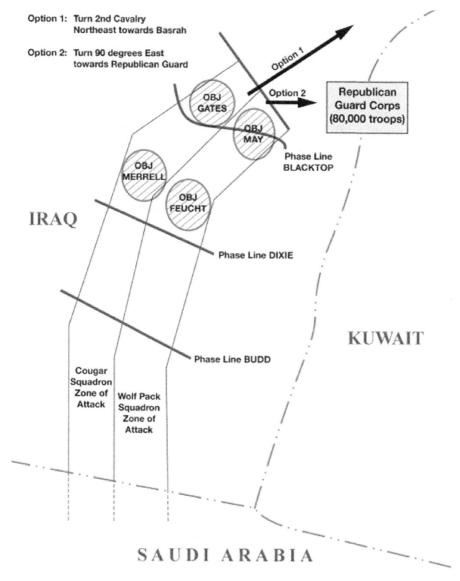

The 2d ACR's plan of attack, December 1990–January 1991. The "Right Hook" maneuver initially had two options: drive on to Basra or turn right to destroy the Republican Guard.

"terrible twos," it could certainly withstand the harsh environment of the desert.

As it turned out, he was correct.

While other troopers had to contend with sandy and broken Walkmans, Moller's Playskool tape deck never gave him a moment's trouble. "Built to last," Chafee snickered.

Pat Bledsoe, meanwhile, stayed busy on his Nintendo Gameboy.

"*Batman* was my favorite game," he recalled. His mother had also sent him a few analog handheld games—including pinball and Waterfuls. "I read a lot of Tom Clancy," he added, "especially *The Hunt for Red October*." In fact, throughout Desert Shield, Ghost Troop had become its own de facto book club. "A lot of people had books," said Ruben Cardosa. "One of the books we had was *The Godfather*"—which got passed around until nearly every person in Ghost Troop had read it. "And that was one of the best books I'd ever read!" he added. While enjoying their recreational literature, men like Cardosa also devised ways to shield themselves from the immense heat of the desert—suspending tarps from tent poles to make impromptu sunshades.

Although writing and receiving letters was their only contact with the outside world, it was often painful because it reminded them of life beyond the desert. Still, Brian Foley was touched by the random letters they received from school children, offering words of encouragement and the unshakable optimism of grade-school youth. These sentiments were also reflected in the many care packages that Ghost Troop received. During the early days of Desert Shield, care packages addressed to "Any Soldier" flowed into Saudi Arabia by the thousands. Filled to capacity with baked goods, toiletries, and magazines, these packages came from families and civic organizations across the US. From the content and quantity of these packages, it seemed as though Americans collectively felt bad for how they had treated their Vietnam veterans, and were determined to make up for it. Inevitably, some of these packages were pilfered by rear-echelon soldiers before being delivered to the frontlines. The untouched packages that did arrive in Ghost Troop, however, (especially those containing muffins and brownies) brightened the otherwise dull routines of the desert cantonment.

Waylan Lundquist, for instance, received care packages from his wife and mother. "Oddly enough," he said, "my mother sent me toilet paper and mouthwash,"—all the items that the news media had said soldiers needed—"and of course candy, nuts, and beef jerky."

Aboard Ghost 16, the first care package that Don Chafee received from his family contained chocolate bars, none of which held up well in the desert heat. Indeed, by the time he opened his package, the candy bars had liquified. Undaunted, Chafee simply scooped it out with an MRE spoon. "It was like pudding," he said. Enjoyable, "but it was awfully messy." Terry Lorson, meanwhile, received a care package from a female friend back home. "Her father was in Vietnam with the 24th Infantry Division," he said, "and his sister had sent him cookies when he was in country." When Lorson received his package, he discovered that his friend had included an identical batch of cookies, with a handwritten note saying:

"This is the exact same recipe that my father would get from my aunt."

Lorson later said that it was "kind of neat to be on deployment and get a care package that had some historical background to it."

Pat Bledsoe, however, received the most exuberant care packages of anyone in Ghost Troop. "My mom owned a deli shop," he said, "and she also helped a friend do local fairs; they had a popcorn cart, so I was always getting bags of popcorn and caramel corn for everyone in the Troop." Sometime later, Bledsoe got an even bigger care package. "My sisters and my mom knew that I missed Mexican food more than anything. And so I got a box that had taco shells, chili beans…and we made tacos that night! That box was pretty legendary."

Sometimes, however, the monotony of desert life broke itself in unexpected ways. On one occasion, a contingent from the British Army arrived in the VII Corps sector, showcasing their tactical vehicles and offering rides to any interested American troops. The British, like the Americans, had committed forces to the growing coalition. Among their showcased vehicles were the FV101 Scorpion (a tracked reconnaissance vehicle similar to the M2 Bradley) and the Challenger Main Battle Tank (a NATO stablemate of the M1 Abrams). According to Rick Michalec, however, this "dog-and-pony show" was likely a preventative safety measure. Some British vehicles, at first glance, resembled the Soviet-built wares used by the Iraqi Army. Michalec mentioned the British Fox Reconnaissance Vehicle as one such example. "It looked like a BRDM." Thus, a field familiarization tour might prevent cases of unwitting fratricide.

Another unexpected break in the monotony occurred during one of the regiment's alert drills. "Colonel Holder had instituted a series of alerts, under the name 'Quickstrike,' designed to posture the combat elements of the squadron for deployment to Saudi Arabia's border with Iraq. With no warning at all, the squadron would be required to get its combat elements moving within fifteen minutes and the rest of its supporting elements moving within thirty minutes." One January morning, the squadron received word that an Iraqi battalion of T-55 tanks had crossed the Saudi border and was headed towards King Khalid Military City. "Soldiers literally tumbled out of their cots and into their vehicles," Major Macgregor recalled. "The tanks turbine engines roared and mini-sandstorms kicked up behind their armored fighting vehicles," as they pulled into fighting positions. Over the squadron radio net, each of the troops reported their combat power. Macgregor responded with "Battle stations, battle stations, this is Cougar 3, battle carry sabot, over." For many, this was the first time they had loaded main gun rounds in anticipation of a real tank battle. "I could hear the excitement in the soldiers' and officers' voices."

In Ghost Troop, Jeff Geoffroy and his gunner were on the edge of their seats. "We didn't have time to be scared," he recalled. "We were all thinking about the mission and not letting anyone down. We were thinking about the tank and making sure it was fit to fight." Geoffroy was certain that he was about to engage a battalion of T-55s—obsolete tanks that would, presumably, make easy fodder for an M1 Abrams.

But the alert proved to be a false alarm.

Indeed, aerial surveillance confirmed that these "Iraqi tanks" had been nothing more than a herd of camels. Still, the experience had been electrifying and the troop commanders agreed that their soldiers could "walk the walk."

Christmas 1990 was as enjoyable a holiday as one could have in the Saudi cantonment. For the occasion, Ghost Troop made its own Christmas tree, improvised with tent poles and green camouflage netting, decorated with red Solo cups. "It was one of the most memorable Christmases I had ever had," said Pat Bledsoe. On that Christmas Eve, he received another popcorn-laden gift box, which he happily disbursed to his comrades in Ghost Troop. "I volunteered for KP [Kitchen Police]* on Christmas, which was cool because we got to eat first…and we probably ate better than anyone else," he chuckled. "We had shrimp that night… all sorts of good food." Some troopers even hung their green socks from the inside of their vehicles, filling them with MRE candy as impromptu Christmas stockings.

A few days after Christmas, Ghost Troop received orders to guard LOGBASE Echo, thirty miles southeast of TAA Seminole. It was one of many logistical support bases that VII Corps had established throughout the region. But amid growing concerns of Arab spies and saboteurs, the Corps commander, General Fred Franks, wanted to give his LOGBASE network an armored security force. However, because there were not

---

* "Kitchen Police" refers to a rotating group of soldiers who assist Army cooks in cleaning and maintaining a unit's kitchen and its dining facilities.

enough residual armored forces in-theater to guard the LOGBASE, VII Corps rotated the guard mission amongst the nearby cavalry troops and tank companies.

Occupying LOGBASE Echo, Sartiano sent Ghost Troop's Bradleys to guard the perimeter while the tanks stayed in the center as a Quick Reaction Force. However, two scout platoons and two tank platoons gave the LOGBASE only twenty armored vehicles to cover a 24-square-mile perimeter. Spread out over that much of a distance, the only way they could stop a suspicious vehicle would be to give chase with a tank or Bradley—neither of which were good pursuit vehicles. But the bigger problem, it seemed, was the presence of female soldiers at the LOGBASE. Unlike their forefathers in World War II and Korea, Ghost Troop served in an Army where women played a more integrated role in the forward area. This often led to commanders issuing strict rules against fraternization.

Luckily, no spies, terrorists, or romantic liaisons came to LOGBASE Echo.

Ghost Troop did, however, make several noteworthy memories of their time guarding the LOGBASE. On the first day of their guard mission, for example, Paul Hains told himself: "You know, I feel like I should drive around and check this whole place out…find out how big it is…maybe meet some of the people we're supposed to be guarding."

While exploring the LOGBASE in his M2 Bradley, Hains suddenly saw something that caught his eye.

"Driver, stop!" he yelled.

As the Bradley lurched to a halt, he cast his gaze upon a shipping container whose back door had been curiously left open. "I see toilet paper!" he exclaimed. Toilet paper was a luxury item Ghost Troop hadn't seen in weeks. In fact, since their arrival at TAA Seminole, many troopers had gone to using MRE napkins as toilet paper.

"Wait here," he told his crew. "I'm going to check this out."

Dismounting his Bradley, he happened upon a group of soldiers lingering in front of the shipping container.

"Who's in charge here?" he asked them.

They pointed in the direction of a female supply officer, and Paul attempted to work his charm as a means to solicit toilet paper for his unit.

"Hi there!" he exclaimed. "Nice to meet you. I'm Paul Hains, Ghost Troop, 2/2 ACR."

Initially unimpressed by the sudden appearance of a sweaty cavalryman, the female officer became a bit more receptive when she learned that Paul was guarding the LOGBASE from any potential spies or saboteurs. "Say, I couldn't help but notice that you guys have all this toilet paper in the back of the container," he said.

"Yeah. What about it?"

"Well, could I get some for my guys?"

"I don't know," she replied. "It's not mine to give away. It's for a lot of people at the LOGBASE."

Sensing that she was about to deny his request, Paul suddenly had an idea. He looked to the supply soldiers guarding the container; he could tell that they were hot, tired, and none too happy to be standing in front a metal container in the afternoon heat. Despite their seemingly low morale, however, they seemed fascinated by the sudden appearance of a Bradley Fighting Vehicle in their sector. "Say, I've got an idea," Paul interjected. "Would it be all right to offer your guys a ride in a Bradley Fighting Vehicle? That's my Bradley right there. And maybe you could get us some toilet paper?"

The young female officer's face suddenly lit up.

"You can do that?!" she beamed. "That would be great! I think my folks would love that! You can take as many rolls as you can carry!" A half-hour, and one joyride later, Paul Hains happily trotted off with enough toilet paper for all of Ghost Troop. When he sallied his M2 Bradley back onto the perimeter, he called First Sergeant Roark over to his vehicle.

"Hey, Top, I've got something for ya!"

Paul then dropped the back ramp of the Bradley, precipitating a small avalanche of toilet paper. "Holy crap," said Roark, "where did you get this?!"

Hains' daily expeditions around the LOGBASE earned him another chance encounter with a rare luxury item: shower trailers equipped with running water. Just as he had done with the toilet paper stores, Paul dismounted his Bradley and approached the nearest ranking officer. But whereas the last commander had been a receptive young lady, the officer in charge of the showers was a crotchety, older captain.

Still, Hains didn't miss a chance to deploy his "Aw shucks" charm and demeanor. "Sir I couldn't help but notice you have showers. I was wondering if my guys could use it?"

"Absolutely not!" thundered the old captain.

"Not every passerby can just use the showers," he continued. "My guys work hard, and they work a lot of shifts. We have a schedule for the showers and we can't have people tracing through." Paul repeated his request, asking for a one-time use so his troops could get clean—many of them hadn't showered since leaving Germany. "No," repeated the captain. "I can't set a precedent. Because then every other clown who comes through here is going to want to use it."

By now, Paul was growing tired of the captain's reluctance. "You know, sir," he said, "it's really hard to see out here at night. I'm telling you it'd be a damn shame if I ran over that shower in the middle of the night." In hindsight, Hains admitted that his response was "completely inappropriate," but it nevertheless persuaded the irascible captain into letting Paul's platoon use the shower.

The most memorable moment at the LOGBASE, however, was Waylan Lundquist and Keith Garwick accidentally stumbling onto an A-10 pilot's radio net. While guarding the LOGBASE, a scout section from Garwick's 1st Platoon had teamed up with a tank section from Lundquist's 2d Platoon, covering the farthest edge of the LOGBASE closest to the Iraqi border. One night, Garwick and Lundquist were hopping frequencies when they happened upon two unfamiliar voices using unfamiliar terms. The voices were distinctively American and, after a few moments, Garwick and Lundquist realized that the voices belonged to a couple of A-10 pilots. Somehow, Ghost Troop's radio had bounced on to the pilots' frequency. The two wingmen were returning from a reconnaissance mission, and were jovially calling each other by their first names—"Bill" and "Bobby."

Not wanting to alert their new radio hosts, Garwick and Lundquist remained silent as the two pilots laughed and joked with each other. At one point, Bill told Bobby:

"Hey, do you see that? It looks like a weird hole in the ground."

Bill then vectored his A-10 to investigate the newfound hole.

"I'm not sure what it is," Bill said, "but hey, you got any missiles left?"

"Yea, I got one," Bobby replied.

Bobby then fired his missile into the unknown hole, and both pilots yelled "Holy Sh*t!" when that hole erupted into a massive fireball measuring nearly one-kilometer wide. "The next thing you know," said Lundquist, "Bobby and Bill are trying to get out of there because this explosion is so horrific."

Indeed it was.

Keith Garwick could feel the rumble of the explosion even though it was several kilometers away. As it turned out, the pilots had destroyed an Iraqi ammunition dump.

On the morning of January 15, 1991, Ghost Troop awoke to the news that Saddam Hussein had reached his deadline—and had made no effort to withdraw from Kuwait. The next day, President Bush announced the start of the military campaign to eject the Iraqis from the war-torn emirate.

Operation Desert Shield had just become Operation Desert Storm.

On January 17, at 2:38 AM, Baghdad time, the first wave of the coalition's air campaign destroyed Iraqi radar sites near the Saudi border. For the next five weeks, coalition air forces pounded away at key targets within Iraq and Kuwait. For the men of Ghost Troop, watching the action overhead from TAA Seminole was the greatest thrill they had had since arriving in the desert. Paul Hains was sleeping atop his Bradley, Ghost 31, when suddenly one of his soldiers jolted him awake.

"Sir! Sir! Wake up! You've got to come see this!"

"What is it?" Paul replied.

Wiping the sleep from his eyes, Hains was shocked to see what looked like "a huge lightshow on the horizon." Because the action was so far away, he couldn't hear the explosions, but he could see the tracer rounds from Iraqi air defense guns lighting up the sky. Watching the air campaign unfold from atop his Bradley, Paul said aloud: "Well, I guess the war's started." Waylan Lundquist, who was blissfully sleeping atop his own vehicle, was jolted awake by the sudden sound of coalition jets flying at full afterburner. "I remember it waking me up in the middle of the night," he said. He could see the running lights of the coalition aircraft as they thundered into the black horizon; and he could feel the concussion wave from the explosions happening on the other side of the border. Meanwhile, Pat Bledsoe and Tony Harrison marveled as they saw the horizon light up with the telltale glow of exploding ordnance. As daylight approached, Ghost Troop could see the contrails of the various Allied aircraft flying overhead—including B-52s, F-15E Strike Eagles, F-111 Aardvarks, and F-4 Wild Weasels. Listening to news reports of the air campaign over BBC Radio, many in Ghost Troop wondered: "Is the Air Force going to win this whole thing for us?"

On the Iraqi side of the border, however, the feeling was much different. This around-the-clock bombardment whittled away at Saddam's ground forces and destroyed much of his air force before it even got off the ground. Meanwhile, Saddam tried to fracture the coalition along religious lines by firing Scud missiles into Jerusalem and Tel Aviv. However, the Iraqi Scuds were notoriously inaccurate; many of them landed in the Mediterranean or were shot down by Patriot missiles. On one occasion, General Schwarzkopf bantered that he was more afraid of being struck by lightning than being hit by a Scud missile.

At the same time, Jeff Geoffroy took to his diary, writing his own musings of the conflict:

"January 18—AFN [Armed Forces Network] reported a Scud missile launch, and a Patriot missile intercepted it. Score one for the Army. This isn't too bad because we're out of their [Scuds'] range and we have air superiority. Against a stronger foe, it might not be so neat. 10 Scuds were launched at Israel and Syria; 5 people died from asphyxiation due to wearing gas masks improperly. The air campaign is ongoing and, from what we know now, it's going very well. Egypt and Syria said it's OK for Israel to defend herself, but don't escalate."

Geoffroy was also thrilled to hear that coalition planes had dropped more than 30 million tons of ordnance, and that several Iraqi SAM sites had been disabled because "Wild Weasels are knocking the crap out of them!"

Before making their final move to the border of Iraq, the 2d ACR held one more Tactical Exercise without Troops (TOCEX) to rehearse its advance across southern Iraq. As the spearhead of the VII Corps' advance, 2d ACR would lead the follow-on divisions deep into southern Iraq, then turn ninety degrees to meet the Republican Guard head-on.

At the end of the TOCEX, the normal round of AARs followed with the two lead squadron commanders, the 3d "Wolfpack" Squadron commander, and Sullivan, the 2d "Cougar" Squadron commander, briefing their movements out to Phase Line Blacktop, "an asphalt road ninety miles inside Iraq running northeast out of Kuwait." Reading from his notes, the 3d Squadron commander remarked that he anticipated taking fifteen percent casualties by the time he reached Phase Line Blacktop. "These figures," the Wolfpack commander said, "are the result of force ratio calculations based on the Iraqi enemy template by our intelligence officers."

Major Macgregor, listening intently, was incredulous. "Where in the hell did this come from, I wondered?" Indeed, Macgregor's own intelligence had reported the heaviest concentration of enemy forces being much farther east. Sullivan was equally surprised by his fellow commander's remarks, but not for the same reasons as Macgregor. In fact, Sullivan thought that Macgregor had let him down by not providing him with similar data on casualties.

Macgregor quickly reassured him, "Sir, don't worry about it. We aren't going to have any casualties, at least not until we attack the Republican Guard. This is preposterous."

Sullivan did his portion of the AAR according to the script and Colonel Holder seemed pleased with the presentation. But the one thing Macgregor noticed throughout the TOCEX was the lack of any bold maneuvers. He likened it to a plodding, World War I-style attack where slow-moving, linear formations would crash headlong into an enemy force under the cover of artillery fire. The bigger problem, however, was that many of the officers had resigned themselves to the idea that US forces were going to take heavy casualties. In fact, other units along the Saudi border had come to similar conclusions. The 24th Infantry Division, for example, estimated as many as 2,000 killed or wounded, while the XVIII Airborne Corps projected as many as twenty percent casualties on the first day.

Many of these fears, however, subsided on the morning of January 29, 1991, when the Iraqi Army's 5th Mechanized Division attempted an attack on the Allied position at Khafji, a small Arab town on the coast of the Persian Gulf. However, after only two days of fighting, the Iraqis were repelled by US Marines accompanied by two Saudi Arabian National Guard battalions and a Qatari tank company (equipped with French-built AMX-30 tanks). According to Major Macgregor, this poor showing by the Iraqi Army confirmed what he had suspected all along: Saddam's frontline forces were far weaker than the coalition's leadership made them out to be. Apparently, the Iraqis couldn't maneuver, couldn't coordinate their fires, or even shoot effectively. Furthermore, they seemed to lack the stomach for a real fight. Hearing this assessment of the Iraqis' performance at Khafji, Macgregor beamed, "We are up against the Italian Army of the 90s. What we have now is the greatest opportunity an armored force has had since the Germans seized Tobruk in '42."

But while the Iraqis' defeat at Khafji showed the unsuitability of their regular army, the jury was still out on the Republican Guard. More than 100 miles beyond the Iraqi border, the Tawakalna and Hammurabi Divisions had dug in along a defensive line surrounding Kuwait, waiting silently for the coalition's ground forces to come their way.

A few days later, Squadron moved Ghost Troop from TAA Seminole to the staging area astride the Saudi-Iraqi border. Simultaneously, VII Corps began situating its forces along the border, making their final preparations for the ground assault into Iraq. Senior leaders, meanwhile, gave instructions while flying overhead in their Blackhawk helicopters, telling one unit or another to readjust their position for the initial attack.

Their move to the Saudi border, however, required crossing Tapline Road. The road itself wasn't an obstacle, but there was no feasible way to get around the Trans Arabian Pipeline, for which the road was named. Tanks, Bradleys, and other armored vehicles were too heavy to drive over the pipeline, so the combat engineers had to build earthen bridges to protect the structure. These sand bridges, about forty in total, were nothing more than mounds of dirt piled over the pipeline, packed with enough density to protect the ductwork from the weight and vibrations of the VII Corps' armored vehicles.

During the move to the border, Ghost Troop encountered something unexpected and entirely out of place—an overturned Pepsi truck. Indeed, along the side of Tapline Road, a bottle-carrier truck emblazoned with the Pepsi logo (written in Arabic) lay on its side. From the condition of the vehicle and its cargo, Ghost Troop could tell that the truck had been wrecked for only a few hours. Whatever the reason for the accident, the driver had abandoned the vehicle, leaving behind several dozen cases of Pepsi Cola. Not wanting to let this serendipitous find go to waste, Ghost Troop happily carried off several cases of Pepsi to enjoy before the ground war started.

In mid-February, the regiment's officers assembled for one final discussion on the upcoming offensive. The air campaign had devastated much of the Iraqi defenses but, from what VII Corps' intelligence estimated, the enemy's ground forces remained combat effective. The meeting at the Regimental TOC was capped by the appearance of General Fred Franks. Pointing to his map, Franks briefed that the Air Force was continuing to bomb Iraqi positions along the Saudi-Kuwaiti border and that the Republican Guard lie several miles north, waiting to engage the enemy. Franks then discussed the regiment's "impending advance around the flank of the Iraqi defensive line and its movement in front of the Corps towards Objective Merrill and Phase Line Blacktop." Franks also noted the Republican Guard's disposition and the possibility of an Iraqi counterattack against the VII Corps' open flank.

Before the start of the ground war, Lieutenant Colonel Sullivan selected John Mecca to lead a reconnaissance of their attack zone along the Iraqi border. Satellite imagery, and reports from the local Special Forces teams, indicated that some Iraqi elements had set up observation posts within range of the Saudi borderlands. Squadron, however, wanted to fully assess the enemy's disposition and capabilities. John Mecca thus took some mine detectors along with a Bradley, a few dismounts, and a tank platoon to probe the border. With their combined optics, Mecca's scouting team could certainly assess and report the enemy's presence, if any.

Joe Deskevich, however, had already been keeping a close eye on the Saudi-Iraqi border. "I sat staring at the Iraqi border for probably a good ten days," he recalled. But what truly concerned him was the apparent lack of activity on the Iraqi side of the berm. From his viewfinder aboard the FIST-V, he could see, literally, for miles—yet there was no sign of activity. For a country that had the world's fourth largest army, and a pending Allied invasion on its doorstep, Joe found it odd that there was no sense of urgency along the western border of Iraq.

It was too quiet for comfort.

He wondered if, beyond the horizon, there was an Iraqi scout team or a battalion of dug-in T-72s. But of late, the only thing he had seen through his FIST-V optics was an abandoned outpost building (probably a border patrol station) and a derelict ZSU 57-2 antiaircraft vehicle. John Mecca's scouting team ventured out to inspect the abandoned curiosities, but none yielded any actionable information. From their appearance, both the outpost and the air defense gun had been derelict for quite some time.

But as D-Day approached, it was clear that VII Corps wasn't taking any chances: overkill was the name of the game. In fact, "as late as February 21, VII Corps had requested 35,000 TOW-2 missiles and half a million hand grenades." While these numbers seemed excessive, it showed that VII Corps was anticipating exactly what Saddam had predicted—"the Mother of All Battles."

Tacking down a date for D-Day, however, seemed a battle in itself. Initially, the ground campaign was set for February 13. Then it was rescheduled to February 17; and then rescheduled again for the 18th. This was to allow the 1st Infantry Division to occupy its position behind 2d ACR as the main-body force of VII Corps' attack. "People were getting on edge," Cardosa remembered. Tony Harrison agreed. "I just wanted to get this over with," he said. "My birthday was on February 22, and I wanted to be done with the fight by then."

The waiting finally came to an end, however, on February 21, 1991. That evening, President Bush issued his final ultimatum: Saddam Hussein had twenty-four hours to withdraw from Kuwait or face destruction at the hands of coalition forces. Despite this ultimatum, however, the

Iraqi dictator dug in his heels and told his troops to prepare for combat. From these developments, one thing was certain—VII Corps would soon meet its foe on the other side of the border.

On the night of the 21st, Ghost Troop was visited by a technical support team, running diagnostics on the new Bradleys before they went into combat. "Since these were new and untested Bradleys," said Don Chafee, "they wanted to test the TOW systems. And my TOW system failed!"

Incredulous, Chafee demanded an explanation.

"It needs a new firing card," the technician replied.

To make matters worse, there were no replacement cards anywhere in theater. Andy Moller and Don Chafee were livid. They were about to take Ghost 16 into combat, and their most powerful defensive armament was now broken. "We'll get you another card as soon as we can," the technician assured him.

But Ghost 16 couldn't wait that long. They were going into battle tomorrow.

"Well, what's going to happen if I try to fire the missile?" Don asked.

"One of two things: it will either fire two missiles at a time, or it won't fire at all."

Chafee was not impressed.

At least the 25mm gun was still operational. "But throughout the entire 100-hour ground war," he continued, "I had no TOW missile capability. It was a decoration. Pretty hard to go against a tank when you have nothing to kill him."

Preparing for the initial assault into Iraq, Lieutenant Colonel Sullivan ordered every man in the squadron to wear their chemical protective suits. These dreadfully thick, charcoaled-lined garments were a necessary nuisance to safeguard the troops from a chemical attack. Still, wearing them in the desert only amplified the daytime heat. Some troopers noted that when the order came to don their protective suits, the reality of war finally sank in—there was no turning back now.

Gathering around their commander for the Operations Order, Ghost Troop listened intently as Captain Sartiano outlined their portion of the attack. Their mission, as many of them had known all along, was to find and fix the Republican Guard. Tomorrow, the combat engineers would plow a passageway through the sand berm that marked the Iraqi border. Ghost Troop would then assume its position on the right apex of the squadron diamond, with Fox Troop in the lead and Eagle Troop on the right. Ghost Troop itself would assume a troop wedge formation. Under this configuration, the scouts would assume the lead—Keith Garwick's 1st Platoon on the left; Paul Hains' 3d Platoon on the right. Joe Deskevich and the rest of his team aboard the FIST-V would tie in with 1st Platoon. Just behind the lead scouts would be Sartiano's tank, Ghost 66, with enough room to give him visibility of the entire troop formation. Following Ghost 66, the tank platoons would assume a similar configuration to their Bradley counterparts—Andy Kilgore's 2d Platoon on the left; Jeff Geoffroy's 4th Platoon on the right. Trailing behind the tank platoons, John Mecca would maneuver the troop trains. These included the maintenance personnel, Mecca's own Bradley, and the M577 mobile command post.

According to Sartiano, the troop would maneuver with the squadron across the border through a series of "phase lines" en route to Objective Merrell. In military parlance, "objectives" are graphic measures placed on a map indicating the site (or suspected site) of an enemy position; "phase lines" are graphic references laid out every few kilometers, designed to keep track of a unit's forward movement. Phase lines were often given colorful names, depending on how creative a higher headquarters could be. For the 2d ACR's advance into Iraq, their phase lines were named after famous beer brands. For instance, to reach the suspected enemy on Objective Merrell, Ghost Troop would have to cross Phase Line Bud, Phase Line Busch, Phase Line Coors, and Phase Line Corona. However, after crossing Objective Merrell, Ghost and her sister troops would have to advance to Objective Gates, where the outpost units of the Republican Guard were presumably waiting. The final phase line, and proposed limit of advance along Objective Gates, was Phase Line Blacktop, a long and winding asphalt road that ran north from Kuwait into Iraq.

The day before D-Day, Colonel Don Holder, the Regimental Commander, came down to 2d Squadron's assembly area. In a bold gesture, the commander gathered his troops in front of him and drew a line in the sand. "Whoever doesn't want to go to war," Holder said, "can cross this line, and you won't have to go. We'll put you off somewhere in the rear." The Ghost Troopers looked at each other; then at their Squadron mates. "I was waiting for someone to cross that line," said Ruben Cardosa. "But no one did."

"Very well," said Holder. "Good hunting!"

Ghost Troop erupted in a chorus of cheers.

Camp Harris, near the Czech border in West Germany, 1990. As part of the ongoing Cold War mission, Ghost Troop did several border guard rotations to Camp Harris. By the summer of 1990, however, the Inner-German border had opened and guard duty was suspended. *Photo courtesy of Chris Hedenskog*

Ruben Cardosa and family pose alongside the Inner-German Border, 1988. *Photo courtesy of Ruben Cardosa*

Jeff Geoffroy visits the Inner-German Border on his Kawasaki Ninja motorcycle. *Photo courtesy of Jeff Geoffroy*

Invasion of the Trabants, 1990. The Trabant was a compact, two-door, two-stroke automobile manufactured by the East German government. When the Inner-German border fell, East Germans flooded the countryside in caravans of their Trabants, trying to reunite with families on the Western side. *Photo courtesy of Randy Trahan*

American tanks are loaded onto flatbed railcars, November 1990. Responding to Iraq's aggression, President Bush announced the deployment of more than 400,000 troops to Saudi Arabia for Operation Desert Shield. *Photo courtesy of Randy Trahan*

Ghost Troop's tanks stand silently in the cargo bay of their transport ship en route to Saudi Arabia. *Photo courtesy of John Mecca*

After sailing across the Mediterranean Sea and into the Suez Canal, the American tanks arrive in Saudi Arabia just in time to meet their incoming troopers at the port of Al-Jubail. *Photo courtesy of Randy Trahan*

Paul Hains (bottom left) and his comrades pose with their Pan Am stewardess en route to Saudi Arabia. Pictured in the photo are John Gifford (center), the Executive Officer of Eagle Troop, and TJ Linzy (right), a scout platoon leader in Fox Troop whose M2 Bradley led the charge into Iraq on February 22-24, 1991. Coincidentally, John Gifford later married the stewardess in this photo. The couple is still married to this day.
Photo courtesy of Paul Hains

Ghost Troop arrives at the airport in Dharan, Saudi Arabia, December 1990.
Photo courtesy of John Mecca

A Ghost Troop Bradley sallies off its ship at the port of Al-Jubail.
Photo courtesy of John Mecca

Ghost Troop's tanks line up in front of a VII Corp "paint tent."
Photo courtesy of John Mecca

A Ghost Troop tank receives its conversion from woodland green to desert tan.
Photo courtesy of John Mecca

The unofficial Ghost Troop "logo," as seen from Don Chafee's vehicle. Inspired by Rommel's Afrika Korps, Ghost Troop stenciled its own logo featuring a palm tree superimposed over the US Cavalry insignia. *Photo courtesy of Don Chafee*

Corporal Kenn Parbel, the gunner from Ghost 34, wrings out his laundry at the Dew Drop Inn. As Don Chafee recalled, Ghost Troop used one industrial-sized pail to wash all their clothes. *Photo courtesy of Kenn Parbel*

Captain Joe Sartiano, Ghost Troop commander. Sartiano was awarded command of Ghost Troop on the eve of their deployment to the Persian Gulf.
Photo courtesy of Joe Deskevich

The crew of Ghost 66, Joe Sartiano's tank. From left to right: Staff Sergeant Wood (gunner); Specialist Pike (driver); Specialist Green (loader). *Photo courtesy of Andy Kilgore*

TAA Seminole, December 1990. *Photo courtesy of Jeff Geoffroy*

Joe Deskevich (left) and Jeff Geoffroy (right) pose in front Ghost Troop's sector of TAA Seminole, which the Troop had affectionately nicknamed "Ghost Town."
Photo courtesy of Jeff Geoffroy

Kenn Parbel shows off his captured scorpion. Many Ghost Troopers wrangled scorpions and pitted them against one another in shoebox death matches.
Photo courtesy of John Carpenter

The crew of Ghost 44, commanded by Sergeant First Class Mark Currier. December 1990. *Photo courtesy of Jeff Geoffroy*

Ghost Troop's impromptu Christmas tree, constructed from tent poles and camouflage netting, adorned with red Solo cups. *Photo courtesy of Brian Foley*

Ghost Troopers gather around their Christmas tree for a yuletide celebration, December 24, 1990. *Photo courtesy of Jeff Geoffroy*

Other troopers enjoy a leisurely game of volleyball, Christmas Day, 1990.
Photo courtesy of Randy Trahan

Waylan Lundquist takes a moment of introspection at TAA Seminole, December 1990. Note Ghost Troop's Christmas tree in the background. *Photo courtesy of Andy Kilgore*

In the days leading up to the air campaign, Ghost Troop's 4th Platoon stays busy in their tent. *Photo courtesy of Jeff Geoffroy*

Jeff Geoffroy and the crew of Ghost 41. Geoffroy had nicknamed his tank "Guns & Ammo"—a nod to the first letter of his last name, and the last name of his gunner, Sergeant JW Adams. *Photo courtesy of Jeff Geoffroy*

Craig Simo, Joe Sartiano's Humvee driver, poses with the Troop mascot, "Ham Slice." The dog was one of many stray animals that Ghost Troop found in the Saudi wilderness. It had likely been the lost pet of a Bedouin tribe. *Photo courtesy of Craig Simo*

Andy Kilgore poses in front of his fully-loaded tank, Ghost 21. Aside from the bags of personal gear, Kilgore's tank is affixed with a tactical plowing blade, designed to clear enemy mines and other mobility obstacles. *Photo courtesy of Andy Kilgore*

Rick Michalec and the crew of Ghost 36—nicknamed "Guardian Angel." Michalec's crew poses with their own dog, "Blue." Like "Ham Slice," this dog was another stray found in the desert. Coincidentally, Blue accompanied Ghost 36 into battle, riding in the backseat of the Bradley as Michalec and his gunner fired on Iraqi targets. Michalec nearly brought the dog back to Germany, but the Army-appointed customs agents wouldn't allow it. Sadly, the crew of Ghost 36 had to leave Blue behind.
Photo courtesy of Tim Tomlinson

The men of 4th Platoon. *Photo courtesy of Jeff Geoffroy*

Joe Deskevich (far right) and his fellow Field Artillery officers in 2d Squadron, January 1991. *Photo courtesy of Joe Deskevich*

Andy Kilgore (far right) and the crew of Ghost 21, including Caesar Franco (left) and Terry Tennant (middle). *Photo courtesy of Andy Kilgore*

The crew of Ghost 22. Sergeant James Leofsky (far left); Corporal Tony Harrison (seated in driver's hatch; head is visible); Staff Sergeant Abraham Guillermo (center standing); and Private Patrick Sargent (far right). *Photo courtesy of Andy Kilgore*

The crew of Ghost 24. Sergeant Jerry Michaud (left, standing); Staff Sergeant Waylan Lundquist (right, standing); Private First Class Brian Foley (left, seated); and Private First Class Anthony Pritchett (right, seated). *Photo courtesy of Andy Kilgore*

A colorfully-decorated HEAT round aboard Andy Kilgore's tank. This HEAT round was the first main gun round fired from Ghost Troop during the Battle of 73 Easting.
Photo courtesy of Andy Kilgore

Kenn Parbel prepares his M203 grenade launcher, affixed to his M-16 assault rifle. As VII Corps prepared for combat, "overkill" became the name of the game. Units were issued massive quantities of AT-4 bazookas, hand grenades, and claymore mines.
Photo courtesy of Kenn Parbel

Kenn Parbel and John Carpenter show off their "field-expedient" haircuts. *Photo courtesy of John Carpenter*

The crew of Ghost 34, commanded by Sergeant Fist Class Joe Woytko. *Photo courtesy of John Carpenter*

Paul Hains, still sporting his hastily-tailored Desert BDUs, stands in front of his vehicle, Ghost 31, before crossing the berm into Iraq. Whereas most of Ghost Troop painted the palm tree with sabers emblem, Hains opted to paint a scorpion on his vehicle.
Photo courtesy of Paul Hains

Paul Hains and his gunner, Sergeant Steven Wunder. Considering Wunder's name, and the fact that he liked to wear dark sunglasses, many troopers began calling him "Stevie Wonder." Noticing that Paul Hains also preferred to wear dark sunglasses, the troopers simultaneously referred to Hains as "Ray Charles." *Photo courtesy of Paul Hains.*

The crew of Ghost 42. *Photo courtesy of Jeff Geoffroy*

The crew of Ghost 43. Ruben Cardosa and his so-called "skeleton crew." Cardosa had been the gunner of Ghost 43, but was unexpectedly promoted to tank commander while deployed to Saudi Arabia. His gunner was an in-theater replacement sent from another unit. Although the new replacement was a capable crewman, he had no prior experience as a gunner. Moreover, Cardosa's loader wasn't even a tank crewman, but a cavalry scout who had been sent to the tank platoon because the scouts were overstrength on manpower. *Photo courtesy of Ruben Cardosa*

John Mecca poses with his fiancée, Lieutenant Kelly McGinley, a fellow Army officer assigned to the 1st Armored Division. The New Jersey natives met in Germany the previous spring and married after the Gulf War. At this writing, they have been married for nearly thirty years. *Photo courtesy of John Mecca*

2d Squadron's howitzers moving across the Iraqi desert. *Photo courtesy of Joe Deskevich*

John Mecca's Bradley Fighting Vehicle captures two Iraqi MTLBs. John Mecca was one of the few executive officers to ride into battle atop an M3 Bradley. Whereas most of 2d Squadron turned in their base-model M3 Bradleys in favor of the M2A2s, Joe Sartiano asked to keep a few of the older Bradleys on hand to give to his headquarters crews. Thus, John Mecca received a "hand-me-down" M3 Bradley, which he turned into a "fighting command post." Otherwise, Mecca would've had to ride into battle in his M577 Mobile Command Post, a clumsy and lightly-armored M113 variant.
Photo courtesy of John Mecca

Joe Deskevich's mortar teams in action. February, 26, 1991. *Photo courtesy of John Mecca*

An Iraqi T-55 explodes from American fire in the opening volleys of 73 Easting.
US Army photo

The smoldering remains of an Iraqi T-55 following the Battle of 73 Easting.
Photo courtesy of Tim Tomlinson

From aboard Ghost 43, Ruben Cardosa photographs a destroyed Iraqi tank immediately following the Battle of 73 Easting. *Photo courtesy of Ruben Cardosa*

A T-72 destroyed by American tank fire at 73 Easting. Looking closely, one can see the charred remains of the Iraqi tank commander slumped over the turret. Both pictures show the same tank, photographed at different angles. *Photos courtesy of Paul Hains*

A member of Ghost Troop inspects a partially destroyed BMP within its defensive position following the Battle of 73 Easting. *Photo courtesy of Paul Hains*

Two Iraqi BMPs destroyed by Ghost Troop, February 27, 1991. One BMP is situated on the reverse slope of a sand dune. Although most of the terrain surrounding 73 Easting was flat and featureless, Ghost Troop's area had several dunes and spur lines which made it easier for some vehicles to hide. *Photo courtesy of Joe Deskevich*

An Iraqi T-72 destroyed by Ghost Troop at 73 Easting. *Photo courtesy of Tim Tomlinson*

Amidst the chaos and confusion of battle, this ill-fated BMP collided with a T-55. *Photo courtesy of Bill Virrill*

Vectoring past another destroyed Iraqi tank. *Photo by John Mecca; courtesy of Bill Virrill*

Shell-shocked Iraqi POWs following the Battle of 73 Easting. *Photo courtesy of Paul Hains*

The bodies of dead Iraqi Republican Guardsmen give mute evidence of the horrific battle. *Photo courtesy of Tim Tomlinson*

Rick Michalec after the Battle of 73 Easting. The highlight of Rick's participation in the battle was rolling into a minefield covered with surface-laid mines. This situation necessitated him firing his 25mm main gun onto the landmines and, literally, blazing a trail for his Bradley to escape the minefield. *Photo courtesy of Rick Michalec*

Andy Kilgore and his tank crew celebrate their victory following the Battle of 73 Easting. Note the battle damage on the gun tube of Kilgore's tank.
Photo courtesy of Andy Kilgore

John Mecca and Chris Harvey, one of Deskevich's Fire Support soldiers, embrace for a celebratory photo on February 27, 1991 – both elated that they had survived the horrific battle. *Photo courtesy of Chris Harvey*

Paul Hains and Steven Wunder take pause for a photo on February 27, 1991. Their forays into the Battle of 73 Easting were marked by taking on a handful of T-72s while trying to re-establish contact with neighboring Eagle Troop. *Photo courtesy of Paul Hains*

John Mecca's gunner, Sergeant Honeycutt, aboard the "fighting command post" Bradley. February 27, 1991. *Photo courtesy of John Mecca*

Ghost Troop's First Sergeant, Dwight Roark, and his .50 cal gunner, Specialist Greer. February 27, 1991. *Photo courtesy of John Mecca*

The remains of Ghost 16. Although disabled from an enemy BMP round, the vehicle remained intact until it was fired upon by a friendly tank from Hawk Company. *Photo courtesy of Don Chafee*

The Regimental Commander, Colonel Don Holder, visits with Joe Sartiano and the crew of Andy Kilgore's tank following the Battle of 73 Easting.
Photo courtesy of Andy Kilgore

General Fred Franks, the VII Corps Commander, visits with Ghost Troop on the battlefield following their firefight against the Republican Guard.
Photo courtesy of Andy Kilgore

Ghost Troop poses for a group photo following the Battle of 73 Easting. *Photo courtesy of John Mecca*

A young Arab boy flashes an American flag to Ghost Troop as they make their way into Kuwait. *Photo courtesy of Andy Kilgore*

To occupy their defensive position in Kuwait, Ghost Troop had to travel down Highway 80—the infamous "Highway of Death." Trying to escape the jaws of the coalition, the Iraqi Army commandeered a horde of Kuwaiti vehicles, driving them up Highway 80 back into Iraq. However, these retreating Iraqis were stopped dead in their tracks by US air squadrons, leaving the highway littered with burned-out vehicles and blackened carcasses. *US Army photo*

The burning oil fields in Kuwait. *Photo courtesy of Tim Tomlinson*

Sergeant Macom, Ghost Troop's Communications NCO, sits atop an abandoned Type 69 tank in Kuwait. *Photo courtesy of John Mecca*

On their way to An-Nasiriyah for occupation duty, Ghost Troop passed several distance markers along Highway 1, indicating just how close they were to Baghdad. *Photo courtesy of Danny Davis*

Jeff Geoffroy makes new friends along the screen line outside of the city of An Nasiriyah. Many Iraqi children were fascinated by the sudden appearance of American GIs and were eager to approach them as playmates. *Photo courtesy of Jeff Geoffroy*

Specialist Travis Ellis gives food to some of the local Iraqi children.
Photo courtesy of John Mecca

The iconic ziggurat, symbolizing the ancient city of Ur. Ghost Troop's position along the UN Demarcation Line near An Nasiriyah put them alongside this ancient landmark. While it made for great photo opportunities, John Mecca recalled that some scouts found abandoned caches of chemical weapons in and around the site.
Photo courtesy of Andy Kilgore

Andy Kilgore (left) promotes one of his soldiers to his next rank atop the ancient ziggurat. *Photo courtesy of Andy Kilgore*

In between their regular checkpoint duties, Tim Tomlinson and Kenn Parbel mingle with a local Iraqi family. *Photo courtesy of Tim Tomlinson*

Ruben Cardosa's collection of Iraqi Dinars – the local currency. While fleeing the post-war chaos, several Iraqis offered their local dinars in exchange for cigarettes and MREs. Although the currency held no value back in the United States, many Ghost Troopers were happy to accept dinars as souvenirs.
Photo courtesy of Ruben Cardosa

The officers of Ghost Troop stand ready on the tarmac of King Khalid Military City, awaiting their flight back to Germany. From left to right: Paul Hains, Jeff Geoffroy, Andy Kilgore, and John Mecca. *Photo courtesy of Jeff Geoffroy*

Celebrating Ghost Troop's triumphant return from the desert. From left to right: Jeff Geoffroy, Joe Deskevich, Paul Hains, and John Mecca. *Photo courtesy of Jeff Geoffroy*

At the 2d ACR's Regimental Ball, Joe Sartiano (right) is inducted into the Order of St. George, a prestigious honor society for American tankers and cavalrymen. Summer 1991. *Photo courtesy of Andy Kilgore*

The lieutenants of Ghost Troop prepare for the Regimental Ball, held only a few months after their return from the Persian Gulf. From left to right: Andy Kilgore, Jeff Geoffroy, John Mecca, and Keith Garwick. *Photo courtesy of Andy Kilgore*

Sergeant Andrew Moller's memorial gravesite. As Jeff Geoffroy recalled: "We were lucky to have him." Moller was a friend to many in 2d Squadron and was universally liked throughout the unit. *Photo courtesy of Jay Augustus*

INTO IRAQ

It was late afternoon on February 22 when Ghost Troop and the rest of 2d Squadron drove up to the border of Iraq. After two months of waiting, and several weeks of false starts, the ground phase of Operation Desert Storm was now less than thirty-six hours away. Within minutes of Ghost Troop's arrival at the border, VII Corps Artillery began its preparatory strikes—launching hundreds of MLRS rockets and 155mm artillery shells into Iraqi territory. Even though the VII Corps batteries were several kilometers behind them, the men of Ghost Troop could still feel the ground tremble in the wake of the MLRS' missile launch. As the squadron assumed its position along the Saudi border, the VII Corps Artillery continued its bombardment, determined to destroy any forward Iraqi elements lying in wait.

Saudi Arabia's border with Iraq was nothing more than a man-made sand berm that stretched for miles across the desert. To clear a pathway wide enough to accommodate the squadron's vehicles, a team of combat engineers brought in their M59 Armored Combat Earthmover—the military's version of a standard bulldozer—and plowed a clearing all the way through to the Iraqi side. Along Ghost Troop's section of the border, however, the engineers were less successful. For whatever reason, that tactical bulldozers simply couldn't clear a passage through the border berm. But Joe Sartiano, not wanting to stall the momentum of Ghost Troop's attack, waved off the bulldozers, and proceeded to mount the berm with his own M1 Abrams. Ghost Troop then watched in both awe and amusement as Sartiano pivot-steered his tank back and forth atop the berm, grinding it down in a manner similar to a drill bit barreling through the topsoil.

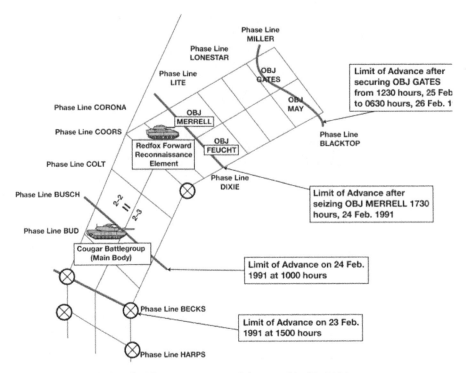

The 2d "Cougar" Squadron's movement on February 23–25, 1991.

Over the squadron radio net, each of the cavalry troops—Eagle, Fox, and Ghost—called in, confirming their combat power, verifying their battle loads, and reporting ready to fight. As Ghost Troop's 2d Platoon sallied across the open berm, however, Waylan Lundquist nearly broke his ribs. As his tank cleared the berm, his driver hadn't anticipated the steep drop-off on the reverse side of the slope. The sudden braking launched Waylan against the rim of the commander's hatch, knocking the wind out of him. Breathless, but otherwise unharmed, he advised the tanks behind him to watch their steps as they cleared the breach.

Just as they had practiced during the squadron's rehearsals, Ghost Troop vectored to the right, allowing Fox Troop to take the lead in the squadron's diamond formation. Meanwhile, Keith Garwick maneuvered his six Bradley vehicles into the lead, followed closely by Joe Deskevich in his FIST-V and the mortar carriers. Behind these lead elements, Sartiano's tank travelled near the center of the formation. Directly behind Ghost 66, the tank platoons arrayed themselves into an inverted V-shaped formation—Kilgore's platoon on the left; Geoffroy's on the right. Farther to the right of Geoffroy, and travelling a few hundred meters ahead, Paul Hains' 3d Platoon sallied forth in their own tactical formation. "Our formation was tighter than it normally would have been," said Lundquist. "Normally, when you do an advance, you have the scouts way out, but in the desert there was nowhere for them to hide if they got heavily engaged." Thus, the tanks in Ghost Troop kept within close visual contact of the forward Bradleys.

Across the border and into Iraq, however, the Ghost Troopers were shocked by what they saw.

There was no enemy in sight.

Many troopers had anticipated meeting some enemy resistance as soon as they crossed the border. Yet, with every step, Ghost Troop continued its march unmolested by enemy fire. Instead of meeting the Iraqis, however, Ghost Troop was greeted by some unusual sounds. "It was the psychological operations (PSYOPs) team," said Major Macgregor—playing rock music from their vehicle-mounted speakers in the hope of demoralizing the enemy. When the PSYOPs team had initially joined the squadron, Macgregor's only guidance was to abstain from that "whiny, peacenik crap of the 1960s"—any of which was certain to inspire memories of Vietnam. The PSYOPs team happily obliged and were now playing "Ride of the Valkyries" along with "Hells Bells" by AC/DC and Tin Lizzy's "The Boys are Back in Town."

But as the PSYOPs team blared their music, Ghost 16 drove across the berm while listening to a different soundtrack. Like many of his comrades, Terry Lorson had figured out how to daisy-chain his Walkman into the Bradley's intercom system. A fan of the 1960s rock group The Doors, Lorson played "Break on Through (To the Other Side)" to his crewmates as they scanned the horizon, looking for any sign of enemy activity. Meanwhile, from the backseat of the Grateful Dead, Terry Lorson looked longingly through the Bradley's observation ports—fixed periscopes mounted on the side of a Bradley from which a soldier could observe enemy activity. Looking out into the desert from his periscope, Lorson saw nothing but sand and the same monochromatic landscape he had seen in Saudi Arabia. "I didn't exactly have the best seat in the house," he joked.

Within minutes of crossing the border, Sartiano gave the call to test fire their weapons. Everything from the 7.62mm machine gun to the 120mm main gun would be test-fired to ensure its operability. These combat test fires required strict synchronization among the vehicles. All calibers of weapons had to be fired in turn, and each volley had to be fired in unison. This synchronized firing pattern helped conceal the number of weapons in play, so a listening enemy couldn't detect how many guns belonged to an opposing force.

During this test fire sequence, Chafee requested permission to test his TOW missile. He wanted to see if the situation was as dire as the maintenance staff had predicted. "They gave me permission to test fire the TOW," he said. "We raised the hammer up, armed it, fired, and… nothing."

Deflated, Chafee radioed to Keith Garwick that the TOW was still inoperable.

"That was the second time I knew my TOW was busted," he later recalled. "We were hoping to fire two missiles at the same time"—which the maintenance staff had predicted as a possible outcome—"but it wouldn't fire anything."

All he could do was hope that Ghost 16 wouldn't meet an enemy tank.

As the test fire concluded, Ghost Troop watched as the regiment's AH-1 Cobra and OH-58 Kiowa helicopters flew forward into the zone of attack. Then, without warning, the squadron's movement stopped at Phase Line Becks.

At 4:30 that afternoon, having made no enemy contact, the regiment instructed them to advance no farther. For Ghost Troop, February 22 had been an uneventful day. "We were moving at only eight miles per hour from phase line to phase line," said Jeff Geoffroy. While it seemed counterintuitive to move so slowly in the wide-open desert, it was prudent given the experience of American commanders during the North African campaigns of World War II. According to General Harmon, who had commanded the 1st Armored Division in North Africa, maneuvers had to be slow and deliberate. "We get a false sense of speed in maneuvers," he wrote. "We have been guilty of rewarding officers and men for grandstand moves that would be impossible to make on the battlefield, and which give false impressions of what can be accomplished." Still, the deliberate pace only heightened Ghost Troop's sense of anxiety and anticipation. They were, by every measure, the "tip of the spear," but as Jeff Geoffroy noted, "it wasn't exactly a Blitzkrieg at eight miles per hour." Nevertheless, Ghost Troop was collectively in good shape. The enemy was more than one hundred miles away and, as Major Macgregor noted, "nothing of significance would happen until the coalition ground invasion officially started the next morning."

At 7:00 AM on the morning of February 23, the squadron received orders to advance fifteen kilometers to Phase Line Busch, where they would establish a defensive line until the following day. Meanwhile, news came over the squadron net that two Marine divisions had broken through the Iraqi defensive line near the coast of the Persian Gulf. "A battle the Marines had expected to last for thirty-six hours," Macgregor said, "was over in less than three." This meant that the main thrust of the coalition's attack, spearheaded by VII Corps and the XVIII Airborne Corps, would soon follow. This attack would envelope the Iraqis' frontline defenses with a decisive "left hook" flanking maneuver—of which the 2d ACR was a lead element. If this left hook maneuver went according to plan, the squadron would cut a path clear across the desert and into the forward elements of the Republican Guard.

Finally, at 2:30 PM on the afternoon of February 23, Regiment gave the order to attack in zone, focusing on Objective Merrell. For the first time, Ghost Troop and the rest of the squadron would be attacking in the diamond formation as they had practiced. Fox Troop took the lead at the apex of the diamond "with Eagle Troop a little behind on the left, Ghost Troop a little behind on the right, and Hawk Company in the center as the squadron reserve." The Howitzer Battery also occupied the center, two thousand meters forward of Hawk Company with two sections split alongside the flanks. This would provide a flexible and rapid artillery suppression should Fox, Eagle, or Ghost Troop require it.

As Ghost Troop moved out, reassuming its troop wedge formation, Sartiano heard Lieutenant Colonel Sullivan pipe in over the squadron net, criticizing him for Ghost Troop's movement formation. Riding behind Ghost Troop in his own command tank, Sullivan announced: "Ghost 6, Cougar 6 [Sullivan's call sign], you are not executing a proper zone reconnaissance, over." Sartiano politely acknowledged the call, but Major Macgregor, sensing that Eagle Troop was next on the hit list, preempted Sullivan and said "Cougar 6, this is Cougar 3. I can vouch for Eagle Troop, they've got it right." He later added that "I did not think that critiquing movement at the troop level on our way into our first combat action was the right focus."

As Ghost Troop sallied forward, Major Macgregor heard Major John Rogler, the squadron's forward air controller and Air Force liaison (call sign: Bethel 1), announce over the squadron net that a group of A-10 Thunderbolts, referred to as "nails" in radio-speak, were in the air and looking for targets.

"Roger Bethel 1," Macgregor responded. "Can the nails fly up to Objective Merrell and tell us what's there?"

"Sure, this is Bethel 1, out."

About a minute later, Rogler returned on the radio saying "the Nails are over Objective Merrell. They see ten or twelve tanks parked behind trenches and bunkers, with hundreds of little guys running around on the ground. There are fifteen or twenty artillery guns with little guys manning them."

Amused by Rogler's used of the term "little guys" to describe enemy infantry and artillerymen, Macgregor asked the forward air controller to direct the A-10s' firepower onto Objective Merrell but to stay mindful of the squadron's forward scouts. The regiment couldn't afford a case of fratricide, especially this early into the war.

"Roggggerrrr," the air controller replied, "we can do that."

After a few minutes of silence, Rogler re-appeared on the radio: "Cougar 3, Bethel 1, we have positive ID with the scouts. We struck the tanks and artillery several times. We think that stuff is gone but the little guys with rifles disappeared into their holes, over."

Macgregor acknowledged Rogler's report and asked him to keep the A-10s over Objective Merrell until Fox Troop arrived and then fly forward to Objective Gates. Rogler responded that he could only keep the A-10s aloft for five more minutes as they were running low on fuel. Normally, Macgregor and Sartiano wouldn't have minded losing the A-10 coverage, but because Regiment had placed their attack helicopters on a ten-kilometer leash, the A-10s were 2d Squadron's only viable air asset.

As the A-10s raced back to their refueling station, Fox Troop came on the radio recommending a bypass as their lead scout platoon had encountered a field of volcanic rocks that they described as "boulders the size of bowling balls." Macgregor approved it and Sartiano relayed the command to Ghost Troop. From his driver seat aboard Ghost 22, Tony Harrison welcomed the change in direction. For hours, he had been fighting boredom, trying to stay awake as the featureless desert scrolled by his periscope. Similar to a motorist who becomes hypnotized by the passing yellow lines, the tank drivers in Ghost Troop tried to stay focused as the mass of monochromatic dirt passed underneath their tracks. The adrenaline could only keep them awake for so long and, as the hours passed without enemy contact, the much-maligned "adrenaline dump" was taking over.

Aboard their Bradley Fighting Vehicles, John Carpenter and Pat Bledsoe were battling the same conditions. They wondered where the enemy was, and why Ghost Troop hadn't made contact yet. But whereas these Bradley drivers sat upright in their seats, the tank drivers were at a disadvantage because they sat in a reclined position. Thus, when the hours of boredom and repetitive scenery began to take their toll, a tank driver had to fight his own physiology to stay awake while his body lay in a position that facilitated sleep. During these times, Tony Harrison and the other drivers often kept themselves busy by checking the gauges on their instrument panels. To the left of their throttles stood the indicator lights for the tank's transmission, oil pressure, and engine temperature. The tank's engine was a fickle beast and the driver was the only crewman who had a real-time link to monitor the engine's status.

As Ghost Troop cleared the volcanic rock field, and vectored itself back on course to Objective Merrell, Fox Troop began taking small arms fire from a platoon of Iraqi infantry. With an unmistakable tone of excitement in his voice, Fox Troop's commander, Captain Tom Sprowls, reported over the squadron radio net that his scouts had made first contact. The announcement electrified every troop in the squadron. All across the squadron front, tank and Bradley commanders hurriedly jumped onto the net, eager to listen as Fox engaged the enemy, and wondering if more enemy lie waiting in the wings.

But this first contact was over almost as quickly as it had started. A few moments after sending their first contact report, Fox Troop returned on the radio confirming that two Iraqi soldiers had been killed in the exchange. However, when the second Iraqi soldier fell from Fox's fire, the rest of the enemy platoon surrendered. "When I heard the report," Macgregor said, "I breathed a huge sigh of relief." Ghost Troop, however, was surprised to hear that the enemy had surrendered so quickly. They hadn't anticipated taking prisoners this early in the war. Eagle, Fox, and Ghost had rehearsed *ad nausem* what to do when meeting enemy prisoners of war (EPWs): they were to be properly searched, silenced, and sped to the rear where the nearest Military Police unit would take them into custody.

When the troops stopped to intercept these EPWs, they saw first-hand just how miserable the Iraqis looked. Many of them had been forcibly conscripted and they hadn't eaten in days. Their officers—political appointees from the higher ranks of the Ba'ath Party—had abandoned them days ahead of the coalition's ground assault, leaving these forsaken troops to fend for themselves.

After a few minutes, Jack Waldron, Fox Troop's Executive Officer, radioed that he was tossing bottled water to the Iraqi prisoners and pointing them in the direction of the squadron's main body, some fifteen kilometers behind them. Meanwhile, all remained quiet on Ghost Troop's sector. But as the three cavalry troops rode forward, Fox radioed to Ghost and Eagle to be wary of a "reinforced company-sized element of infantry" that Fox had bypassed. True to Fox's hunch, when Ghost and Eagle Troop came into sector, the Iraqi dismounts opened fire with some automatic weapons, and ducked quickly behind some rocks after every volley. Major Macgregor admitted that the shooting was more of a nuisance than an actual threat, but nevertheless he was concerned that these dismounts might have larger-caliber weapons like RPGs or other anti-tank rockets. Thus, Macgregor called to Cougar Forward, the squadron's "command-and-control" Bradley, and asked them to open fire with the 25mm gun. Sergeant Rusty Holloway, the gunner on Cougar Forward, answered the call with a 25mm shot that killed one Iraqi armed with an AK-47.

The impact of the round sheared off the enemy's entire upper torso.

It was crack shooting from a distance of 1,100 meters but it was the first time many of the men had ever seen an enemy soldier killed in action. At the same time, it was both gruesome, yet eerily satisfying. Seeing the lethality of American armor up close and personal "was both terrifying and reassuring," Macgregor recalled. If there had been any doubts over the killing capacity of the M2 Bradley, this dreadful scene had surely put those doubts to rest.

"Farther on," said Major Macgregor, "we encountered about a hundred Iraqi troops in defensive positions, and these would not surrender. Recognizing that we had rolled up on an infantry company in dug-in positions, Sartiano directed his scouts and tanks to open up on the Iraqi troops." As Keith Garwick made contact, Joe Deskevich's mortars sprang into action. "As Keith brought his Bradley online," said Joe, "I called back to Sergeant Newman"—the chief mortarman.

"Shake and bake!" Deskevich yelled into the radio.

This command triggered the mortarmen to fire High Explosive (HE) rounds, followed by a round of White Phosphorous ("Willie Pete") onto the same target. "It was a pretty vicious thing to do to infantrymen," Joe admitted, but such was the nature of war.

Garwick, meanwhile, positioned his Bradleys to the left and right of the Iraqi trench—preparing to blaze the enemy with 25mm gunfire.

But Joe's mortarmen had already beaten him to it.

The "shake and bake" mission was doing exactly that—shaking the enemy with the high explosive rounds, then "baking" him with the torturous heat of the White Phosphorous. As it turned out, Keith Garwick was in such a hurry to get to the trenchline, that his M2 Bradley nearly outran the mortar fire. Indeed, one of the mortar rounds landed only twenty meters in front of his vehicle. "He was none too happy about that," said Joe. But Deskevich's response was simple: "Well, back the hell off, and let the rounds do what they're supposed to do. Then go clean up."

But as it turned out, there wasn't much to clean up. "We ground these guys up like hamburger meat." Of the several dozen light infantrymen who had occupied the trench, only two of them had survived. "And they were so terrified," said Joe, "that they wet themselves."

Later that afternoon, as Ghost Troop continued moving towards Objective Merrell, the turret hydraulics on Jeff Geoffroy's tank abruptly failed. Without a functional hydraulics system, the M1's turret could not traverse at even half of the speed necessary for effective target engagement. True, the gunner could traverse the turret manually, but the time delay would cost him precious time in a firefight—where mere seconds could mean the difference between life and death. For the rest of the day, Geoffroy's tank was out of commission as the maintenance team attempted to troubleshoot the hydraulics. Although it was a monumental task, especially in the wide-open deserts of Iraq, the Troop maintenance team had his tank up and running within the next eight hours. Geoffroy's mount finally returned to Ghost Troop at 3:00 AM the following morning.

At about 4:30 PM on the afternoon of the 24th, Ghost Troop finally arrived on Objective Merrell. The A-10s had done a lot of damage but there were still some enemy trucks that had escaped the bombardment. Minutes before Ghost Troop's arrival, however, Fox Troop's scouts had disabled these trucks with 25mm gunfire. After firing just a few rounds, these Iraqis, too, had quickly given up. Throwing up their hands in terror, many of these war-weary conscripts were shouting "President Bush! President Bush!"

Evacuating this newest batch of EPWs to the rear, 2d Squadron halted for the night. In the past twenty-four hours, they had covered more than seventy kilometers. Meanwhile, Regiment would initiate an artillery strike on the farthest end of Objective Merrell. But some troopers wondered if this artillery strike was even necessary. After all, the squadron battle group was already on the objective and most of the enemy was surrendering without a fight. Nevertheless, Ghost hunkered down for another night of watching and waiting.

Over the squadron radio net, Lieutenant John Hillen, one of Macgregor's Assistant S-3 officers, sent new waypoints to Eagle, Fox, and Ghost Troop for the following morning. As it turned out, the regiment's artillery prep had included several cluster bomblets, which tended to be more of a liability than an asset. Frequently, they didn't explode on impact and became a hazard whenever friendly formations moved through the area—disabling vehicles or blowing off feet and legs. The new waypoints, therefore, directed the troops about a kilometer and a half around the impact zone. Ironically, Joe Deskevich had warned his colleagues against firing cluster bombs this early in the campaign. "In soft sand," he said, "they tend not to explode." A good rule of thumb, therefore, was never to fire cluster bombs into sand or snow.

Shortly after Hillen signed off the radio, Major Macgregor decided to pay a visit to Ghost Troop. By now, Fox Troop was evacuating its POWs and Eagle Troop seemed to be well in control of its sector. "Ghost Troop is the one element about which I know nothing," he told the squadron commander, "and I want to make sure things in Ghost Troop are in good shape." In the bustle of the day's activity, Macgregor had yet to assess how Ghost Troop had fared during its initial foray into Iraq.

"I went over to the TOC, where my lightly-armored hardtop M1025 Humvee was parked," said Macgregor. "I did not want to waste fuel driving the tank around the neighborhood, especially when the enemy was surrendering in droves. A staff sergeant in the S-3's fire support section volunteered to man the .50-caliber heavy machine gun while I rode next to the driver. He also brought along a [GPS] unit that would guide us through the open desert over to the left flank where Ghost Troop was setting up a screen line for the night."

After driving for about fifteen minutes, the GPS brought them within a few meters of John Mecca's Bradley. "Sartiano and Mecca were inside Mecca's Bradley reviewing map positions of the scouts and the maintenance posture of the troop," Macgregor continued. "Lieutenants Garwick and Hains walked in during the visit and described their screen lines and what, if anything, was happening. Ghost was extremely alert, morale was good, and I was satisfied with what I saw."

For the rest of the night, all remained quiet on Ghost Troop's front. Eagle Troop had engaged some probing Iraqi scouts, and Fox had intercepted some more truck-mounted infantry trying to escape from the battlefield. But by this point, Ghost Troop had been in Iraq for nearly forty-eight hours and its one "Shake and Bake" mission had been the only action they'd seen. So far, they had encountered a mishmash of Iraqi Army units, most of whom surrendered after first contact. The Republican Guard, however, was still out there.

At 6:00 AM the following morning, February 25, Sartiano and his crew awoke for another day of maneuver. By 7:00 AM, as the squadron continued its move beyond Objective Merrell, Ghost Troop encountered even more surrendering Iraqis. Whereas other units were taking on POWs and speeding them to the rear, Ghost Troop initially followed only one order:

"Don't stop. Take away their weapons. Give them some food or water. Then drive off."

Some troopers simply pointed the POWs to travel in the opposite direction, where they could be processed by the nearest Military Police (MP) unit. In Eagle Troop, HR McMaster recalled: "Many of the enemy greeted us with thumbs up signs and waved to us wildly. Some seemed to actually cheer us on." Initial interrogations revealed that many of these Iraqis had no love for Saddam, but felt compelled to fire a few rounds just for the sake of defending their homeland. Many of them had been conscripted at gunpoint by Saddam's secret police—an ever-popular recruiting strategy for the Iraqi Army.

Jeff Geoffroy, for example, encountered one POW who spoke impeccable English. As it turned out, this conscript had attended the University of Chicago on a student visa. Upon his return to Iraq, he had been forcibly enlisted by Saddam's Fedayeen agents, all of whom threatened to kill his family if he didn't fight for the Ba'athist regime. Don Chafee, meanwhile, noticed that many of these POWs were teachers and farmers—well-spoken and well-meaning individuals who were caught in the wrong place at the wrong time by the Ba'ath Party strongmen. But Chafee was even more astounded to see that their vehicles were combat ineffective. "They had no track underneath them and no engines," he said. "They were just left out there to shoot at whatever came at them." In fact, these conscript vehicles had been given piecemeal loads of ammunition and were expected to be little more than "speedbumps" in the path of the coalition's advance. Jeff Geoffroy noticed that their firearms were in even worse shape. "Their machine guns had rusted," he said—some to the point where they were no longer operable.

Because these POWs had been without food or water for several days, Chafee mercifully threw them some MREs. As the MREs landed at the Iraqis' feet, they didn't seem to care that the meals contained ham and pork ribs. Indeed, without any regard to their Muslim diets, they tore open the packages and devoured the contents, looking slightly more dignified than a pack of ravenous wolves.

John Carpenter, meanwhile, encountered a POW whom he described as the "skinniest guy I had ever seen—like a walking skeleton." The gaunt and sickly POW reached inside his shirt and pulled out a gold necklace adorned with an ornamental cross. "He was trying to tell me he was a Christian." Catholic and Orthodox Christians were among the largest minorities in Iraq, and several of them were drafted into the Iraqi Army alongside their Muslim countrymen. Perhaps this frail soldier thought that his faith would give him some common ground with the American troops, many of whom were at least nominally Christian.

As Ghost Troop advanced onto Objective Gates unopposed, they suddenly found themselves under a curious downpour—black, greasy, rain. As it were, the Iraqi Army had resorted to its own cruel version of a "scorched earth" policy. In the wake of their retreat, they had set fire to Kuwait's oil fields, hoping to disrupt the advancing coalition. The smoke from these oil fires had drifted northward and had begun showering frontline forces with droplets of crude.

Wiping these black droplets from their goggles, Ghost Troop's advance was halted yet again by Regimental Headquarters. The squadron was ordered to form a hasty defensive line stretching forty kilometers north to south along Phase Line Blacktop. Ghost Troop took its position on the far right, tying into 3d Squadron.

All remained quiet until 2:00 PM when Ghost Troop reported on the squadron net that they had engaged a company of Iraqi motorized infantry mounted atop MTLBs—tracked, lightly armored, Soviet-made vehicles that served as the Eastern Bloc counterpart to the M113. The exchange of fire was brief, as only two Iraqis were killed before the rest of the company gave up. While rounding up the Iraqi prisoners, however, John Mecca, decided to parade his newest war trophies—a group of brand-new MTLBs that looked like they had just rolled off the Soviet assembly line. Calling Major Macgregor on the radio, Mecca beamed:

> "Cougar 3, this is Ghost 5, you have to come over and see this equipment. It's all new and in great condition, over."

Macgregor politely declined. He had to stand fast to maintain comms with the regiment. Undaunted, Mecca simply replied:

"Cougar 3, Ghost 5, understand. I will come to your location, over."
"Ghost 5, what you mean, over?"
"Cougar 3, I will bring the MTLBs to your location for your inspection, over."
"Roger, Ghost 5, look forward to it, out."

But as Macgregor signed off the radio, he realized that Mecca would be driving an enemy vehicle right into the squadron's kill zone. "If Mecca brings those MTLBs over here, somebody might mistake him for the enemy." Scrambling for his radio, Macgregor blared:

"Battle Stations, Battle Stations, this is Cougar 3, Ghost 5 is moving a group of MTLBs to my location. Do not engage them. Acknowledge, over."

Luckily, all radio stations acknowledged the order, and none fired on Mecca as he brought the captured vehicles into view. Squadron Headquarters laughed as Mecca brought his commandeered Iraqi vehicles across the squadron front—"saluting like a Russian commander at a May Day Parade." It was refreshing to see that, even in the midst of war, American GIs could still keep their sense of humor. For John Mecca, it was his first exposure to a Soviet-made vehicle and, admittedly, he wasn't impressed. Its eight-gear manual transmission was difficult to operate, and it was obvious that the Soviets had paid little attention to ergonomics when designing their vehicles. For lack of a better term, this MTLB was a thinly-armored, poorly-designed "death trap."

But while John Mecca wrangled his MTLBs, the rest of Ghost Troop suddenly found itself straddled with an impromptu guard mission. As it turned out, the MP units were getting so overwhelmed by the sheer number of surrendering Iraqis, that Ghost Troop had to assume temporary guard of the newest POWs until the MPs could clear their backlog. As Don Chafee recalled: "We were given responsibility to guard these POWs until the MPs got there to take them." The crew of Ghost 16, and their wingman crew aboard Ghost 15 were thus given the task of guarding a group of 30-50 POWs. Like their comrades elsewhere along the frontlines, these wayward Iraqis were reluctant conscripts—fearful of Saddam, and much happier to be in the presence of an American cavalry unit than a Ba'ath Party hit squad.

"We took the tarp from our Bradley, some poles, and made a lean-to shelter for the POWs," recalled Chafee. Emerging from the back of

Ghost 16, Terry Lorson was among the many crewmen in Ghost Troop tasked to wrangle the growing horde of POWs. "They were actually happy to see us," he marveled. "They were begging for food and their uniforms were ragtag."

Suddenly one of the POWs asked Lorson for a pen and paper.

"All right," thought Lorson, "maybe he's going to give us some information."

Lorson handed the POW his pen and notepad. After about ten minutes, the Iraqi came back with a hand-written note (in Arabic), and began reading it aloud to Lorson. "I couldn't understand what he was saying, but he reached out to shake my hand and smiled. Who knows what the hell he wrote?" For all Lorson knew, the POW could have been cursing him in Arabic. Lorson wanted to get the piece of paper translated after the war, but it was lost during the Battle of 73 Easting.

Throughout the night of February 25, Ghost 15 and Ghost 16 took turns guarding the POWs in two-hour shifts, while the rest of Ghost Troop pulled back to refit and rearm their vehicles for tomorrow's operation. At some point during the night, however, Chafee's routine was disrupted by the sudden appearance of artillery fire. The crews of Ghost 15 and 16 both startled at the sound of incoming shells. Chafee could hear the impact of the rounds, but he could tell that they were landing several thousand meters away. Looking through his thermal sights, Chafee could see the cloudbursts of sand and confirmed that this artillery was indeed too far to be a threat.

But for the crew of Ghost 15, even this distant artillery was too close for comfort.

The commander of 15 promptly started his vehicle and drove full reverse back to Ghost Troop's assembly area—leaving the Grateful Dead alone to fend for themselves.

"So I'm sitting there with at least 30 POWs," Chafee said, "and my wingman has just left me." To make matters worse, the sudden onslaught of artillery fire had spooked the POWs, and nearly every one of them began charging towards Ghost 16 in a fit of panic. "Saddam is going to kill us! Saddam is going to kill us!" they shouted.

Chafee and Moller went into survival mode.

Moller with the handle of his mattock axe, and Chafee with the spare antenna, began beating back the hysterical Iraqis, trying to get them off the Bradley. While trying to subdue these panicking prisoners, Ghost Troop called on the radio for Chafee to pull back due to the incoming artillery fire. Incredulous, Chafee shouted back into the radio that these frantic POWs were the real problem, not the distant artillery.

About five minutes later, Ghost 15 returned to the Grateful Dead, and both crews finally got the POWs settled down and back into their lean-to shelter. It turned out that the artillery fire was from an American unit on a bracketing fire mission. The following morning, Chafee was ordered to abandon the POWs. Although the MPs were still overwhelmed by the massive influx of enemy prisoners, 2d Squadron had to move to its next waypoint. All 2d units were ordered to leave the surrendered Iraqis in place, where the MPs could pick them up as the lines continued moving eastward. From among the huddle of Iraqi prisoners, Chafee ferreted out the POW with the best command of the English language. "Look," he told him, "you can either stay under this shelter, and another unit will come get you, or you can move in that direction," he said, pointing west. The POWs elected to stay under their shelter—"because it was out of the sun," Chafee added. "I never found out what happened to those POWs."

Between midnight and 2:00 AM on the morning of February 26, Joe Sartiano and the other troop commanders were summoned by Major Macgregor to the squadron's makeshift command post. This *ad hoc* command-and-control center had been thrown together a few hours earlier after the squadron's latest halt and consisted of a headquarters Bradley, the forward air controller's M113, and Macgregor's own tank. Macgregor had just received word from Lieutenant Colonel Sullivan that the latter was headed back from a meeting with Colonel Holder, the Regimental Commander.

Squadron was about to get a change-of-mission.

As Sartiano and the other commanders strolled up to the command post, they buoyed themselves with excitement. Perhaps Sullivan would bring news of a pending attack.

Sadly, it was not to be.

Sullivan greeted them with news that they had been re-assigned to the Corps reserve. "We've done our job," he said. "It's now the mission of the divisions to pass through and take on the Republican Guard."

Sartiano was incredulous.

Since taking command of Ghost Troop last fall, Sartiano had been preparing his men for this showdown in the desert. Now it had come to a very anti-climactic end. A reserve force? The cavalry regiment's sole purpose was to find and fix the enemy; and thus far they had neither

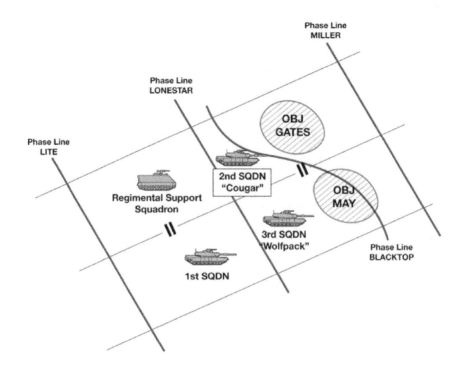

Hasty defensive positions along Phase Line Blacktop. Ghost Troop and the rest of 2d Squadron held these positions from 11:00 AM on February 25 until daybreak on February 26.

"found" nor "fixed" anything except a few listless Iraqi regulars. The Republican Guard was now within striking distance and apparently VII Corps didn't think 2d ACR had the resources to stand toe-to-toe with the enemy.

Sullivan further added that the engineers would be online to dig defensive positions for the tanks and Bradleys. More information would be announced over the squadron radio later that night, Sullivan said. With that, the squadron commander departed—leaving a group of disappointed and deflated captains in his wake. Macgregor recalled that: "Joe Sartiano stared at me for a second, then turned and left in silence."

But little did he know that by the time Sullivan had convened the meeting, General Franks had rescinded the order and no longer planned to keep the 2d ACR in reserve. Meanwhile, Squadron put out a net call instructing all three troops—Fox, Eagle, and Ghost—to change the orientation of their defense to the east. Fox Troop would occupy the northern flank; Eagle in the center; and Ghost Troop to the south.

On the morning of February 26, Ghost Troop repositioned to its new defensive sector. Paul Hains' platoon remained on the southern flank while Keith Garwick's platoon tied in with Eagle Troop to the immediate north. The tank platoons, meanwhile, occupied the middle of the formation in depth where they could support the scouts and react forward if necessary. By now the oil-saturated rain had given way to a dense fog, limited the Troops' visibility as they established their fields of fire.

Meanwhile, at Squadron Headquarters, Major Macgregor and his staff were frustrated over the newest limitations regiment had just placed on them. The 2d ACR's new operational graphics gave the squadron "a ten-kilometer front…half the frontage we had on the way up from Saudi Arabia." Maneuvering across that small of a front would render the diamond formation impractical—they would have to revert to the dreaded "box" formation. "None of us like the box," Macgregor said. "Configuring the squadron in a box, without any forward reconnaissance element, meant that we would unavoidably crash like a Napoleonic column into the enemy. It also prevented the majority of Cougar Squadron's tanks and armored fighting vehicles from being employed quickly when we did make contact."

Conferring with his assistant S-3 Lieutenant John Hillen, Macgregor agreed that this box was "the least desirable formation for a maneuver battle, but the only one that will give each of the two lead troops five-thousand-meter fronts. Otherwise, our soldiers will be so hemmed in, they may accidentally shoot themselves." For this two-troop lead, however, Ghost Troop and Eagle Troop were the units he had in mind. The order for the final attack was coming soon, and when it did, he wanted Ghost and Eagle leading the way.

At the same time, many miles away, the Tawakalna Division massed its armored formations against the pending VII Corps assault. As the coalition continued its drive into Iraqi territory, Saddam's general staff suddenly realized that if they were to have any effect on the advancing VII Corps, the elite divisions of the Republican Guard would have to move forward and replace the poorly-trained conscripts of the regular army. These "ash and trash" frontline forces had been expected to absorb the brunt of the coalition's ground assault, inflicting enough damage against the Americans and leaving enough time to mobilize the Republican Guard for a massive counterattack. But after seeing the ease with which the US was tearing through Iraq's defenses, the Republican Guard was frantically preparing itself for action.

The Iraqi version of the T-72 tank, known as "The Lion of Babylon," had a 125 mm main gun that could destroy targets at more than 2,000 meters. Weighing in at forty-one tons and covered in armor up to twelve inches thick, the Iraqi T-72 could reach speeds in excess of forty miles per hour. Despite the aggressive air campaign, Saddam still had more than 1,000 of these tanks sitting combat-ready along the Iraqi defensive lines. These T-72s were supported by hundreds of lighter armored vehicles including the Soviet-made BMP.

Headed straight for them was the VII Corps, with more than 1,000 of their own tanks and hundreds of Bradley Fighting Vehicles. Their M1 Abrams tanks were more than thirty tons heavier than the T-72, but just as fast, and with better armor protection. By sunrise on the morning of February 26, these two opposing forces lay only nine miles apart.

DAY OF BATTLE

At 7:30 that morning, Ghost Troop assumed its position on the northern edge of the "box formation," with Eagle Troop directly south. Almost simultaneously, Ghost and Eagle oriented their vehicles facing east, ready to take on any Iraqi elements that crossed their path. Going into battle, Sartiano would deploy Ghost Troop in its own unique formation. While staying within the Squadron's "box" movement, Sartiano put Ghost Troop into a modified "wedge." First Platoon's scouts and 2d Platoon's tanks would be on the left-hand side of the wedge, while 3d Platoon's scouts and 4th Platoon's tanks would be on the right-hand side. Paul Hains's 3d Platoon would be on the extreme right, maintaining contact with Eagle Troop along its route of advance. Eagle and Ghost would be leading the assault into the frontline formations of the Republican Guard, and Paul Hains had been ordered to maintain radio and visual contact with Eagle Troop at all times. It was a tall order but, in a fierce firefight, tight communication and situational awareness would help carry the day.

Currently, the squadron was positioned along the 50 Easting and had received orders to move ten more kilometers east to the 60 Easting. "Meanwhile, the lead scouts in Ghost and Eagle Troops continued to reconnoiter by fire, sending 25mm high-explosive incendiary rounds into anything that looked suspicious," said Macgregor. "There was no return fire. Ghost Troop reported finding some abandoned Iraqi equipment, while Eagle Troop assumed its new obligation to quickly establish contact on its right [i.e. southern] flank with 3d Squadron."

At 8:00 AM, however, Ghost Troop engaged the first probing elements of the Republican Guard. As it turned out, three Iraqi MTLBs had wandered into the Eagle-Ghost sector of 2d Squadron's front. Eagle

Troop made first contact, with HR McMaster blasting one of the enemy vehicles with a 120mm sabot round. "For once," said Major Macgregor, "the Iraqi soldiers reacted quickly. The remaining two MTLBs fled north before Eagle Troop could inflict any more damage, only to find Ghost Troop waiting in ambush for them. This made the Iraqi MTLBs perfect targets for Garwick's Bradley gunners."

As Garwick recalled: "The fight started the way any fight starts—with the smallest engagement." And Keith Garwick was about to launch the opening rounds of the squadron's fight against the Republican Guard. "I'm looking through my sights and I see this vehicle with at least twenty people on it." This oddly-shaped vehicle looked out of place to Garwick, and its occupants seemed unaware that they were fleeing right into his kill zone. "I was trying to figure out what the hell I was looking at," he continued, "because it looked like an MTLB but it had antennas all over it. And with all the people on top, you almost couldn't see the track."

It was, in fact, an MTLB—one of the two Iraqi mounts that had just fled from Eagle.

Garwick then realized that, with all its antennas, this MTLB had to be a reconnaissance track, or a command track.

"This thing had to go," he said. "I gave the platoon orders to open fire."

First Platoon answered the call with a salvo of 25mm gunfire, halting the heavy-laden MTLB in its tracks. The few Iraqi soldiers who survived the incoming burst of gunfire jumped off the MTLB and started running. But then, unexpectedly, a few of the fleeing Iraqis changed course and started running back towards the MTLB—either in attempt to salvage its comms or relay a transmission that the Americans were coming. Either way, Keith Garwick wasn't going to let the vehicle survive.

"Gunner. Missile. PC!"

The Bradley shuddered to a halt as Garwick's gunner, Sergeant Steve Rogers, deployed the TOW missile launcher, lining up the MTLB under the glowing red crosshairs of his thermal sights.

"On the way!" yelled Rogers as he depressed the trigger.

It was the first time either man had fired a missile in combat. The entire Bradley trembled as the TOW erupted from its housing tube, hissing as it hurtled towards the Iraqi vehicle.

"That ended the problem of any radio transmission," Garwick chuckled.

Whatever forward elements they had just engaged, there was now no way for them to alert their higher headquarters or any follow-on forces.

Meanwhile, Joe Deskevich's mortar teams dropped their 4.2-inch heavy rounds right onto the second MTLB, destroying the evasive vehicle in a brilliant flash of searing metal. Some of the Iraqis who had fled the scene took their sidearms and disappeared into the ground, no doubt jumping into their hastily-dug trenches and spider holes, waiting for the Americans to come within small arms range. But Keith Garwick, not wanting to let these dismounts get away, called for another mortar strike.

Joe's mortar teams were happy to oblige.

Strafing the trenchline with the same "Shake and Bake" mission they had done earlier, Ghost Troop's mortars ripped through the bodies of the fleeing Republican Guardsmen. After the immediate area was deemed "clear," Ghost Troop rolled forward to inspect the battle damage.

"That's when I saw the markings of the Tawakalna Division," said Garwick.

It was their first indication that 2d Squadron was now fighting the Republican Guard.

Moments later, Major Macgregor appeared on the radio. "Battle stations, battle stations, this is Cougar 3. Eagle Troop is now in the main attack. Ghost is the supporting attack. Hawk follows Eagle in support. Fox Troop follows Ghost in support. Cougar forward will issue waypoints. Acknowledge, over." The announcement came like a clarion call: the 2d ACR would turn ninety degrees and attack eastward to fix the main body of the Tawakalna Division. However, the regiment was to avoid any decisive engagement with the enemy, assuming that was possible. The idea was to "hold the line" against the Republican Guard before handing off the battle to the 1st Infantry Division, whose armor battalions would deliver the crushing blow. Meanwhile, the 3d Armored Division would swing north to envelop the enemy along his flanks.

Keith Garwick, meanwhile, pondered the feasibility of these orders. As expected, 2d ACR would be performing a "movement to contact" operation. But, performing this maneuver with scouts in the desert wouldn't be the same as doing it in the German countryside. If engaged by enemy tanks, his Bradley would have nowhere to hide. "I had studied enough, and I had been on the border enough times to realize how vulnerable scouts could be," said Garwick. "And no matter how fancy your tactics are, no matter how great your optics, nothing is going to stop that 125mm round from a T-72. If it hits you, you're done."

Thus, if Ghost Troop expected to survive first contact with the Republican Guard, the Bradleys would have to hand off the battle to the tanks before the first shots were fired, or let the tanks lead the way into the fight. Come what may, Ghost Troop was happy to be on the move again. The staccato stop-and-go rhythm of VII Corps' advance had taken its toll on the men. For three days, Ghost Troop had yet to fight a major engagement and, with the Republican Guard only a few hours away, the troopers just wanted to get on with the attack.

Battlefield visibility, however, continued to be a problem.

For the morning fog soon gave way to an intense sandstorm. In fair weather, Ghost Troop had visibility for seven to eight kilometers. But on this day of the sandstorm, even with their thermal sights, the tanks and Bradleys could barely see four kilometers to their direct front.

Taking their position along the northern flank of the Squadron's box formation, Ghost Troop arrayed itself into its tactical wedge configuration. Pairing together the scout and tank platoons across the forward slopes of their troop "wedge," Ghost sallied forward with Joe Deskevich's FIST-V tying in with 1st Platoon's scouts. By now, every man in Ghost Troop was eager to get his first taste of combat.

But as Major Macgregor admitted: "Time dragged while we crawled forward. As we reached the successive limits of advance, [John Mecca] had to endure my relentless calls for immediate frontline 'traces,' marked up maps, showing where all of our lead combat elements were on the ground." At first, Macgregor noted that Mecca seemed to be taking longer than the other executive officers to relay information. "What I did not know," said Macgregor, "was that the delay in Ghost Troop was the result of [Paul Hains'] excessive enthusiasm." As it turned out, Paul thought he had to provide Mecca with GPS coordinates for every vehicle in 3d Platoon. Thus, during every short halt, Paul would go to all six Bradleys in his platoon, asking for their GPS grid coordinates. "When Hains explained what he had been doing, Mecca made it clear that he did not need to provide a six-digit grid coordinate for each of his vehicles," said Macgregor. "Left, right, and center vehicle grids would suffice. After that, our reporting process sped up somewhat, making all of our lives a little easier. Hains' exuberance, however, would soon find a positive outlet along the 73 Easting."

The sun peeked through the clouds but the sandstorm continued with its dusty fury. As Ghost Troop moved forward, they met their first contact of the afternoon—airburst artillery. Like most enemy contact thus far, this artillery fire was more of a nuisance than a true threat. Moreover, the Iraqis typically couldn't adjust their fire quickly enough to keep pace with the coalition's movement. Still, this artillery was precise enough to get Ghost Troop's attention. Aboard Ghost 34, John Carpenter and his gunner, Corporal Kenn Parbel, noticed the incoming burst of white smoke registering just above their vehicle. But, because the terrain offered no impediments to their mobility, Ghost Troop simply maneuvered around the incoming fire. Other vehicles in 3d Platoon had similar encounters with the nuisance artillery, some having shells land within a few meters of their tracks. The concussion waves were enough to shimmy the Bradleys, but the vehicles remained intact and fully functional. Nevertheless, it seemed that the closer Ghost Troop got to the Republican Guard, the more precise their artillery fire became.

"As the [enemy] artillery fire fell intermittently among the advancing armor," added Macgregor, "Ghost Troop reported finding and destroying Iraqi outposts in the billowing sand." Keith Garwick recalled: "We started running into enemy patrols at about the 60 Easting, so we were in contact, on and off at different levels, for at least ten kilometers before we got to the 73 Easting." Indeed, as Ghost Troop sallied upon the 65 Easting, Rick Michalec encountered a pair of BMPs, both of which he handily destroyed with a multi-round burst from his 25mm main gun. Joe Sartiano, meanwhile, moved his tank back and forth between the scout platoons, trying to maintain situational awareness in the poor visibility. "Simultaneously, Sergeant Honeycutt, Mecca's gunner, kept telling Mecca what he could see through the thermal sights, helping Mecca to keep track of where the scout platoons were."

But as Ghost Troop continued to scan its sector, enemy contact suddenly erupted along Eagle Troop's front. Aboard Ghost 36, Rick Michalec had been trying his hardest to maintain contact with Eagle Troop but, in the fog of war, it was a task easier said than done. "When Eagle came across enemy formations," said Michalec, "they did their charge and went into a wedge"—the famous "tanks front" formation that paved the way for Eagle Troop's victorious firefight against the Tawakalna Division. "I stayed with them…I wasn't engaging anything; I was just reporting what I was seeing. I was letting my guys [in 3d Platoon] know what was going on out there."

But once Eagle Troop had cut its swath of destruction across the battlefield, Michalec had to work his way back to Ghost Troop. Ghost's platoons were still in contact with enemy patrols, and he sensed that more contact was on the horizon. But as Michalec vectored Ghost 36 to rejoin his comrades, he ran into a different problem.

"I got stuck in a minefield!"

Indeed, dozens of surface-laid mines were scattered in front of him. "They looked like green beakers with yellow stripes," he said. "I had never seen anything like this." At best, they could be conventional antivehicular mines, designed to immobilize tracks. At worst, they could be gas mines—loaded with VX, Sarin, or Mustard Gas.

Thinking quickly, Michalec radioed the combat engineers and explained his predicament. The engineer replied that, given Michalec's description of the landmines, they weren't likely to contain chemical agents. But with the rest of Ghost Troop on the advance, Michalec knew there was only one way to get out of this minefield.

He would literally have to blast his way out.

He directed his gunner, Sergeant Michael Strong, to swing the gun tube over the back deck of the Bradley and shoot the mines until they exploded. "We essentially blazed a trail—Bam! Bam! Bam!—and blew up all the mines in our way." In total, Michalec and his gunner force-detonated nearly a dozen landmines.

As Ghost 36 emerged from the minefield, Michalec looked back, gazing upon the tracks left in the sand by his M2 Bradley. He was horrified to see that, in between the tread marks, lay several of the surface-laid mines that Ghost 36 hadn't hit. "We were lucky," he said. Ghost 36 had missed running over some of these landmines by mere inches. Paul Hains, meanwhile, had gone back to look for Ghost 36 and was relieved to see that Michalec and his crew had emerged from the minefield unscathed.

But amidst the minefield detour, Ghost Troop had lost contact with Eagle. Sartiano, therefore, sent Paul Hains and Sergeant Kevin Merriweather in their respective Bradleys to re-establish contact. A few moments after breaking away from Ghost Troop, however, Hains suddenly saw a group of heat signatures populate in his thermal sights.

"Vehicles," he told himself. But was it Eagle Troop?—he wondered.

Suddenly, as the heat signatures grew bigger and brighter, Hains spied a group of dismounted soldiers scurrying across the battlefield. Then, out of the corner of his viewfinder, he saw a giant diesel plume erupt from the ground, followed by a T-72 emerging from its dug-in position.

"Ah, that must be enemy," Hains said with a cool nonchalance.

But this T-72 wasn't alone. Hains suddenly noticed that the other heat signatures had morphed into a platoon of T-72s, all of which were pointing their turrets in his direction. Now his nonchalance had turned to panic.

"Oh sh*t!" he cried. "Where is Eagle Troop?!"

Hains immediately went into survival mode.

Spying a nearby dirt mound, Hains told his driver to pull the Bradley up to it and prepare for combat. An M2 Bradley couldn't stand toe-to-toe with a T-72, but its twin-mounted TOW missiles could take out at least one or more of the enemy tanks before they closed in on him. If Hains was going down, he would go down swinging. As soon as the Bradley shimmied to a halt on the mound, Hains' driver yelled, "Tanks! Front!"

Hains, already looking at a T-72 nearly fifty yards to his front replied, "I got it, thanks."

"No, no," the driver replied, "there's a tank to our immediate front!"

Hains, thinking that his driver was referring to the same T-72, replied "I see it!"

"No, no," the driver repeated, "You don't understand, there's a tank to our immediate front!"

Puzzled by his driver's remarks, Hains lifted himself out of the hatch and looked over the right side of his vehicle. Sure enough, dug into a fighting position just below the Bradley, was a T-72 tank. The "mound" that Hains had just driven on was the displaced sand from the T-72's hiding hole.

Much to his horror, Hains dropped back into his hatch and swung the turret around, depressing the 25mm gun and firing frantically at the T-72. Realizing that he was in over his head, Hains ordered his driver to pull back. But suddenly he realized that, in the open desert, he had nowhere to run. Because the Bradley couldn't fire its TOW missiles on the move, Hains stopped the vehicle yet again and deployed the twin-mounted missile launcher. Laying his gunner onto the nearest T-72, Hains shouted "Gunner, Missile, Tank!"

"Identify, T-72 tank!" replied the gunner.

"FIRE!"

With a violent hiss, the TOW missile escaped from its tube, hurtling dead-center into the enemy tank. As the T-72 exploded in a brilliant flash of yellow sparks and molten armor, Hains realized that there were now eight enemy tanks in the area.

"Ok," he told himself, "these guys all know that I'm here and they're probably a little pissed off about it." Ordering his gunner to fire the second TOW missile, Hains expected to hit one more Iraqi tank before going down in a blaze of glory. However, halfway through the second TOW missile's trajectory, Hains' heart sank when he saw the missile sputter and fall to the ground. Preparing to back his vehicle up again, Hains was relieved to see Merriweather's Bradley pull up next to him and fire another TOW missile, killing the closest T-72, and promptly fire another missile for a second kill.

With the two Bradleys having fired both their missiles, Hains kept his vehicle in front to cover the other Bradley crew while they reloaded their TOWs. However, there were still at least five T-72s out there, and they were closing in fast. Out of desperation, Hains ordered his gunner to fire the 25mm cannon until it could fire no longer. The gunner responded with a volley of 25mm rounds, all of which simply bounced off the nearest T-72.

"We're just pissing it off, sir" the gunner protested.

From the looks of the situation, it seemed that the gunner was right: the T-72 was moving its turret in the direction of Hains' vehicle and its gun tube was slowly settling onto an azimuth, meaning that they had acquired Hains as a target. Thinking that the end was near, Hains suddenly heard Merriweather shout "Up!" and raced his Bradley in front, firing his reloaded TOWs into the offending tanks. The quick reload undoubtedly saved Hains' life.

Moving forward through the smoke and out of the sandstorm, Hains finally spotted two of Eagle Troop's Bradleys—Eagle 16 and Eagle 12. As Eagle 16 pulled up to Hains, its vehicle commander popped open the hatch and yelled: "There's tanks over there!"—pointing in the directions from which Hains had just come.

Incredulous, Hains shouted back: "I know!"

But, for now, Hains had accomplished his original mission to re-establish contact with Eagle Troop. Now that he could see Eagle 16 and was speaking face-to-face with its commander, he was happy to radio to Sartiano that the gap between Eagle and Ghost Troop had been closed—with no fewer than five T-72s destroyed along the way.

"Ghost Troop had encountered scattered enemy elements," said Major Macgregor, "but not the large concentration of enemy that Sartiano was sure was lurking somewhere to his front. Sartiano figured that the short, sharp engagements on the way up to 73 Easting represented encounters with forward outposts for larger, defending enemy forces."

As he would soon find out, Sartiano's hunch was correct.

"With the weather clearing," Macgregor continued, "it was finally possible for Sartiano to see more than just hotspots in the thermal sights. Listening to the troop net, he and Mecca both knew that Garwick's 1st Platoon scouts still had no contact in the north, and that Hains' 3d Platoon scouts on the southern flank were busy regaining coherence."

Within sight of the 70 Easting, Garwick realized that his platoon was looking at the frontside of an uphill berm. The regiment had given them orders to halt, but Garwick and Sartiano knew better. "There's no way I'm going to stay on the backside of this terrain and having no visibility in front of me," Garwick told himself. "So, I just kept pushing forward and told Sartiano that we can't stay here—we gotta keep moving." In the featureless deserts of southern Iraq, a rise of only ten to twenty feet is militarily significant because it can create defilade for the enemy.

As it turned out, the crest of that small berm sat just parallel to the 73 Easting. "It was very shallow," said Garwick. "It didn't show up on the maps and you wouldn't have known it was there." But as Ghost Troop sallied forward to the 73 Easting, Joe Sartiano saw a new heat signature emerging in the green glow of his thermal sight. He couldn't precisely identify it as a tank or BMP, but he could tell from its relative position that it wasn't friendly. Thus, at a range of 548 meters, Sartiano's gunner fired a SABOT into the anonymous vehicle. The target stopped dead in its tracks, but the explosion was less than fulfilling.

A moment later, however, Sartiano detected another vehicle, later confirmed as a BMP. His loader, Private First Class John Green, pulled a HEAT round from the ammunition rack and, within a mere three seconds, rammed the round into the gun breech with his fist. The young loader then artfully pulled his hand away as the breech lock closed. Flattening himself against the turret wall, he wrapped his glove-laden hand around the neck of the arming handle, thrusting it into the "armed" position.

"Up!" he yelled.

By this time, Sartiano's gunner had acquired the BMP at less than 500 meters. Sartiano yelled "Fire!" a half-second before Ghost 66's gun belched a HEAT round into the Iraqi vehicle. Unlike the previous target, this BMP exploded into a flash so bright that Sartiano's crew had to shield their eyes.

"Ghost 5, this is Ghost 6," he called to Mecca. "Just destroyed two targets to my front."

"Target description, over?"

"Ghost 5, I have no f*cking idea, they could be tanks, they could be BMPs, hell it could be a truck convoy for all I know. But they're smoking now."

With a mild chuckle, John Mecca acknowledged the call and reported to Squadron that Ghost had engaged two enemy vehicles in sector.

"Although the sandstorm had diminished to the point where visibility now reached out beyond a thousand meters," Macgregor recalled, "the smoke and fire from the recently destroyed enemy equipment [particularly in Eagle Troop's sector] more than compensated for the disappearance of the sandstorm."

It was now 4:30 PM and, for Ghost Troop, the Battle of 73 Easting was about to begin.

As Andy Kilgore's platoon settled in next to Keith Garwick's scouts along the 73 Easting, he took note of the battlespace in front of him. "It was the worst visibility I had ever seen. We were traversing left and right, using our thermal sights to keep contact with other vehicles because we couldn't see anything." Sallying online with 1st Platoon, Kilgore recalled: "We were inching forward literally about as fast as you could walk. You could almost feel the individual track pads hit the ground."

Suddenly, Kilgore saw the heat signature of enemy troops pop out from their bunkers.

The M1's thermal sights could easily detect them because "their bodies were extremely hot compared to everything around them." These troops were now scrambling to their nearby vehicles.

"Gunner! Coax! Troops!" yelled Kilgore.

From that cluster of troops, only three of them made it to the nearest BMP. The enemy's relief was short-lived, however, as Kilgore promptly fired a HEAT round into their vehicle.* "And that vehicle was literally 300 meters in front of us."

The lingering sandstorm and the smoke from the burning vehicles only added to the apocalyptic aura of the battle scene. "You've still got 70-80 mile-per-hour winds out there, and the hot fire from the

---

* As it turned out, Kilgore's HEAT round was the first main gun round fired from Ghost Troop during the battle.

burning vehicles is washing out your thermals as its going across your direct front," said Kilgore. Because the smoke and fires had obscured Kilgore's visibility, neither he nor his platoon could get a clear visual on the enemy targets. "I could see some hot spot movements here and there behind the smoke, but not long enough to see what it really was."

Vehicles?

Dismounts?

Artillery?

Kilgore didn't know.

But whatever it was, it was enemy—and it had to die.

"So, I radioed the troop commander and asked him to move my platoon forward. I wanted to poke my nose through the smoke because we could see stuff moving behind it."

Sartiano granted his request.

Kilgore then switched his radio from the troop level down to his platoon-level net, meaning that his next radio transmissions would be broadcast only to 2d Platoon's tanks.

He then vectored his tank to the right of the vehicle he had just destroyed. But as soon as he passed the burning Iraqi tank, he saw several bunkers arrayed in front of him. "When I poked through the smoke, I realized we had a company-sized defense spread out in front of us." More to the point, Kilgore's platoon had just wandered into the enemy's assembly area. As Sartiano recalled: "He basically opened the front door and started shooting!"

At that moment, the "muscle memory" of Andy Kilgore's numerous crew drills took over. "I told my gunner to engage. And at about the time we fired the first main gun round, the other tanks in my platoon punched through the smoke."

Kilgore's platoon was now the forward-most element of the US VII Corps.

But because they had gone through the smoke, Sartiano no longer had visibility of 2d Platoon. Still, he could hear the main guns of Kilgore's platoon firing almost in unison—accompanied by coax machine guns and the unmistakable sound of the loaders' M240 hatch-mounted machine guns. Yet even through the haze of the smoke, Sartiano could see the illuminating flashes of the main guns as they pounded away at one Iraqi target after another.

"Once we got through the smoke," said Tony Harrison, "we started opening fire." His tank commander, Sergeant Guillermo, fired the first round of the engagement. From the periscope of his driver's seat, the unfolding battle looked surreal to Harrison. Iraqi vehicles were erupting into flames nearly faster than he could count them.

Meanwhile, as Keith Garwick listened to Kilgore's melee over the platoon net, he could hear the fury in 2d Platoon's voices—shouting their fire commands and punctuating each with the telltale roar of the tanks' main guns. Keith could tell from the battlefield acoustics that Kilgore's men were receiving return fire.

As the first of Kilgore's main gun rounds landed on the offending T-72s, he was thrilled to see the enemy turrets flying several feet into the air, landing on the desert floor with a metallic thud. These catapulting turrets, he said, were attributed to the T-72's internal design. "The Soviets had a different theory on storage of ammo than the Americans," he said. "They've got the ammo stored around their hull. So, if you make the ammo explode on a T-72, or any Russian tank, all that explosive force is funneled up through the turret"—hence the catastrophic explosions Ghost Troop was seeing as they fired on the T-72s.

Meanwhile, aboard Waylan Lundquist's tank, he spied a two-man RPG team, and ordered his gunner, Sergeant Michaud, to engage the coax machine gun. But when the coax jammed after firing only a few rounds, Lundquist knew he had no time to troubleshoot the stoppage before the RPG descended upon his tank.

"Fire the main gun!" he screamed.

In a move seldom seen during combat, Lundquist was about to bring the fury of the tank's 120mm main gun against the enemy dismounts.

"HEAT round's in the tube," yelled Brian Foley.

Waylan's gunner then depressed the trigger, hurtling the massive round right into the enemy's foxhole—"took the head clean off of one guy," Lundquist said. Kilgore, beholding the same sight from aboard Ghost 21, recalled that the HEAT round hit the wayward Iraqi in the center of his chest. "It looked like he just imploded." Parts of his body and uniform simply fluttered into the air like leaves. The other Iraqi soldier simply keeled over, dead from the HEAT round's concussion blast.

From his loader's station, Brian Foley could neither see nor truly hear the battle. But even through the heavily-layered headset of his Combat Vehicle Crewman Helmet, he could detect the sound of the explosions happening all around him. Perhaps the most telltale sign of battle, however, was the smoke from the burning vehicles that kept wafting into his loader's hatch. "Whatever round I grabbed," said Foley, "is what Sergeant Lundquist shot, because any round we had would destroy anything they had."

Fixing his gaze onto the next enemy target, Lundquist ordered his gunner to fire a SABOT into what looked like an enemy pillbox. "It turned out to be a communications bunker"—and as luck would have it, his round landed directly into the enemy's field radio. "It cut off their communications," he said, "so they couldn't call for reinforcements at this point." Little did he know that the Iraqis had already called for reinforcements, which were on their way and would soon be arriving in Ghost Troop's sector.

From his perch atop Ghost 24, Waylan could hardly believe the chaos that was unfolding before his eyes. The enemy was in full panic, and some of the Iraqis had resorted to charging the American tanks in a banzai-style attack. One desperate Iraqi, meanwhile, was running back to his BMP, attempting to retrieve the AK-47 that stood leaning against the side of his vehicle. He almost made it…before being cut down by a well-placed shot from Waylan's Colt 45. As a tank commander, Waylan never truly expected to use his sidearm in combat, but such was the intensity of this battle.

Back aboard Tony Harrison's tank, Ghost 22, his gunner Sergeant James Leofsky was likewise about to down an enemy soldier with the tank's main gun. From the opening rounds of this firefight, Leofsky's Laser Range Finder had been flashing zeroes—indicating that the enemy tanks were less than 200 meters away. By the standards of tank warfare, they were fighting at point-blank range. Calling up to Guillermo and Leofsky, Harrison spotted another enemy soldier with an RPG. Expecting to see this wayward Iraqi cut down by the coaxial machine gun, Harrison jumped in his seat when he heard the main gun go off.

Leofsky had just fired a HEAT round squarely into the chest of the enemy soldier.

And, just as it had done aboard Waylan's tank, this HEAT round literally disintegrated the brazen Iraqi—sending his charred head and pieces of his limbs fluttering into the air.

All the while, Joe Sartiano was frantically trying to get ahold of Kilgore on the radio.

"White 1, Ghost 6, report, over!"

"White 1, this is Ghost 6, what is your status, over?!"

"White 1, this is Ghost 6, answer the goddamn radio, over!"

But it was no use. Kilgore couldn't hear him. And even if he could, his priority was to fight and to win the battle. "Fight the battle, then report," touted Macgregor. "That was Kilgore's thinking, and he was right." But seeing the horrific explosions and hearing all calibers of gunfire, Sartiano simply wanted to know who was winning the fight and who, if anyone, had taken casualties.

Hearing the agony in Sartiano's voice, Sergeant Macom, Ghost Troop's communications NCO, dropped down to Kilgore's platoon net to find out what was happening. Hearing the chaos and fury from 2d Platoon's net, Macom promptly radioed John Mecca: "Sir, Kilgore's platoon is in some serious sh★t, better tell the old man." Mecca relayed that 2d Platoon was fighting an "unknown number of Iraqi troops at point-blank range and was too busy to report." But the radio call only heightened Sartiano's anger and anxiety. "Pushing forward into the smoke and confusion could make things worse, even cause fratricide." At this point, Sartiano knew there was little he could do; Kilgore would simply have to fight his way out.

Andy Kilgore, meanwhile, realized that his current tactics weren't working. He and his platoon had eliminated a company-sized element of tanks and BMPs. But now they were facing a swarm of dismounts. "Neither he nor the rest of his tank commanders could get rid of the attacking Iraqis. Kilgore's tank crews were spraying machine gun fire from every available weapon…to keep the Iraqi soldiers from reaching the tracks, but it was getting damn dangerous and there was no time to think." With his own .50-caliber machine gun, Kilgore was cutting down dozens of Iraqi dismounts. Many of these fanatical Republican Guardsmen were closing within fifteen meters of his tank. "Body parts were flying everywhere"- yet these Saddam loyalists kept on coming.

In many ways, this firefight underscored the level of fanaticism held by the Republican Guard. Unlike the hapless and reluctant draftees whom Ghost Troop had met earlier, these Republican Guardsmen considered themselves to be Iraq's elite—"the best of the best." They were fiercely loyal to Saddam and were expected to fight until the last man standing.

But it soon dawned on Kilgore that his tank commanders and gunners "could not depress their guns low enough to kill the Iraqi infantry." Waylan Lundquist was already drawing his Colt 45 to beat back the onslaught of enemy dismounts. "If any of the Iraqi troops crawled up next to the tanks, Kilgore thought, they could probably plant charges on the tanks without even being seen." Without more standoff distance between his tanks and the enemy dismounts, his tank commanders simply couldn't engage the Iraqi troops with their onboard machine guns.

Without hesitation, he screamed into the radio: "Back up! Everybody back the f★ck up now, over!"

Moments later, Tony Harrison and the rest of the drivers in 2d Platoon thrust their transmissions into full reverse, revving the tank's engines as they bounded back from the melee. During this hasty retrograde, however, some of the Iraqi troops were crushed under the treads of 2d Platoon's tanks. Even over the roar of the tank's engine, one could still hear the Iraqis' bones breaking under the weight of the treads.

As Kilgore's tanks bounded back towards the rest of Ghost Troop, they kept firing their .50 caliber and M240 machine guns, cutting down scores of Iraqi infantrymen in their wake. Surprisingly many of the Republican Guardsmen kept on coming. "Did they think they had driven off the tanks and were winning the battle?" Kilgore had no idea; but he kept on firing the tank's crew-served weapons. A mere sixty seconds later, though—as the tanks gained more standoff between themselves and the enemy—these fanatical dismounts finally buckled under 2d Platoon's fire. Surveying the damage in front of him, Kilgore concluded that there was nothing left alive in his platoon's sector. "Where once green-colored uniforms had darted in and out of bunkers, there were now only heaps of corpses. The Iraqi soldiers had been blown to pieces. This Republican Guard company strongpoint was now a heavy-metal graveyard." Within a mere three minutes, his platoon had destroyed more than a dozen BMPs, T-72s, and at least several dozen enemy dismounts.

But as his adrenaline slowed, he asked himself: "Where the hell is the rest of Ghost Troop? And then, being the lieutenant that I was, I remembered that I should report this." Little did Kilgore know that Sartiano had been trying to get ahold of him all along. Kilgore had intended for Waylan Lundquist, his platoon sergeant, to relay the situation reports. But somehow, in the fog of battle, that request never made its way to Lundquist. Waylan, too, had dropped down to the platoon-level net during the engagement—thus leaving poor Sartiano in the dark about what had happened with 2d Platoon.

"Ghost 6, this is White 1, report follows, over."

Sartiano was furious. "This is Ghost 6. Where the f*ck have you been?!!"

"Ghost 6, engaged and destroyed a dozen BMPs, and unknown number of enemy troops, over."

"White 1, understood. If you ever do that again, I'll shoot you myself!"

"This is White 1, Roger, sir, uh…over."

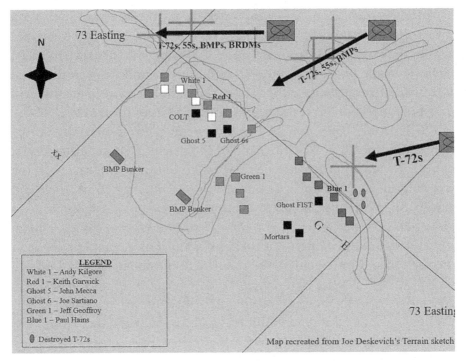

Ghost Troop's position along the 73 Easting, facing eastward as the horde of Republican Guardsmen descend onto their frontline formations. Note that Kilgore's and Garwick's platoons are interspersed with each other, while Paul Hains' "Blue" Platoon is on the right, with Jeff Geoffroy's platoon in reserve. The symmetrical "+" symbols represent artillery targets whereby Joe Deskevich would call for pre-plotted howitzer fire. At one point during the battle, Deskevich had even tried calling for naval gunfire, but Ghost Troop was too far inland from the nearest naval batteries, which coincidentally were aboard the USS New Jersey.

While Sartiano's remark may have been over-dramatic, he nevertheless admitted that Kilgore's maneuver was a bold and "truly great action." Sartiano then ordered Kilgore to pull his platoon back to the rest of Ghost Troop.

"Looking back on the incident," said Kilgore, "I probably should have said: 'No sir, you come up here with me.'" But Kilgore bit his tongue and did as he was ordered.

By 5:00 PM on the evening of February 26, Ghost Troop's tanks and Bradley Fighting Vehicles had consolidated along the 73 Easting. By all accounts, their opening forays into the battle had been superb. Andy Kilgore's tank platoon had cut down nearly a dozen BMPs and had dispatched several more T-72s. On the far-left flank of Ghost Troop's advance sat Keith Garwick's platoon. Shortly after consolidating his six Bradleys online, Garwick called on his scouts to assume their pre-determined sectors of fire. Establishing these sectors of fire was a critical task for any Bradley in a defensive position. Every space on the battlefield had to be covered by a vehicle's armament—be it the main gun, the TOW missile launcher, or the coaxial machine gun. Every Bradley, therefore, had a specified area of the battle space for which it was responsible for engaging targets. The Bradleys on the far left of the formation (Ghost 15 and Garwick's own Ghost 11), scanned their guns from the center of the battlefield to the extreme left of the squadron's sector. For the two Bradleys occupying the center, Ghost 16—the Grateful Dead—scanned from the left to the center while Ghost 14 scanned from right to center. The remaining Bradleys, Ghost 12 and 13, scanned from the center towards the right. But barely a few moments after picking up their sectors of fire, Garwick reported to Sartiano that a dozen tanks and BMPs had appeared over the horizon at a range of about 3,500 meters—and were closing in on Ghost Troop's position.

But since these Iraqi vehicles were in the 3d Armored Division's zone of attack, Sartiano told him to establish "positive identification" before engaging the BMPs. Elsewhere along the coalition's battlefront, there had been some tragic incidents of fratricide involving American Bradleys. Friendly tank commanders and aircraft pilots, many of whom were fighting off delirium because of their lack of sleep, had mistakenly engaged a handful of Bradley Fighting Vehicles, believing them to be either BMPs or ZSU 23-4s. Sartiano was determined not to have any such incidents occur in Ghost Troop's sector. Moments later, John Mecca, came over the radio with confirmation that the advance elements of the 3d Armored Division were still an hour away.

The sector was clear to engage.

At ranges of more than 3,000 meters, Garwick knew that he could not effectively engage the BMPs with his 25mm main gun; he would have to rely on the TOW missiles. As it was throughout most of Saddam's mechanized forces, these incoming BMPs were the base-model BMP-1s, with thinner armor and one-man turrets. Still, the BMP's 73mm main gun could disable a Bradley from ranges out to 1,000 meters. Garwick also kept in mind that he had to save most of his TOW missiles for the priority targets, namely the T-72s.

As Garwick picked up the first BMP in his sights, he began the drill of issuing fire commands. The success of any Bradley crew depended largely on the synchronicity between its gunner and commander, the only two personnel who resided in the Bradley's turret. Within the confines of the turret, the commander and gunner were expected to work interdependently to acquire and engage targets. Both men could acquire and engage a target from his respective station and Garwick, as the commander, had the capability to control the turret and the main gun independent of the gunner. Garwick began the first of his fire commands the same way he had done at countless gunneries on the firing ranges in Germany:

"Gunner, Missile, PC!"

Garwick's gunner, Sergeant Steve Rogers, shouted "On the Way!" as the missile erupted from its cannister. However, the missile prematurely exploded as soon as Rogers fired it—startling the crew and shuddering the Bradley with a raucous concussion wave.

"Have we been hit?!" Garwick bellowed.

Had something obstructed the TOW launcher?

All systems indicated that the launching tube was clear and that there was no external damage to the Bradley. Chalking it up to a simple misfire, Garwick readied the second TOW missile. Steve Rogers happily obliged—sending the missile more than 2,000 meters into the oncoming BMP, halting it with a fiery explosion. For the next several minutes, a medley of "Gunner, Missile, PC!" and "Gunner Missile, Tank!" came over the intercoms of Ghost Troop's frontline Bradley Fighting Vehicles as they engaged their targets of opportunity.

Meanwhile, on Garwick's right flank, Sergeant Garcia, the commander of Ghost 12, calmly deployed the first of eight TOW missiles into a medley of Iraqi tanks and BMPs at a range of 3,600 meters to his direct front. Launching the TOW missile, Garcia issued his fire commands with the calm steadiness of second nature. With a quick "Gunner, Missile, Tank!" Garcia guided the gunner of Ghost 12 onto the targets. Under the eerie glow of the Bradley's thermal sight, the gunner spied the unmistakable heat signature of an Iraqi T-72. Barely three seconds later, the T-72 exploded in a brilliant flash of blue and orange flames. With one T-72 down, Garcia repeated the drill against a BMP with the same result.

From the looks of the battlefield, Garcia and the other Bradley crewmen could tell that the Iraqis were startled and confused by the onset of American armor. Half of the Republican Guard seemed to be counterattacking (albeit unsuccessfully and with no tactical bearing) while the other half seemed to be fleeing the battlefield. Whatever their disposition, though, they were presenting nothing but easy targets for the Ghost Troop Bradley crews. Indeed, several BMPs were travelling *perpendicular* to Ghost Troop's position—offering slow-moving silhouettes that resembled the gunnery targets from the firing ranges in Germany. Engaging targets under these conditions, some Bradley and tank commanders remarked that this part of the battle felt like just another training exercise.

But as Garwick's platoon fired their missiles downrange, he remembered that he could also use indirect fire to kill the enemy vehicles (or at least disrupt their movement) before they got any closer to Ghost Troop's lead echelon. Over the radio net, he appealed for artillery support. Thanks to the squadron's Combat Observation Lasing Team (COLT), mounted atop their M981 Fire Support Vehicle, Garwick confirmed the distance of the Iraqi formation at 3,600 meters. With the distance and direction verified, Joe Deskevich radioed the Squadron's Fire Support Cell to get the howitzers' 155mm rounds on target. At first, however, Fire Support said "no"—the impact area was in the 3d Armored Division's intended zone of attack. Luckily, the Fire Direction Officer (FDO) for 6-41 Field Artillery was aware that 3d Armored Division was still hours behind the 2d Cavalry's advance and overruled the Fire Support Cell. According to Major Macgregor, this FDO had "tactical control" of the Squadron's self-propelled howitzers, even though most of the M109s belonged to the Squadron's battery. Thus, with the FDO's blessing, the 155mm rounds were on their way in a matter of seconds.

From his position aboard Ghost 11, Garwick watched with delight as the rounds disrupted and killed several more enemy BMPs creeping towards his sector. For the scouts in Garwick's platoon, it was the first time any of them had ever seen the 155mm Dual-Purpose Improved Conventional Munition (DPICM) rounds in action. The DPICM were cluster bomb variants used for anti-armor purposes. Despite Joe Deskevich's earlier reservations about using DPICM in the soft desert sand, he now specifically requested them; the growing armor battle necessitated their use. Watching the 155mm cluster bombs fall on their targets, the 1st Platoon scouts were awestruck at the devastating effect it was taking on the Iraqi vehicles. As Macgregor described it: "Imagine a thousand exploding baseballs crashing into a metal box in which you are sitting."

Hearing Garwick's contact reports over the radio, Sartiano moved his tank northward to join Garwick on-line, scrambling the rest of Ghost Troop to provide direct fire support to the 1st Platoon scouts. This scrambling maneuver integrated the 2d Platoon tanks, under

Andy Kilgore, into Garwick's formation, turning the line into the so-called "viper team"—a combined arms firing squad of four tanks and six Bradleys. As Kilgore's tanks settled into the viper team, his tank gunners shot their Laser Range Finders into the offending mix of eleven BMPs and nine tanks. Confirming the range at 3,000 meters, Kilgore's four tanks began firing sabot rounds into the enemy vehicles. But Garwick in Ghost 11, and his wingman in Ghost 15, had their own agenda. Picking up another BMP in his sights, Garwick issued the fire command for yet another TOW missile engagement. Hearing the mechanical choreography of the TOW launcher rise from its retracted position was a delightful sound for any Bradley commander. However, in the heat of combat, the process of deploying the TOW missile seemed excruciatingly slow. This was compounded by the fact that the Bradley had to remain stationary while the TOW was in flight and the gunner had to optically guide the missile to its target with a steady hand. In the years following Desert Storm, the Bradley crewmen were unanimous in their complaints that the vehicle did not have a "fire-and-forget" missile system. But today, the gunners of Ghost 11 and Ghost 15 deployed their missiles with deadly precision. Hearing the hiss of the TOW as it left its launcher, Garwick could feel the 35-ton Bradley shudder in the wake of the missile's deployment. Sergeant Rogers, eyeing the trajectory through the red glow of the thermal viewfinder, maintained his white-knuckle grip on the fire controls as he made steady corrections to the warhead's trajectories. Seconds later, the broad side of a BMP erupted in flames as the vehicle sputtered to a halt.

By this time, Garwick's training had taken over; he was delivering the fire commands with the speed and accuracy that could only be gained through rigorous repetition. Yet seeing that this was his first engagement against live targets that could shoot back, Garwick was understandably shaken. Those listening to Garwick on the radio could sense it, too. From the driver's seat of Ghost 14, eighteen-year-old Private First Class Jason E. Kick recorded his observations in real time. Speaking into a tape recorder he had snuck along for the journey, Kick reported that: "This is chaos here. This is total chaos. Red 1 [Garwick], he's the platoon leader. You can hear it in his voice, he's all shook up." But shaken as he was, Garwick suppressed his emotions and plowed through his fire commands, all while processing the contact reports from the other five vehicles in his platoon.

Meanwhile, by the time Ghost 36 had cleared its minefield, the rest of Ghost Troop had settled into their screen line along the 73 Easting, engaging the relentless onslaught of Iraqi vehicles. Sallying Ghost 36 onto the line, Michalec and his gunner spotted their first T-72.

"Gunner! Missile! Tank!"

Sergeant Strong quickly sprang into action, lining up the enemy tank under the red crosshairs of the Bradley's thermal sights. It was the first time either man had engaged a hostile target in combat.

With their adrenaline pumping at full speed, Michalec and Strong gazed through their sights as the TOW missile hurtled through the air, hurtling towards the enemy tank at full gallop. "It seemed like that thing was flying forever," Michalec recalled. "And we were watching…watching…and I remember thinking that this missile was going to fall to the ground." After all, the TOW's effective range dropped off precipitously after 3,700 meters.

"But then, all of a sudden, we see an explosion."

"Bingo!!" Michalec screamed on the radio.

Aboard Ghost 36, the choreography continued as Michalec and Strong engaged one enemy tank after another. "I saw a few turrets go flying…we're talking 40 or 50 feet in the air. It was just unbelievable." Each of their T-72s had been reduced to nothing more than a smoldering hull.

Still shaken by the element of surprise, the Iraqis were fighting back, but to no avail. "They were definitely returning fire," said Michalec, but the enemy was in a state of panic. "They weren't coming at us in battle formations," he continued. "They were coming at us in hordes." Any discipline that the Republican Guard may have had prior to the engagement had now seemingly disappeared with the opening volleys. In fact, these Iraqi troops seemed to be firing helter-skelter in the general direction of their American attackers—hoping that their volume of fire would eventually halt the Americans' advance.

At the same time, aboard Ghost 34, John Carpenter and Kenn Parbel had adopted an internal "see-and-shoot" strategy as they started firing on enemy vehicles. Identifying their first BMP, Parbel opened with a ten-round burst of 25mm gunfire. Carpenter, while keeping the vehicle at a steady 5-10 miles per hour, spotted and corrected Parbel's sensing rounds:

"Bring it up! Short left! Up Right!"

The teamwork aboard Ghost 34 continued unabated until a round from a T-72 broke their rhythm. As with many incoming Iraqi tank rounds, this round, too, fell short. The misplaced round pelted sand in front of Ghost 34, causing enough of a disruption to get the crew's attention. The short impact also sent a concussion wave that rattled the vehicle's innards. "I turned left so hard, it threw Parbel and Sergeant Woytko [the commander of Ghost 34] out of their seats," Carpenter remembered. "The impact of that round was so close, it was scary." The offending T-72 soon met its demise with a TOW missile. Still, both Carpenter and Parbel were surprised by how many T-72s were missing their targets. With every attempt the Iraqis made to return fire, their 125mm rounds constantly fell short of Ghost Troop. Had the Iraqis been overwhelmed by the element of surprise? Was the problem in their equipment? Were they not adequately trained? All of the above? Whatever the reasons may have been, 3d Platoon continued destroying targets with every bit of ammunition they had.

Although the enemy within Eagle Troop's sector had been destroyed, the enemy in Ghost Troop's sector wasn't done yet. "We started getting these little counterattacks," said Hains. Seeing that the enemy wasn't ready to quit the fight, Ghost Troop brought the full fury of its tanks, Bradleys, and artillery support upon the fledgling Iraqis. Even though it was getting dark, Paul Hains remembered that the sky "was getting brighter and brighter, like a fireworks display," as main gun rounds and artillery shells created a massive screen of fire and molten metal. By this point, "target overkill" had become the name of the game. For even if an enemy tank or BMP had been shot previously, Ghost Troop had no qualms pumping more rounds into the vehicle just to make sure it was dead.

At about 7:00 PM, Ghost Troop detected thirteen more enemy vehicles coming in from beyond the 75 Easting. By now, however, 1st Platoon was running out of missiles. "We had less than 50% of our TOWs left," said Garwick, "and we were going to run out of missiles long before they ran out of T-72s." Squadron, however, realizing that Ghost Troop was running dangerously low on ammo, ordered Hawk Company to move forward for a relief-in-place.

But Keith Garwick wasn't done yet.

Calling on Joe Deskevich, Garwick vectored his attention onto the BMPs and dismounts that were swarming 1st Platoon's sector. Knowing that his mortarmen were the quickest and easiest way to dispatch the impending threat, Joe handed off the artillery coordination to the COLT team while he directed the mortars to drop rounds "danger close" within a few meters of Garwick's frontline trace.

But there was still the problem of the enemy's follow-on forces.

By this point, Deskevich knew that Ghost Troop (and likely the entire squadron) was fighting outnumbered. From what he could deduce, Ghost was holding its own against the first echelon, but he didn't want the Republican Guard to catch its second wind with any follow-on elements. Thus, from the tiny confines of his FIST-V, Deskevich radioed a flight of A-10s from the Louisiana Air National Guard. These "fast-movers" promptly answered the call, flying several kilometers ahead to destroy whatever Iraqi elements lay beyond the horizon.

"Then, all of a sudden, six T-72s started opening up on us," said Joe—targeting his FIST-V and the nearest Bradleys in 1st Platoon. "At this point nothing had hit us, but I could see green tracer rounds going over our heads," meaning that the enemy fire was getting too close for comfort. His FIST-V crew briefly considered firing their smoke grenades, hoping to deploy a smokescreen long enough to obscure the Iraqis' view and facilitate their own withdrawal.

But Joe Deskevich had a better idea.

Determining that these tanks were about 400 meters from the forward edge of the 73 Easting, Joe scrambled for the radio and called for "immediate suppression" from the howitzer battery.

"Fortunately, while I did that," he said, "my mortar section was right behind me." And the mortar section was quite literally throwing every piece of ordnance they had at the incoming tanks. Indeed, from atop the mortarmen's M113, Deskevich could see one crewman pumping .50 caliber machine gun rounds into the Iraqi tanks. And this trigger-happy mortarman seemed unperturbed by the fact that the rounds were simply pinging off the tanks. The other mortarmen, meanwhile, went about their carefully-rehearsed drill of loading and launching mortar rounds—making hasty adjustments as each cluster of rounds landed nearer and nearer to the Iraqi tanks. "And just as we were about to run out of mortar rounds, the artillery came crashing down," said Deskevich. "We hit them four times on a 'repeat mission,' for that immediate suppression. That ended up being eighteen guns of artillery coming down on six tanks."

Keith Garwick, meanwhile, seeing the effects of this immediate suppression, recalled that: "When the artillery hit the Iraqi armor, the drivers just stopped, which was the absolute wrong thing to do. But it worked for us because we could hit them with everything we had."

Although the threat from these six tanks had been neutralized, Joe admitted that his FIST-V and mortarmen had been lucky. The FIST-V had neither the protection nor the firepower to stand toe-to-toe against a T-72 or BMP. But a combination of the Iraqis' poor maintenance, poor gunnery skills, and shock from the sudden onset of American fire had all contributed to their lethargic response. "If those guys had been American gunners," said Deskevich, "we would have been toast."

All the while, Joe Sartiano had kept 4th Platoon in reserve, "as a counterattack force," said Jeff Geoffroy. Though tied in behind 3d Platoon, Jeff Geoffroy's men still engaged whatever targets wandered into their sector. Aboard Ghost 43, Ruben Cardosa's "skeleton crew," as he called them, had been holding up well despite their collective inexperience. From his narrow view of the battlefield, however, Ruben could tell that the fight was becoming a close-quarters engagement. In fact, for every round he fired, he could hardly believe the range feedback he was getting from his gunner. "We were lasing targets at less than 1,600 meters!"—very close by the standards of tank-on-tank warfare.

Back on 1st Platoon's side of the battlefield, several BMPs had now come within range of the Bradleys' 25mm main guns. Taking aim at the nearest BMP, Sergeant Rogers fired a 25mm sensing round. To his and Garwick's surprise, however, the BMP exploded as soon as the round made impact. Rogers knew that his HE rounds were powerful, but he had no idea they were this powerful. Rogers and Garwick did a quick double-take. "Wow, that was a good round!" Garwick said.

Aboard Ghost 16, Chafee and Moller had destroyed two BMPs and an MTLB. Even with their disabled TOW launcher, the Grateful Dead had been holding their own throughout the battle. Lorson, meanwhile, was hard at work in the back of the Bradley, reloading the 25mm rounds and listening to the intense radio traffic of the raging battle. Suddenly, from among the growing cluster of destroyed vehicles, Chafee saw an unusual heat signature. "I spotted an RPG team," he said, "and led Moller onto it." Moller then flipped his selector switch to "coax" and fired a 10-round burst into the enemy dismounts.

But Lorson, fearful that these dismounts would attempt to pry open the back door of the Bradley, activated its "combat lock"—meaning that the ramp could only be lowered from the inside. However, Chafee had instructed him earlier *not* to engage the combat lock since the ramp hydraulics didn't work anyway. Today, however, in the heat of battle, Lorson didn't want to take any chances.

"The coax jammed," said Chafee, "but during the firing, I saw two of them drop. So, I know we hit two." The other RPG bearers quickly fled the scene. After they disappeared, Don Chafee saw no further activity in the area.

Fifteen minutes after Garwick's initial contact report, Ghost Troop's "viper team" Bradleys happily reported that all targets had been destroyed. In the contest of fire, the Bradley had not only proven itself against the BMP, but against the vaunted T-72 as well. But as Garwick and Kilgore's platoons cheered the destruction of the enemy's vehicles, some of the displaced Iraqis were catching their second wind.

Suddenly, after several moments of silence along the battlefront, two 73mm BMP shells struck the desert floor in front of Ghost 16 and Ghost 14—the two Bradleys on Garwick's right flank. But where were these enemy rounds coming from? Garwick and Kilgore had confirmed that all enemy vehicles in front of them had been destroyed, either by direct fire or from the artillery barrage. Had they somehow missed a vehicle? Had enemy reinforcements arrived? Whatever the case may have been, Garwick alerted his platoon for action, scanning for the vehicle that had just thrown grounders into Ghost Troop's sector.

In the turret of Ghost 16, as Moller switched back to the 25mm main gun, Chafee removed the jammed coax from its chamber and handed it back to Terry Lorson, who hastily cleared the stoppage and lubricated the gun. But barely a moment after Chafee reloaded the coax and slammed shut the chamber door, a loud clanging noise rattled the Bradley. As Chafee remembers: "It sounded like two metal chunks had just been slammed together."

Something had just hit Ghost 16.

"What the f*ck was that?!" Moller screamed.

Chafee was equally befuddled. Looking out from his commander's hatch, he saw no entry wounds to the Grateful Dead, but he spied a prominent scratch across the front slope of the Bradley. Whatever had just hit Ghost 16 had ricocheted off the front.

What the crew of Ghost 16 didn't know, however, was that the offending BMP was standing directly in front of them, less than 1,000 meters away in the low ground ahead of the spur line running parallel to 73 Easting. The vehicle had been hit by a SABOT round from Kilgore's tank platoon earlier in the fight. However, since the SABOT was a "kinetic energy" projectile, the round would often slice through a target without making it explode. Such was the case with this lone BMP; the SABOT round from Kilgore's platoon had ripped through the vehicle, killing one or more of the crew, but the vehicle itself remained intact and the 73mm main gun was still operational. Thus, either a surviving member of the original BMP crew (or a surviving member from the RPG team) had climbed into the turret and was now taking aim at Ghost Troop. The first two projectiles had hit the desert floor, which wasn't surprising considering the Iraqis' poor gunnery skills. But the next shots fired from this BMP wouldn't be grounders.

Dropping back down into the turret, Chafee prepared to rearm the machine gun when the second round descended upon Ghost 16. For years, it had been reported that the second round had penetrated the turret and subsequently decapitated Sergeant Moller.

Don Chafee, however, confirms that this was *not* the case.

"That round hit my TOW missile launcher," he said, which was ironic considering it was the only weapon system aboard Ghost 16 that didn't work.*

The resulting explosion brought a massive fireball down into the gunner's hatch which, unbeknownst to Chafee, Moller had propped open for better ventilation. "The explosion came down inside the hatch and snapped his neck instantly." Chafee could feel the heat of the fire and the mild blast of the concussion wave. But a split-second later, he felt the suffocating aroma of the Bradley's Halon Fire Suppression System. The Halon bottles had been automatically triggered to suppress what they perceived as an internal fire. "When the Halon cleared," said Chafee, "I reached over and shook Sergeant Moller, thinking that he was just knocked out. But when I did that, his head flipped sideways."

Chafee then realized that Moller's neck had been snapped.

"Also, on the left side of his head, there was an area of his scalp that had been peeled back [by the explosion]. There was no life there."

Chafee then gave the command to evacuate Ghost 16.

They had just taken direct fire from the enemy, and Chafee surmised that more rounds were on the way. Moreover, the Halon bottles had shut down the Bradley's internal systems.

Ghost 16 was now a dead vehicle.

By this time, however, Pat Bledsoe had already jumped from his hatch and was running towards Ghost 14. From his driver's seat, Bledsoe was just as shocked as his vehicle commander. He had felt the impact of

---

* Tony Harrison also confirmed seeing the BMP round hit the TOW launcher. From his position aboard Ghost 22, Harrison could see Chafee's vehicle through the right side of his driver's periscope.

the residual heat of the second blast as it landed just inches above the driver's compartment. At first, Bledsoe had no indication that any of his crew had been killed, but given the severity of the impact, he wasn't optimistic. At first, he yelled through the intercom to see if anyone was still alive. When he received no answer, he jumped from the driver's seat and ran to Ghost 14 where he pounded on the rear hatch of the Bradley until it opened. Visibly shaken, Bledsoe grimly told the dismounts of Ghost 14, "We just got hit! I think Sergeant Moller's dead."

Watching this situation unfold from the commander's station of the COLT vehicle, Sergeant Foltz, a towering man with a bodybuilder physique, dismounted his vehicle and made a beeline dash to the disabled Bradley, not knowing whether he'd find any survivors. Andy Kilgore, from atop his tank, provided covering fire while Foltz made his way towards the ailing vehicle.

Don Chafee, meanwhile, could still hear the enemy's bullets pinging off the front slope of the Bradley. "But then I heard a loud boom, and the rounds stopped." The BMP firing at Ghost 16 had just been destroyed by a friendly tank.

Scrambling to eject himself from the Grateful Dead, Chafee called out to Lorson but got no answer. Don Chafee had already lost one crewman; he hated the thought of losing another. But, dead or alive, Chafee was determined to get his crewmen to safety. With no response from Lorson, Chafee shimmied himself into the back of Ghost 16 where he found a dazed and confused Terry Lorson crawling on his hands and knees, bleeding profusely from his nose and face. As it turned out, the shock wave from the fireball had blown the turret shield door off its hinges, slamming Lorson in the face and rendering him temporarily unconscious.

Sergeant Foltz, meanwhile, slid to a halt behind Ghost 16. Initially, he tried to open the Bradley rear door. When that proved unsuccessful, he jumped on the back deck of the vehicle, pounding away at the top-rear cargo hatch. There, however, he encountered a different problem. The force of impact from the BMP round had literally jammed the cargo hatch shut. Undeterred by the situation, however, Foltz simply grabbed a nearby "tanker's bar" (a five-foot steel rod that tank crewmen use to lift the M1 Abram's track blocks) and furiously beat and pried the hatch until it opened. Terry Lorson, slowly regaining consciousness, saw the hazy image of Don Chafee lifting him off the floor of the Bradley, and handing him up to Pat Bledsoe who had come back with Sergeant Foltz. Foltz promptly put Lorson onto a stretcher and hastened him back to the Ghost Troop medics. For his actions that day, Foltz was awarded the Silver Star.

John Mecca recalled hearing the announcement of Sergeant Moller's tragic demise: "All of a sudden, the whole troop net went silent." Thus far, it had been a one-sided battle and none of the Ghost Troopers could fathom how quickly and suddenly they had lost one of their own. Despite the shock, however, Garwick was able to take control of the situation. Suppressing his own anxiety, he keyed the radio and announced: "Keep fighting. Don't lose focus! Keep fighting, out!" Ghost Troop was able to rally around Sergeant Moller's death and continued pressing the enemy.

As Chafee pulled himself from the Grateful Dead, he knew he couldn't stay on his disabled track. More importantly, he knew he had to get Sergeant Moller's body out of the vehicle.

But evacuating Moller's remains would have to wait.

Ghost Troop was still taking intermittent fire, "and we couldn't have sent his body with Lorson," said Chafee. "You can't evacuate live and deceased casualties together."

Still in shock from their gunner's demise, Chafee and Bledsoe jumped from Ghost 16 and descended upon the nearby Ghost 15. "They wouldn't let us in at first," said Chafee, but after enough banging and hollering on the back door of the Bradley, the crew finally let Chafee and Bledsoe inside. "At first, they wouldn't even let me use the radio to listen to what was going on," Chafee recalled. Ghost 15 was one of the few vehicles in 1st Platoon with access to the troop net. But then, the Ghost 15 commander handed Chafee the mic and asked him to send the official casualty report. Of course, by now, everyone in Ghost Troop knew that Sergeant Moller had been killed. For the sake of battlefield formalities, however, Chafee keyed the microphone and reported:

"Loader MEDEVAC'd…gunner KIA…driver, minor wounds and burns."

Chafee himself had also sustained some mild burns. The entire left sleeve of his uniform was singed and blackened from the fireball that had descended into Ghost 16.

By 10:00 PM, Ghost Troop had expended nearly all of its ammunition; and their vehicles were running on fumes. Suddenly, Joe Sartiano came back on the radio.

"Blue 1," he said, referring to Paul Hains' callsign, "you are to go back and link up with Hawk Company, and lead them back to our forward position for a relief-in-place."

Ghost Troop's mission at 73 Easting was complete.

Hawk Company was en route to relieve Ghost Troop and occupy its position along the 73 Easting, ready to counter any further resistance and prepare for the forthcoming passage of lines with the 1st Infantry Division. Ghost Troop would then rearm and refuel, while going into its much-needed rest cycle, and recover the remains of Sergeant Moller from Ghost 16.

"We had done link-ups like this in training," said Hains, "but never in real life. And it was pretty scary." Hains didn't want a trigger-happy crewman from Hawk Company to mistake his oncoming Bradleys for BMPs.

"They do know I'm coming, right?" asked Hains on the radio.

"Roger," said Sartiano.

He then gave Hains the radio frequency for Hawk Company's command net so he could liaise with them directly. Taking Sergeant Meriweather's Bradley with him, Hains radioed Hawk Company, advising them that two Bradley Fighting Vehicles were entering their sector, identifiable by their turrets facing backwards. Under the cover of darkness, it was the most conspicuous and expedient way to make his Bradley stand out among the battlefield clutter.

Hains met Hawk Company without incident, but as Hains brought the tanks onto Ghost Troop's position, his worst fears came to pass. Somehow, a tank from Hawk Company saw the remains of Ghost 16 and, mistaking it for a BMP, fired a main gun round right into its rear—splitting Ghost 16 down the middle and charring the remains of Sergeant Andrew Moller.

Tony Harrison saw the tragedy unfold from his driver's periscope. He had been monitoring the radio and had expected to hear some incoming calls from Hawk Company. But as of yet, he had heard no transmissions. The relative lull was abruptly shattered, however, when Tony saw a main gun round fly past the right side of his periscope.

Another enemy round?—he thought.

No. This round was coming from friendly lines.

"It was a HEAT round," he said grimly.

Harrison's heart sank as he saw the round hurtling into the rear of Ghost 16. At that moment, Harrison knew that Hawk Company had just fired on the Grateful Dead.

Aghast by the sudden onset of friendly fire, Sartiano jumped onto Hawk Company's net, shouting: "Cease fire! Cease fire! You just engaged one of my Bradleys!" While some Ghost Troopers recalled seeing only one round from Hawk Company strike the Grateful Dead, Don Chafee and others distinctly recall seeing *two*.

"The first round was a SABOT; the second round was a HEAT," he said.

Because Ghost 16 had been packed to the gills with TOW missiles, C4 explosives, and Claymore mines, the resulting explosion was horrific. Even though the Bradley weighed more than 30 tons, the explosion hurtled the vehicle nearly six feet into the air. "The vehicle sat there and burned for hours," Chafee remembered. "That broke my heart. It still hurts me very much." Sergeant Moller's body was burned beyond recognition.

Forensic reports never confirmed which of Hawk Company's tanks fired on Ghost 16 but, given the metrics of military law, Hawk Company could not be charged with fratricide. Ghost 16 had already been disabled, and Sergeant Moller was already dead.

Viewing the aftermath of the firefight, Waylan Lundquist recalled: "It looked pretty horrific. There were bodies that had been burnt to a crisp. You don't realize how deadly a force you have on the ground until you drive through the battlefield and you see what you've done."

With the battle effectively over, and a pending passage of lines, John Mecca began consolidating Ghost Troop's vehicles and personnel, and hurried them to the rear, "where fuel and water were waiting." For Mecca, however, an irate Sergeant Major Chapman was waiting for him. "Why did you leave Sergeant Moller's body up there, lieutenant?" Chapman screamed. "You never leave a man behind like that. What the hell were you thinking, lieutenant?"

Mecca was not impressed.

"Sergeant Major, it was too dangerous to bring up the M88 and the ambulance."

All told, Mecca was right. Ghost Troop was still under enemy fire, and there was a risk that the remaining TOW missiles aboard Ghost 16 would have exploded inside the vehicle.

But Chapman would have none of it. He kept pressing until Mecca finally exploded.

"Sergeant Moller's body was in pieces. Do you want me to draw you a picture? Now that's f*cking it. You have no right to question my decision in the middle of combat."

Chapman, realizing he had pushed Mecca too far, respectfully withdrew.

Despite the tragic loss of Sergeant Moller, Ghost Troop had emerged victorious from the Battle of 73 Easting. Fighting outnumbered, they had killed more than three dozen enemy vehicles, with minimal losses to their own ranks. The feral BMP round that disabled Ghost 16 was a proverbial "lucky punch." By that time, Ghost Troop's tank and Bradley platoons had made short order of the BMPs and T-72s in the immediate area. They had achieved a lull in the battle; and they were regaining their bearings when the lone BMP suddenly sprang back to life. This BMP, like many other vehicles on the battlefield, had been engaged with a 120mm SABOT round—a kinetic energy round that can often slice through a thinly-armored vehicle, leaving an exit wound but no explosions or catastrophic kills. Either a surviving member of the original crew, or a wayward dismount, had re-entered the BMP and fired upon the nearest Bradley it could find. Nevertheless, the Bradleys in Ghost Troop engaged and destroyed numerous BMPs—many of which were obliterated by only a few-round bursts from the 25mm Bushmaster. These Bradleys also had the distinct pleasure of destroying a number of T-72s.

In the final analysis, the factors that contributed to Ghost Troop's victory were both technological and metaphysical. The M1 Abrams and M2 Bradley were technologically-superior vehicles, but their success at 73 Easting was attributable to the superior tactics, training, and comparative resources of the US Army.

In the game of tank and mechanized warfare, the rule is "see first, fire first, hit first"—and the winner is typically the one who fires first. To that end, the M1 Abrams' and M2 Bradleys' optics ensured that they would see the enemy long before the enemy saw them. Moreover, the Iraqis' training programs were primitive by NATO standards and the Iraqis' maintenance system did not stress the same level of due diligence as the Americans'. Thus, when the ground war began, it was not surprising to see many Iraqi tanks and BMPs miss their targets, break down, or move sluggishly across the battlefield.

At the tactical level, Ghost Troop's vehicles were mobile and operated on a wider frontage. The Iraqi defenses, meanwhile, were hastily-constructed and nearly all of their BMPs and T-72s had been dug into static fighting positions. This, coupled with their inferior optics, defeated the purpose of having armored vehicles in the frontline defense. Because their hastily-dug fighting positions did not allow for freedom of traversing, the T-72 and BMP crews had to waste precious time getting their vehicles into a suitable position to return fire. During the Battle of

73 Easting, the tanks and Bradleys in Ghost Troop had paired themselves into the hunter-killer teams to create a "see-and-shoot" combination. Because the Bradley's Integrated Sight Unit could see farther and clearer than the M1 Abrams's thermal viewer, the Bradleys would spot targets for the M1s so that the tanks could destroy them with their 120mm main guns. No such teamwork existed between the Iraqi BMPs and T-72s.

Ultimately, the Battle of 73 Easting demonstrated the veracity of American-made equipment against their Soviet counterparts. Although untested in combat, Ghost Troop's tanks and Bradleys had proven themselves against the best armored vehicles the Soviet Union had to offer. However, the qualitative differences among the M1 Abrams, M2 Bradley, BMP, and T-72 were only part of the equation. The deciding factor lay in the human realm: better training and better tactics had paved the way for Ghost Troop's victory at 73 Easting.

CEASE-FIRE

At around midnight on February 27, the 2d Armored Cavalry passed the battle on to the 1st Infantry Division. The so-called "Big Red One" passed through the 2d Cavalry's lines to destroy what remained of the enemy's defenses farther east. "All night," said Hains, "it was a parade of armored vehicles coming through our position." Farther back, the MLRS batteries began firing their missiles deeper into Iraqi territory.

From the driver's seat of Ghost 34, John Carpenter could see the settling of the battlespace in front of him. "I remember seeing those MLRS rockets through my driver's night vision scope," he said. "It was the most beautiful thing I had ever seen. The rocket trails looked like glitter through the green screen."

Meanwhile, the rest of Ghost Troop began rounding up the Iraqi prisoners. Once again, the PSYOPs team came forward. This time, instead of playing contemporary rock music from their speakers, the PSYOPs crew handed the microphone to their Kuwaiti interpreter. Broadcasting his message in Arabic, the Kuwaiti appealed for any remaining Iraqis in the area to surrender quietly. All told, Ghost Troop was surprised by the horde of surrendering enemy. Falling into a single file line, the Iraqis solemnly marched towards Ghost Troop with their hands held high and their heads hung low. The Iraqis, however, were genuinely surprised by the humane treatment they received. Saddam had told them that the Americans would torture and kill them.

As more surrendering Iraqis turned themselves in, Ghost Troop was shocked that many of these Republican Guardsmen—the so-called "elite" of Iraq's armed forces—were in deplorable health. Ruben Cardosa recalled one POW who removed his boots and socks, revealing two feet that were covered in blisters and oozing pus. Nearly gagging at the sight, Cardosa ran to his tank and tossed a bottle of foot powder, along with some fresh socks, to the hapless Iraqi. For Ruben Cardosa, it was a heartbreaking sight—even Saddam's "elite" fighters couldn't get access to basic needs like extra socks or foot powder.

After being pulled from the wreckage of Ghost 16, Terry Lorson remembered only what he could see during his intermittent spurts of consciousness. For instance, he remembered being put onto a stretcher and hastened away from the smoking wreckage of the Grateful Dead. During a brief moment of lucidity, Lorson reached up to wipe away what he thought was sweat from his brow. But when his red-stained hand returned to his side, he realized that he was bleeding from his face. The flying turret shield door had impacted the left side of Lorson's face, giving him a prominent laceration that stretched from the base of his nose up to his left eye.

Sergeant Foltz off-loaded Lorson from the COLT vehicle into the back of First Sergeant Roark's M113. As Lorson's consciousness slowly came back to him, he gazed up to see the M113 driver looking back at him, with an unmistakable look of terror etched on his face. Although barely conscious, Lorson found the driver's expression unsettling.

"How bad do I look?" Lorson wondered.

It didn't help when First Sergeant Roark chimed in, saying: "You're getting a Purple Heart for this, son!"

"What the hell is going on?" Lorson wondered.

Lorson was then helped onto a MEDEVAC chopper and taken to a field hospital. The doctors initially cleaned his wounds with Q-tips and put a gas mask next to him on his cot—still wary of a potential chemical attack.

"They put me under [anesthesia] for surgery to fix my nose."

But Lorson still didn't know what had happened to his crew from the Grateful Dead. "I remembered Don and Pat getting me out of the vehicle," he said, "so I know they had survived whatever had hit the vehicle." Still, "there was this nagging feeling that something bad had happened." No one at the field hospital could tell him anything; they had no knowledge of his unit, nor had they been in contact with anyone at 73 Easting. "But a few days later," said Lorson, "Colonel Holder came in with the Sergeant Major." Holder delivered the painful news that Sergeant Moller had been killed in action.

Lorson tried to stifle the raw emotions as best he could.

The hospital chaplain soon followed, offering any words of solace. "He gave me a little Bible. I still have that Bible. Even though I'm not a religious man, I'll keep that forever."

As he continued convalescing, Terry was visited by the head nurse. "She was in her late thirties, early forties," he recalled. "She was a really nice lady." While making her rounds, she sat down next to Lorson and gave him some touching words of encouragement. "Having that human contact," he said, "meant so much." She told him the story of why she became an Army nurse. Her young husband had been killed in Vietnam and she decided to become an Army nurse to help soldiers in need, and perhaps save a wounded man who might otherwise have been a KIA like her late husband.

At that moment, Terry Lorson was reduced to tears.

He shared a lingering hug with the nurse, who then continued making her rounds, tending to the other patients. "Even after all these years, it's still such a powerful moment," he said.

Meanwhile, Don Chafee and Pat Bledsoe were hoarded onto a Humvee and sent to Squadron Maintenance, where a "floater" M2 Bradley was waiting for them, along with a replacement gunner from another unit. But Bledsoe, still shaken from his encounter aboard Ghost 16, refused to enter the new Bradley. "Not that I blame him," said Chafee. "Most people wouldn't go back if they had been up there in the battle, and had just had a vehicle blown out from underneath them, with machine guns firing all around." After a few minutes, Chafee finally coaxed him onto the new Bradley. The new Ghost 16 arrived back at the frontline just in time for Sergeant Moller's memorial ceremony.

Over the next few days, Chafee and Bledsoe were in a scramble to gather as many personal sundry items as possible—having lost all their gear in the explosion aboard the Grateful Dead. Several troopers gladly donated their spare uniforms. Specialist Robert Goepp, for example (one of Chafee's friends in 3d Platoon), gave him an extra set of Desert BDUs that, while not "government issue," still bore a resemblance to the desert camouflage pattern. "It was some Chinese knockoff," he chuckled. Goepp had purchased it at a local store prior to their deployment.

As luck would have it, Don Chafee did recover one item from the wreckage of the Grateful Dead—his duffle bag. "Somehow there had been a miscommunication with the casualty recovery team, and they thought that they were looking for *my* body out there." Somehow, it had been reported through the MEDEVAC channels that Chafee had been killed alongside Moller. When the supply and medical staff discovered that Chafee was indeed alive, they gave him his recovered duffel bag. It had been blown from the vehicle when Hawk Company fired on Ghost 16. "It didn't actually burn," he said, "but it was shredded with shrapnel—completely ruined."

As it turned out, the rest of 1st Platoon's duffel bags had befallen a similar fate. "All of our duffel bags were shot beyond belief," said Keith Garwick. "Everything had holes in it. Half of our personal gear had been burned up. When we opened our sleeping bags, shrapnel was falling out of them."

Following the demise of Ghost 16, the Army asked Chafee, Lorson, and Bledsoe to itemize the personal belongings they had lost at 73 Easting, so each man could be reimbursed for the fair market value. The three surviving crewmen made a composite list of their destroyed items—including a Coleman stove, camera, and assorted reading material.

"And you know how much we got reimbursed?" said Chafee. "Nothing. Absolutely nothing!"

Moreover, the Army didn't re-issue him even half of the field gear he had lost in the explosion. In fact, the Army re-issued him only two sets of fatigues, his Kevlar helmet, and his load-bearing vest. All other items, including his sleeping bag and tactical raincoat were written off as "field losses"—meaning that if he wanted those items replaced, he would have to pay for them out of pocket.

At the same time, Don Chafee began reflecting on Moller's final days with the unit. In the days leading up to the ground invasion, "Sergeant Moller started having dreams," said Chafee. "These dreams came to him during the night and during the daytime." According to Moller, he dreamt that he was in the middle of a great battle, surrounded by flames and the sound of gunfire. While relating these macabre visions to Don Chafee, Moller also said that there were two "heavenly bodies" that came down to speak with him.

"He never called them 'angels,'" said Don. "He called them 'heavenly bodies.'"

Whoever these two celestial figures may have been, they told Moller that his life would be taken in battle. Beyond that, these celestial figures gave him no further details.

Chafee assured Moller that it was just his imagination, and perhaps a case of the pre-combat jitters. Chafee then re-iterated that he would do everything in his power to keep Moller and the rest of his crew safe. Yet Chafee couldn't shake the feeling that Moller had just foreseen his own destiny—almost as if he were counting on his own demise.

Don Chafee later maintained that only the grace of God had saved his Bradley from a worse fate at the hands of the BMP. That the first round simply ricocheted off the front of Ghost 16, said Chafee, was a miracle. "That first round should have killed us." For even the strongest part of the Bradley's frontal armor couldn't stop a BMP round at such close range.

However, Chafee and his crewmen never understood how the erroneous report had surfaced, indicating that the BMP round had penetrated the vehicle and decapitated Sergeant Moller.

"No round penetrated that vehicle," said Chafee.

Other vehicle crews that were standing nearby Ghost 16 have since confirmed this. Likewise, these same crewmen confirmed seeing the second round's impact on the TOW missile launcher.

As the 2d ACR cleaned up its portion of the battlefield, President Bush announced a cease-fire to the ground war. Barely one hundred hours after the start of the Allied invasion, the Iraqis were in full retreat and Saddam was desperate to sue for peace. The "Mother of All Battles" had come to pass—but it was the Iraqi Army that had been routed. In their disastrous retreat, the Iraqis had fled Kuwait, leaving a devastated country in their wake. The fires from the oil fields were still burning out of control and much of Kuwait's antebellum wealth had been plundered. It would take a massive reconstruction effort to get the emirate back on its feet; but for now, the savagery of Iraq's occupation had ended. On March 3, 1991, General H. Norman Schwarzkopf, commander of UN Forces, met with several Iraqi generals in Safwan to discuss the terms of surrender.

A few days later, news of the UN's victory reached Terry Lorson at the field hospital. The news brought unparalleled joy to the men and women still suffering from their wounds. As Lorson reflected on his time in the hospital, he noted that his injuries were minor compared to those he saw in his ward. "There was a guy in the bed next to me," he remembered, "who had stepped on a landmine and lost both his legs."

The hospital staff soon approached Lorson, asking him if he would like to return to his unit, or if he preferred a few more days of convalescence.

"No, I want to get back to my guys!"

He then hopped aboard a Blackhawk helicopter that, coincidentally, was also carrying mail to the VII Corps front. "So, I take a ride on a Blackhawk while sitting on top of these mailbags!" Gazing out from the helicopter's side door, Terry could see the blurry mass of coalition vehicles, interspersed with destroyed Iraqi tanks, BMPs, and other Soviet-made wares.

Jumping off the helicopter with 2d Squadron's mail in tow, Lorson made his way back to Ghost Troop's assembly area—where he was greeted with an outpouring of hugs, handshakes, and well wishes. By this point, everyone knew that the young Lorson had been critically injured and they were glad to see him back. He returned to his crew to find them aboard the new Ghost 16, alongside the replacement for Sergeant Moller. Just like Chafee and Bledsoe, Lorson had lost everything in the explosion aboard the former Ghost 16. Now, the only thing he owned was what he was wearing: a blood-stained Nomex coverall suit. "All of my equipment was gone…so guys were giving me uniforms and things out of their duffel bags."

Shortly after the cease-fire was announced, Ghost Troop and the rest of 2d ACR moved into a defensive position in northern Kuwait. Staging their vehicles for the long-haul down Highway 80, Ghost Troop finally caught a glimpse of the infamous "Highway of Death." In their desperate retreat from the advancing coalition, the Iraqi Army had commandeered thousands of civilian vehicles—including buses, utility trucks, and private automobiles—to escape the onslaught of the US military. However, the coalition's air forces were determined not to let them get away. Throughout the night of February 26-27, scores of US Navy, Air Force, and Marine attack squadrons strafed the Iraqi columns as they tried to escape in the night. By sunrise, all that remained were several thousand charred automobile frames and many more dead Iraqis.

When Ghost Troop passed through the Highway of Death, it was almost surreal. Using the front ends of their tanks and Bradleys, they had to push several of the abandoned Kuwaiti vehicles to the side of the road. Inside many of these commandeered vehicles, the charred remains of their drivers gave mute evidence of the bombing campaign. These gruesome corpses appeared frozen in time, their hands still affixed to the steering wheels of the vehicles they had stolen.

As it turned out, Ghost Troop's brief stay in Kuwait wasn't much better than their journey to arrive there. Their defensive positions inside the ravaged emirate were only a stone's throw from the burning oil fields. They had seen the black rain during their initial drive into Iraq, but nothing could have prepared them for the suffocating aroma of gas fumes and the intermittent blacked-out skies. "You couldn't even see the sky," said Jeff Geoffroy. "It was like a black and gray blanket." For Ghost Troop, these scenes in northern Kuwait were almost apocalyptic.

Joe Sartiano, meanwhile, called the officers and NCOs together for an after-action review (AAR) of the battle. It was a heart-rending moment, as they knew they would have to discuss the demise of Ghost 16 and the tragedy of Sergeant Moller. But the more pressing task, it seemed, was trying to recall the details of the battle itself. For many, it had been a blur—a chaotic episode of massive explosions, fire commands, near-misses, and cheers of confirmed kills. But for now, they could determine that despite the loss of Ghost 16, they had emerged victorious against a numerically-superior enemy. Countless hours of crew drills, maneuver drills, and gunnery had paid off. Their victory at 73 Easting (a nominal gridline in the featureless desert) had been a nod to the old adage: "The more you sweat in peace, the less you bleed in combat."

Their AAR was abruptly halted by the sudden appearance of a Blackhawk helicopter. As it settled into their assembly area, the men were surprised to see General Fred Franks, the VII Corps commander, emerge from the passenger bay. Franks had been flying into different troop areas, checking on his soldiers' health and morale. A smile played upon John Mecca's face when he saw Captain Toby Martinez following General Franks out from the helicopter.

Toby Martinez had been the Assistant Squadron S-3 under Major Macgregor before being selected as General Franks's aide-de-camp. Mecca and Martinez had a long-standing friendship, and an underground business relationship of sorts. Like many young officers, they enjoyed smokeless tobacco—including dips, chews, etc. Martinez's wife, however, had forbidden him to purchase tobacco following their marriage. However, the industrious Martinez simply sidestepped the technicality of "purchasing" tobacco by getting free samples from his friend, John Mecca. Almost on cue, Martinez approached Mecca: "Hey man, you got any dip?"—to which Mecca happily produced a can for his friend's picking.

"And when General Franks showed up," Mecca recalled, "we decided to do a troop photo together." In all, it was a welcome break from the more painful aspects of the AAR, and a reminder that the US had won a decisive victory over the fourth-largest army in the world. Moreover, they were elated at the prospect of going home. After all, the cease-fire was still in effect and Saddam's war machine had been trounced after a 100-hour ground war. Ghost Troop thought they'd be in Kuwait for only a short while before moving back into Saudi Arabia for the return flight to Germany.

Sadly, it was not to be.

"Instead, as Saddam dragged his feet on signing the permanent cease-fire accord, it was deemed necessary to send a combat force back into Iraq to put pressure on that government to sign." Thus, the 2d ACR was ordered back into Iraq to occupy new defensive positions near An-Nasiriyah. This defensive posture could facilitate future combat operations if needed.

None of the troopers were thrilled at the prospect of going back to Iraq. Some felt that the unit needed more time to decompress from the horrors of combat. But alas, Ghost Troop had no say in the matter. They had a mission to accomplish and, as they would soon find out, the occupation of An-Nasiriyah would give them far more trouble than they had expected.

Every war produces its own refugees. Some wars also give rise to various guerrilla factions. In the aftermath of the UN cease-fire, Saddam Hussein had to contend with both. In southern Iraq, a Shiite rebellion had erupted, and An-Nasiriyah was one of its focal points. Farther north, the Kurds had also taken advantage of the post-war chaos by initiating their own rebellion against Saddam. Meanwhile, civilians from every walk of life flooded the Iraqi highways, trying to get away before the residual violence claimed their lives, too. Many of these refugees were headed straight towards An-Nasiriyah—looking for the quickest way out of Iraq and into the safety of the American occupation zone.

On March 23, 1991, the 2d ACR crossed the Kuwaiti border and turned west onto Highway 1, a six-lane superhighway that some troopers had dubbed the "Iraqi Autobahn." Driving towards An-Nasiriyah, Ghost Troop once again saw the devastation of the Allied air campaign. Every so often, they would pass a lone tank or armored car that had been killed in place or abandoned by its crew. Though the damage along Highway 1 was far less than what they had seen on the Highway of Death in Kuwait, it was still a grim reminder of the realities of war.

The 2d ACR's new defensive position was currently occupied by the 82d Airborne Division. As the 82d Airborne's relief force, John Mecca recalled: "I remember they just popped out of their foxholes and starting walking. It was really weird because we came up cruising in our Bradleys and tanks, and these guys had been living in the mud for a week along the screen line facing north towards An Nasiriyah." Just before making the turnoff, Ghost Troop passed a huge blue sign that read, both in English and in Arabic: "Baghdad—243 km." It crossed many a trooper's mind to drive straight into the Iraqi capital. "The crazy part is that most of us wanted to continue," said Mecca. "We wanted to finish off the Republican Guard."

Ghost Troop turned off near the ancient city of Ur, the birthplace of Abraham and the site of the famed Ziggurat built during the reign of King Nebuchadnezzar. "We then set up a standard screen line as if we were back on the East German border," Mecca continued. From there, Ghost Troop set up various checkpoints and observation posts (OPs) along the east-west thoroughfares, giving them a clear view into the city of An-Nasiriyah and the Euphrates River.

Duty along these various checkpoints, however, was far from pleasant. In fact, manning these checkpoints gave Ghost Troop a chance to see some of the darker aspects of Arab culture. For instance, several Iraqi men treated their wives and daughters as disposable commodities. Joe Deskevich recalled one incident were a Muslim family rolled up to his checkpoint driving a rundown Chevy Caprice. The male driver, an elderly Iraqi, emerged from the car with two women, one of whom was badly injured. All of her fingers were gone, save one thumb on her right hand, and an index finger on her left hand. "She had picked up a landmine, and it basically blew her hands off," said Joe. The Iraqi man had been taking care of her for a few weeks, but her wounds had become infected and gangrene was travelling up her arm. When Deskevich brought over Ghost Troop's medic, Sergeant Costa, the Iraqi man suddenly changed his mind.

"I'm not going to do that," he said, "I've got another wife."

With that, he promptly shoved the wounded woman back into the car and started driving away. But Paul Hains, witnessing the debacle from atop his M2 Bradley, would have none of it. Hains chased down the fleeing Iraqi, vectoring his Bradley right in front of the old Caprice as it tried to leave the area. Training his 25mm gun directly onto the car's windshield, the old driver wisely backed down and let Hains take the ailing wife to the medic station. Now that the war was over, men like Hains had no patience for the callous metrics of an Iraqi polygamist.

"I just couldn't let that pass," said Hains.

In fact, it seemed that Arab society at large disregarded and trivialized their women. Aside from the fleeing Iraqis, Ghost Troop encountered several Bedouin tribes that lingered near the Euphrates River. "We tried to give the girls MREs," said Don Chafee. "But every time we gave something to the girls, the boys would come and take it away. That was their custom."

But after seeing a few iterations of this gender-based strong-arming, Ghost Troop decided to work up a diversion. The tank and Bradley crews would take the boys on a walkaround tour of their vehicles, while other troopers would tacitly slip cookies and MRE entrees into the hands of the Bedouin girls. "But as soon as they started walking back to their tents, their moms would come out, take it away from the girls, and give it to the boys. So, it defeated our purpose."

Still, many of those who passed through the American checkpoints were well-meaning civilians who were simply trying to escape the Ba'athist regime. "I remember giving a lot of our MREs to Iraqi civilians," said Ruben Cardosa. "A lot of water, too." These were, after all, desert people, who valued potable water more than gold. Some Iraqis tried bartering personal items for MREs, but most troopers were happy to give their spare rations for free.

"They needed them a lot more than we did," one trooper recalled.

Other civilians exchanged Iraqi Dinars, the local currency emblazoned with Saddam's face, for GI rations. Although it was worthless currency back in the States, the troopers gladly accepted them as war souvenirs.

On other occasions, Ghost Troop encountered several of the Shiite rebels who were now fighting what remained of the Republican Guard. In the city of An Nasiriyah proper, just beyond the UN demarcation line, Shiite rebels would conduct nightly raids against the Republican Guard and the Fedayeen. "At night, we would watch this through our thermal sight, and you would see Saddam's secret police wreaking havoc through the homes and buildings," Paul Hains recalled. Hains would call in the spot reports to his higher headquarters, describing the horrific scenes unfolding on the other side of the demarcation line. Yet all he ever heard in response was:

"Roger, out."

For as much as 2d ACR wanted to stem the tide of sectarian violence, they were bound to the UN's official cease-fire line. Hains later recalled the irony of the situation: "We had just spent decades patrolling the East German border, and it was normal to call in spot reports every time we saw something. Here we were doing the exact same thing, yet unlike the East German border, where reportable incidents were few and far between, here they were happening every night, and we couldn't intervene." Some of the Shiites even begged Ghost Troop to join the rebellion against Saddam.

"We are trying to kill the Saddam police," they would say in broken English.

"We want to kill them."

"You should be killing them as well."

"You should be joining us."

Yet, every time, Ghost Troop had to remind these rebels that the US Army had strict orders not to cross the cease-fire line.

The rebels, meanwhile, would hide behind Ghost Troop during the day before engaging Iraqi troops at night. Andy Kilgore also noticed that the Shiites would dig trenches to store their weapons in between their nightly forays into An Nasiriyah. At times, though, it seemed that this Shiite rebellion was a march of folly. For even in the midst of Iraq's defeat, Saddam's henchmen still operated with a brutal efficiency and lethality. But because these retaliatory and repressive killings were happening beyond the UN's demarcation line, American troops could not intervene. "We could sit on our vehicles and watch the firefights all night long," said Joe Deskevich, "and in the morning, they would bring back their dead and camp behind us." Indeed, after their night-long battles, the Shiites would bring their wounded into Ghost Troop's aid station for medical care. "A lot of these people were so badly maimed," added John Mecca. Seeing these mangled and desperate Iraqis—victims of their own repressive government—bothered him far more than the horrors he had seen in combat.

But whether the Iraqi civilians fled in panic or joined the Shiite rebellion, many of their children carried on with playtime as usual. In fact, the Iraqi children seemed fascinated by the American GIs and were eager to approach them as playmates. The soldiers reciprocated somewhat by giving them candy bars and other spare goods. Jeff Geoffroy noted that some of these children were well-dressed by Iraqi standards. "They had clean clothes and designer socks," he recalled. Still, some within Ghost Troop were wary to mingle with the Iraqi children. "I had heard a lot of stories from Vietnam," said Geoffroy, "where the VC would give kids hand grenades. So, we had to be careful to make sure they didn't drop grenades into the tank or shoot us in the back. Luckily, these were just kids trying to survive."

While continuing to man their checkpoints, Ghost Troop saw the return of a familiar nuisance—flies. And this time, they were accompanied by mosquitos. "It got so bad," said Ruben Cardosa, "that we got issued mosquito nets to put over our tanks." Cardosa recalled many an interesting night manning his checkpoint with Ghost 43, scanning the horizons of An Nasiriyah while peering through the mesh of the mosquito net adorned atop his tank. One pleasant aspect of the checkpoint duty, however, was the influx of mail. "A lot of mail caught up to us after the ground war ended," said Andy Kilgore. And because Kilgore had so many teachers in his family, they sent him numerous school-sponsored packages—nearly enough for everyone in Ghost Troop. Not wanting to horde the treasure trove of homemade goods and snacks, Andy happily distributed the extra packages amongst his fellow troopers.

After nearly a month on the An-Nasiriyah checkpoints, Iraq signed the permanent cease-fire agreement. The ink on the armistice had barely dried when the 2d ACR received the orders they had longed to hear: "Move south back into Saudi Arabia, prep your vehicles, and prepare for redeployment back to Nuremburg Airport."

On the day before Ghost Troop departed its checkpoints, one of the Shiite rebels approached Joe Deskevich.

"Where are you going?" the rebel asked him.

"We're leaving," Joe replied.

"What do you mean you're leaving?!"

"We have our orders."

"What about us?"

Painfully, Deskevich realized that without an American presence, the Shiite rebels would likely lose their fight against the Ba'ath Party regime. But orders were orders; and Ghost Troop had little choice but to leave the Shiites to their own devices. "I wonder if a fair amount of those guys ended up in the mass graves around Basra and An Nasiriyah," he lamented. "So many of the Iraqi civilians wanted us to go to Baghdad and kill Saddam."

From their checkpoints in Iraq, 2d ACR drove a long convoy down Highway 80 into King Khalid Military City in Saudi Arabia. Surprisingly, not a single tank or Bradley from Ghost Troop broke down along the 600-mile convoy. They did, however, have to make frequent stops to clean the tanks' air filters. When the troop finally arrived in Saudi Arabia, they were greeted by an even more oppressive heat than when they had landed the previous December. It was now April 1991, and the spring heat was in full force—with temperatures tipping the scale at 125 degrees Fahrenheit.

"Before we got to King Khalid," said John Mecca, "we set up a gunnery range in the middle of the desert basically to get rid of all our ammunition." VII Corps had directed all units to expend their excess ammunition. Indeed, nothing that had been uploaded in the desert could return to Europe. Thus, every caliber of round from 7.62mm machine gun bullets to 120mm tank rounds had to be fired off in a free-for-all gunnery range. "It was a mad hour and a half," Mecca continued, "just shooting off sh*t. It was amazing; we fired off every piece of ammunition we had…although we may have kept a few 9mm bullets," he chuckled.

Life at King Khalid Military City was the best Ghost Troop had had since touching down in Saudi Arabia four months prior. The complex itself was a multi-force base that offered the best amenities then available to the US military. Swimming pools, arcades, lounges, fast food joints, and movie theaters were just a few of the accommodations that soldiers could enjoy at King Khalid. The stores at King Khalid also sold quality goods at bargain basement prices. Terry Lorson bought a CD player—the first one he had ever owned—and a few compact discs to replace the cassette tapes he had lost aboard Ghost 16.

Ghost Troop also had to go through several counseling sessions with the military psychologists. Vietnam had exposed the horrors of Post-Traumatic Stress Disorder (PTSD) and the difficulty that veterans had endured while reintegrating into society. Determined not to let their Gulf War veterans suffer through the same afflictions, the Army put several thousand of its troops through counseling and emotional resiliency courses. Ghost Troop had certainly seen some horrific images of modern warfare—bodies vaporized by high-caliber weapons, civilians maimed, enemy soldiers crushed under vehicles, and the unforgettable stench of burning bodies. Although many Ghost Troopers still wrestle with these images (and still suffer from mild levels of PTSD) they nevertheless satisfied the metrics of the Army's postwar psychological program, and were given a clean bill of mental health.

Ironically, as Ghost Troop prepared for its flight home, the Army issued them a new pair of Desert Camouflage uniforms—and finally gave each of them a pair of tan desert boots. Every trooper then received instructions to wear their desert regalia for the homecoming flight. "I had to laugh at the irony of that," said Paul Hains. "I went through all that sh*t, and *now* you're going to give me a brand-new uniform and boots for a plane ride home?!!"

After what seemed like an eternity, Ghost Troop's return flight finally arrived on the tarmac at King Khalid on May 5, 1991. "We sat on the airfield for like eight hours waiting for the airplane to come get us in the middle of the night," said Joe Deskevich. "And we ended up sleeping on our bags." As the troopers settled into their Pan Am flight, they noticed that the flight attendants were much older than those who had accompanied them to the Gulf six months earlier. "It made sense," Paul Hains remembered. The average age of these flight attendants was no younger than 60 years old. Even after months without female contact, no young trooper would make passes at a woman who was old enough to be his grandmother.

While most of Ghost Troop came back from Saudi Arabia straight away, some troopers had to stay behind for a few more days - loading their vehicles onto the same cargo ships that had taken them to the Gulf months earlier. Waylan Lundquist was in charge of the detail to ferry the tanks and Bradleys back onto the ships at Al-Jubail. "We took a few drivers with us. They loaded us onto a C-130 and flew us down to the port, landing right onto the desert floor. It's the worst ride you've ever had. Then the back opens up, and all this dust and sand starts blowing inside." During these onloading days, Waylan recalled that: "I couldn't sleep for more than four hours a night." Every night throughout Desert Shield and Desert Storm, he had had the same shift for radio guard—3:00-5:00 AM—so he could wake up the platoon. "Your body gets used to that."

Before they could load the vehicles, however, each one had to be inspected for contraband. Several GIs had returned from the Gulf carrying enemy berets, helmets, and other uniform items. Normally, Army officials looked the other way when it came to these war trophies, but, as Jeff Geoffroy recalled, "we were told not to bring back any weapons,"—including bayonets, grenades, and AK-47s. Nevertheless, a few clever troops tried to sneak these items past the Army-appointed customs agents. However, because VII Corps was still flush with victory, many of these "stowaways" were forgiven and discarded without incident.

Circling the Nuremberg airport during their final descent, Ghost Troop marveled at the colors of the city and the German countryside. It was springtime and, as Jeff Geoffroy noted, "everything was in bloom." When they had left Germany the previous December, the winter had rendered everything gray. After nearly six months in the desert, they had seen nothing but monochromatic sand. Now, their eyes were nearly overwhelmed by the infusion of springtime colors. On the tarmacs of the now-reunified Germany, Ghost Troop returned to a heroes' welcome. The 2d Squadron families had turned out en masse (along with several well-wishers from within the local community) to welcome the troops home. For many Ghost Troopers, it was a bittersweet moment—for this warm welcome was a far cry from what their forebearers had received after Vietnam.

After returning from the Gulf, the regiment gave every trooper a thirty-day furlough to decompress from the war and spend time with family. For the married troopers like Don Chafee, Rick Michalec, and Ruben Cardosa, it was a welcomed opportunity to pick up where they had left off. For the single men like Pat Bledsoe and Terry Lorson, the time was ripe to sow their wild oats. The German nightlife hadn't slowed down, and the local *fraulines* were ablaze with intrigue at the victorious American GIs who were filtering back into the Fatherland.

That summer, the 2d ACR held its final regimental ball in Nuremberg. The evening was capped with Champaign and regaling tales of their victory in Desert Storm. Over the past two years, the regiment had seen a world transformed. From their perch along the Inner-German Border, they saw the Cold War end right before their eyes. Years of intense border duty and close encounters with their Communist "mirrors" had ended without a shot being fired. As the military drew down its Cold War stance, it rose to fight a Middle Eastern dictator who commanded the world's fourth-largest army. While the Iraqis had strength in numbers, their equipment and skills couldn't keep pace with the US military and its coalition partners. However, the celebration was tinged by the somber news that the post-Cold War drawdown would continue unabated. Among the bureaucratic casualties of this "peace dividend" was none other than the 2d Armored Cavalry Regiment. Since the Cold War was over, the US no longer saw the need to keep a heavily armored footprint in Western Europe. Thus, the 2d ACR was slated to deactivate within the year and return stateside for conversion into a light reconnaissance regiment. Under the command of the XVIII Airborne Corps, this lighter, leaner ACR would be equipped with nothing more than Humvees until a better armored platform came along.

However, this somber news didn't prevent Ghost Troop from carrying on with business as usual. Following the regimental ball, 2d Squadron returned to Grafenwoehr for another round of gunnery. "You wanna talk about the best gunnery ever?" said Joe Deskevich. "Here we have an entire cavalry squadron that just fought the biggest tank battle of the late 20th Century, and now you're sending us to Grafenwoehr to shoot paper targets?" War had definitely sharpened their skills—nearly every tank and Bradley in Ghost Troop fired a perfect 1,000-point engagement. Following their brilliant gunnery, Ghost Troop participated in its final "force-on-force" maneuver of the Cold War era. Along what had been the Inner-German Border (which was still being dismantled and demilitarized) Ghost Troop took its tanks and Bradleys into the area surrounding Coburg for movement-to-contact drills and tactical surveillance missions. This time, however, the missions were almost surreal. There were no more border guards, and the tanks could move freely into the previously-forbidden territories of East Germany.

In Ghost Troop, young men from every walk of life had come together to serve their country. Unlike many of their forefathers, these young soldiers had joined voluntarily. Some joined for the college money; some joined for the romance; others joined simply as a means of "growing up." Whatever their reasons, they all came with a sense of duty and love of country. These young men demonstrated the vitality and professionalism of America's post-Vietnam Army. Collectively, they showed what any unit can accomplish when it has realistic training, individual initiative, hard-nosed leadership, and pride in the mission. Although the men of Ghost Troop went their separate ways after 1991, their legacy lives on as the frontline heroes of America's greatest tank battle.

EPILOGUE:
AFTER THE STORM

At this writing, less than a handful of Ghost Troopers remain on active duty. Of the officers in Ghost Troop, Paul Hains and Andy Kilgore stayed in uniform the longest. By the time he redeployed from the Gulf, Paul Hains had been a scout platoon leader for twenty-six months. As the regiment began drawing down, Hains transferred to the Military Intelligence Corps and reported to Fort Huachuca, Arizona for the Military Intelligence Officer Transition Course. By this time, however, the active-duty Army was trimming its ranks—offering incentives for its personnel to leave or, in some cases, meting out mandatory separations. Sensing that the Army was no longer a "growth industry," Paul Hains voluntarily transferred to the Texas Army National Guard, where he spent the rest of his career as a full-time Guardsmen. As a newly-minted Intelligence Officer, he was first assigned to 1-124 Cavalry as its Deputy S-2. He then commanded Headquarters Company, 1-141 Infantry, stationed in San Antonio. "I had almost three years in command, and it was great!" he said. "They were a mechanized unit"—so he felt right at home among the unit's M2 Bradleys. "And the maneuver companies all loved the fact that I knew what it took to support a Bradley range. Their biggest annual event was going to Fort Hood, maneuvering a little bit, then shooting gunnery"—all of which he had done in spades during his time along the Iron Curtain.

Promoted to major, Hains then became a Brigade S-2, and supported various training exercises for the Texas National Guard. One such exercise was a high-profile joint maneuver with the Singaporean Armed Forces and the Japanese Ground Self-Defense Force. Like many of his contemporaries in the Clinton-era Army, Hains deployed to the Balkans, where he conducted intelligence-gathering operations in Kosovo. Following 9/11, he deployed with the US III Corps Headquarters to Baghdad where he provided intel support to General Ray Odierno. In this capacity, Hains served on a five-man "Red Team," advising Odierno of possible enemy actions and tactical dispositions. Following another deployment to Iraq as part of a Civil Affairs team, Hains reclassified yet again as an Army Space Operations Officer—one of the rarest career fields in the military. Space Operations Officers act as Army liaisons to NASA and the various missile defense commands, coordinating satellite operations and other space capabilities to support Army operations. Therein, Paul Hains became the inaugural Chief of Special Technical & Space Operations to the 36th Infantry Division (Texas National Guard). It was in this capacity that he deployed to Iraq for the last time in 2010. Hains retired from the National Guard in 2012 and went on to earn an MBA from the University of St. Thomas. He currently works as a business consultant for K. Carpenter Associates in Houston, Texas.

When Andy Kilgore touched down in Germany, he went straight back to Stuttgart, where his old unit had been. As it were, his transfer to the 2d ACR had been processed so quickly, that he still had a Bachelor Officer Quarters (BOQ) billet in his name at Stuttgart. Clearing that billet, Andy discovered that his old platoon in 3-34 Armor was now being commanded by Lieutenant Michael Kirkland, one of his hometown friends from Mississippi. "Small world," he grinned.

After the 2d ACR deactivated, Andy Kilgore remained in Germany for another two and a half years. As one of the last officers to arrive in Ghost Troop on the eve of Desert Storm, Kilgore was, ironically, one of the last remaining officers to close down the regiment. As he recalled: "We were drawing down, giving all our stuff away in Bamberg and in the border camps. There were a lot of hand receipts being swapped." Indeed, everything from uniforms, to mortars, to combat vehicles were being signed away.

As the regiment furled its colors, Kilgore transferred to 3-4 Cavalry, where he was surprised to see that they were organized differently than the 2d ACR. "They had fully-combined platoons," he said. "So, you had tanks, Bradleys, and mortar tracks in each platoon. That was pretty cool…a lot of firepower for a lieutenant to control."

Leaving Germany in the summer of 1994, Kilgore attended the Armor Officer Advanced Course at Fort Knox, and then took command of Fox Troop, 3d ACR at Fort Bliss, Texas. "We were getting ready for a big NTC rotation," he recalled, "but they cancelled it because we were moving the regiment to Fort Carson, Colorado." Every so often, the military conducted a Base Realignment and Closure (BRAC) review—a painstaking process that identified certain units and posts for deactivation or relocation. As part of the ongoing drawdown of the 1990s, the 3d ACR landed at Fort Carson, while the 4th Infantry Division relocated to Fort Hood, replacing the now-deactivated 2d Armored Division.

After commanding Fox Troop and Headquarters Troop, Kilgore prepared for an assignment to the National Training Center as a tactical evaluator. One week before his report date, however, his orders were abruptly cancelled. The Armor Branch assignment officer called him, saying that the Army had decided to send him to Camp Shelby, Mississippi as an Observer-Controller and an active-duty liaison to the Mississippi National Guard. The assignment officer told him: "Look, every time I try to send someone to Mississippi, they threaten to resign from the Army. Nobody will go. But you're from there—will you go?"

"Ok," Kilgore said. "But you owe me."

All told, Kilgore enjoyed being back in his home state. And the assignment to Camp Shelby gave him responsibilities not typically given to an active duty captain: serving as a Battalion S-3 and Brigade Training Officer during the unit's pre-mobilization to Bosnia.

Emerging from Camp Shelby, Kilgore then attended the Command & General Staff College (CGSC) at Fort Leavenworth, while simultaneously earning an MBA from Webster University. Following 9/11, he reported to the 1st Cavalry Division at Fort Hood, whereupon he became the S-3 for a cavalry squadron and deployed to Iraq in 2004. During that deployment, Kilgore's unit maintained control of the Baghdad Green Zone. After five months in theater, he was suddenly promoted to Executive Officer of 3d Brigade, 1st Cavalry Division. "It was extremely challenging because the coalition had transferred authority to the State Department and we had a brand-new ambassador." Nearly every day thereafter, Kilgore had to attend State Department meetings and coordinate 3d Brigade's operations with the diplomatic staff.

Redeploying stateside in 2005, Kilgore moved to Miami, Florida where he was assigned to US Southern Command (SOUTHCOM) as a joint plans officer. Two years later, as a lieutenant colonel, Andy Kilgore became the Professor of Military Science at Appalachian State University. He remembered it being a strong ROTC program because many of its cadets were children of families stationed at nearby Fort

Bragg. Many of their parents were serving in the 82d Airborne Division or the various Special Forces units.

In 2011, when he was due to return to a line unit, he requested an assignment to Afghanistan. Instead, he found himself assigned to the 1st Armored Division at Fort Bliss, where he deployed to Iraq and Kuwait for the final rotation of forces in Operation New Dawn. His final assignment was to Fort Benning, Georgia, where he directed the Army's Counter-IED Task Force, developing and refining doctrines to defeat the perennial menace of Improvised Explosive Devices. He retired in 2014, completing twenty-nine years of service. He currently resides in Hattiesburg, Mississippi where he serves as the director of the Mississippi Defense Initiative at Southern Miss.

While waiting to attend the Field Artillery Officers Advanced Course (FAOAC), Joe Deskevich was assigned to what he described as "the lowest paid unit in the Army"—a tongue-in-cheek reference to their low morale and poor leadership. "I went to be an MLRS Platoon Leader at Fort Sill,"—in a platoon that had just transitioned from being a Pershing Missile unit. "I had gone from watching the Berlin Wall with the 2d Armored Cavalry in 1989," he said, "and now in 1992, I'm with the lowest-speed people you can imagine, who barely know how to operate their own equipment!"

To make matters worse, at the unit's first formal Dining-In, Deskevich drew fire from his battalion commander simply because Deskevich had more medals than he did. Joe, like many of his fellow officers at 73 Easting, had earned the Bronze Star and the Army Commendation Medal with "V" Device for valor. His new commander, however—resentful that he had missed Desert Storm—gave Deskevich a verbal drubbing for wearing all his medals, as if it was somehow ostentatious to wear what the Army had awarded him. Thus, at the next Dining-In, Joe Deskevich chose to wear only his jump wings. Yet when the indignant battalion commander saw Deskevich wearing only his wings, he exploded: "Where are the rest of your medals?!"

"Well, sir, you gave me such a ration of crap last time, I figured I'd just wear the first one the Army ever gave me."

"Go home and put your medals on!"

"Ok, sir."

Deskevich despised that commander; there was simply no pleasing him.

After completing FAOAC, Joe went to the 2d Infantry Division in Korea where he commanded a howitzer battery for twenty-eight months. He then taught ROTC at West Virginia University before becoming an active-duty advisor to an Army Reserve unit at Fort Lewis, Washington. By the ten-year mark, Joe had the option of staying in the Army, or accepting a Voluntary Separation Incentive (VSI)—a lump-sum payout equal to fifteen percent of his annual salary. "They were offering these in the late 90s so they wouldn't have to do another Reduction in Force." Wanting to settle down with his wife and family, Joe took the VSI package and left the Army in March 2001. He currently lives and works in Aiken, South Carolina.

Returning from the Gulf, John Mecca was caught up in the leadership changes that were sweeping the regiment. Lieutenant Colonel Sullivan was being replaced by Lieutenant Colonel JD Thurman, who later achieved four-star rank as the commander of United Nations Command and the ROK-US Combined Forces Command in Korea. No trooper in 2d Squadron was sad to see Sullivan go. In fact, the consensus among the troops was that 2d Squadron was a great outfit not because of Sullivan's leadership, but in spite of it.

One of Thurman's first official acts as commander was to make John Mecca the Squadron Maintenance Officer—in charge of inventorying and maintaining the Squadron's equipment in preparation for its final turn-in and deactivation. During one of their walkthroughs of the Squadron motor pool, Thurman and Mecca happened upon a field generator that looked out of place. Indeed, its unit identifier read "3-32 AR"—an armored battalion with the 1st Cavalry Division at Fort Hood, Texas. Baffled by how a Fort Hood generator could make its way to a European motor pool, Mecca confronted the maintenance shop chief, a warrant officer, demanding an explanation. "I don't know, sir," the warrant officer replied. "But don't worry about it, we'll figure it out. People lost all kinds of stuff in the desert." Amidst the logistical chaos of mobilization and de-mobilization, several pieces of equipment had been lost or placed on the wrong manifests, and ended up in motor pools miles away from their original owners. But because the Army at large was so flush with victory, many of these missing items were written off and purged from the property books.

Upon hearing that this Fort Hood generator had landed in Bamberg, however, Thurman erupted. Coincidentally, he had been the executive officer of 3-32 Armor during Desert Storm, and had done an exhaustive investigation looking for the generator that his unit had lost. While still at Fort Hood, Thurman had to admit to Army officials that his unit had lost the generator and recommended purging it from the supply record. Now discovering that his "lost" generator had serendipitously landed at his new command, Thurman was understandably livid. "But he laughed about it later," Mecca said.

From there, John Mecca had quite the colorful and fast-paced career. "After I left Germany," he said, "I went back to Fort Knox for the Advanced Course." Pondering his next assignment, Mecca chose the 10th Mountain Division. It was an unusual place for an armor officer because the 10th Mountain Division was a light infantry unit whose only "motorized" assets belonged to the Humvee-based cavalry squadrons. Also, Mecca was planning to marry his fiancée, Kelly, and Fort Drum was relatively close to their home state of New Jersey.

However, as Mecca prepared to check in at Fort Drum, Operation Restore Hope kicked off in Somalia. As part of a UN multi-national force, President Bush sent the 10th Mountain Division, among other light forces, to restore order following the collapse of the Somali government. Mecca spent the first half of 1993 in and around Mogadishu—months before the infamous *Black Hawk Down* incident. He returned to the United States just in time to deploy to Haiti for Operation Uphold Democracy. "I got there in October '94. The day I arrived, I looked around…it was the same sh*t, different war; the same smells and the same amount of craziness that was happening in Somalia. It was no fun." Mecca did, however, take command of Troop A, 3-17 Cavalry while in Haiti. He remained in command until well after they redeployed to the United States. Having toured three back-to-back engagements (Iraq, Somalia, and Haiti), Mecca decided that he had had enough of Army life. He left active duty in March 1996 and entered the financial industry. He is currently a senior vice president at Bank of America.

Keith Garwick left the Army in June 1993, amidst the rapid postwar drawdown of the 1990s. Returning to civilian life, Garwick spent the next ten years in Corporate America as a sales representative in the chemical industry. Not satisfied with the life of a corporate drone, however, Keith leveraged his military background to become a police officer in La Verne, California. Having found his new calling in law enforcement, Keith Garwick also served as a Forensic Science Instructor in the local school districts. He currently works as a Drug/Alcohol Compliance and Enforcement Inspector with the Federal Aviation Administration in El Segundo, California.

After the 2d ACR deactivated in Europe, Jeff Geoffroy transferred to the 1st Armored Division. He was a Headquarters Company Executive Officer for one year prior to becoming the Aide-de-Camp to the

Assistant Division Commander. By this time, however, Geoffroy had decided that he did not want to make the military his career. It was now 1993 and he had the option of either continuing to the Armor Officer Advanced Course, or remaining in Germany until the end of his service obligation in 1994.

He chose the latter.

"I was working with the General Staff of [the 3d Infantry Division] in Wurzburg for my last year in Germany." After leaving the Army in 1994, Jeff Geoffroy moved to Boston where he currently works in technical sales and marketing.

Waylan Lundquist departed Ghost Troop in the spring of 1992 and was assigned as a BNCOC instructor at Grafenwoehr. Returning stateside in 1994, he served at Fort Carson, Colorado before returning to Germany in 1998. He finished his career overseas, serving with the 1st Armored Division in Schweinfurt and deployed to Kosovo. After a six-month deployment to the Balkans, Waylan returned to Germany and was promoted to First Sergeant in January 2001. He retired from active duty in 2003 and worked for several years in the Elk River School District in Minnesota before transitioning into the hardware industry. He currently works as a service manager for Lowe's Home Improvement.

Brian Foley's deployment was disrupted by news of a family emergency. While manning his checkpoint in An Nasiriyah, he received a Red Cross message that his mother had undergone triple bypass surgery. After arriving back in Germany with the rest of the squadron, he caught the first plane back to America. His mother was still convalescing from surgery and, when he arrived at her hospital room, he was amazed to see that the staff had decorated her room with Desert Storm memorabilia. Banners, news clippings, and yellow ribbons adorned the walls of Mrs. Foley's hospital suite. Moreover, the doctors and nurses thanked him for his service.

Foley hadn't expected such a warm welcome.

In fact, he was bracing himself to be mobbed by protesters, as had happened during Vietnam. He even told Waylan Lundquist: "When I get off that plane, the first motherf*cker who spits on me, I'm beating the sh*t out of him." But his reception both at the airport and the hospital were a far cry from the animosity endured by the Vietnam veterans. At every turn, he was greeted by smiles and well-wishes.

Foley remained in the Army for the next few years. Departing Germany, he was reassigned to Fort Hunter Liggett, California—not far from the Presidio of Monterey. His assignment was unique in that he belonged to a tank company within a field-testing unit. From the sunny hills of California, Foley then transferred to the plains of Central Texas—assigned to Fort Hood with the 2d Armored Division just as the unit was deactivating and being re-flagged as the 4th Infantry Division. Foley left the Army in 1998, pursuing a career in law enforcement. For the next fifteen years, he served as a patrol officer in the Bridge City Police Department and the Orange County Sheriff's Office in Texas. After nearly two decades on the beat, he pursued a second career as a professional carpenter. He currently lives and works in Orange, Texas.

Tony Harrison, the driver of Ghost 22, likewise left the Army in 1998. He currently works as a foreman in the Water Distribution System for the city of Farmington, Missouri. John Carpenter, the driver of Ghost 34, returned stateside with orders to Fort Stewart, Georgia, where he joined 2-15 Infantry as a mechanized scout. He spent the remainder of his career at Fort Stewart before leaving the Army in 1995. After the Army, he discovered his passion in the food industry as a professional baker. He currently lives and works in the Greater Buffalo, New York area.

Rick Michalec stayed in uniform for another twenty-three years. Reflecting on his career, he proudly says that: "My positive attributes come from what I learned in the 2d ACR. There's no question about it. The standards that you were held to; the way you trained. It was an unbelievable group of people who just did things the right way."

After the regiment deactivated, Michalec arrived at Fort Carson and reported to 2-7 Cavalry. His career took an interesting turn when the local air defense units received the new Bradley-based M6 Linebacker Air Defense System. The Linebacker itself had simply replaced the TOW missiles with four, tube-launched Stinger missiles. However, because the M6 still carried the 25mm Bushmaster, the Linebacker units needed Master Gunners to train the air defense troops on how to operate that main gun. "So I had to take the air defense units through a Bradley Transition Course."

After eighteen months of training the new Linebacker crews, Michalec reported to Camp Casey, Korea for a yearlong tour. He later returned to Germany as a platoon sergeant, and served as a First Sergeant for a Basic Training cavalry troop at Fort Knox. In his last assignment, he was the Senior Military Science Instructor at the University of Minnesota—Twin Cities. "I ran the ROTC program for a year just because I wanted to retire here." He now lives in the Minneapolis-St. Paul area and works in the metal finishing industry.

Ruben Cardosa returned to Fort Bliss, where he became a controller for the various gunnery ranges within the Fort Bliss-White Sands training complex. For the next fifteen years, Cardosa served in a variety of broadening assignments in Germany and Korea, the latter of which put him on the frontlines of the DMZ—the last true "Frontier of Democracy." His final assignment was at Fort Knox as a Tactics Instructor at the Armor Officer Basic Course. Ironically, the Battle of 73 Easting was among the many case studies that he taught to his young charges. Many of his young lieutenants went on to become tank and scout platoon leaders during the inaugural years of Operation Iraqi Freedom. He retired in 2006, serving twenty-four years in uniform. After retiring, he joined the Louisville Metropolitan Police Department, where he served eight years as a patrol officer. He retired for good in 2016 and now resides in his native San Antonio.

Aboard the Grateful Dead, Don Chafee remained in uniform the longest. Returning from the Gulf, he was reassigned to Fort Knox as an instructor at the Bradley Leader Course. During this time, Chafee often fielded questions from the junior enlisted men about the Bradley's performance at 73 Easting. Seeing the 2d ACR patch emblazoned on his right sleeve (indicating that he had seen combat with the regiment), his young students were eager to hear about his toils against the Republican Guard. Although reluctant to share at first, he eventually told the story of how Ghost 16 had met its demise: the vehicle had withstood punishment from a BMP, but the Grateful Dead was destroyed by friendly fire from a Hawk Company tank. However, the story of the BMP, the Halon ignition, and the friendly-fire incident did not sit well with Chafee's command team. Although the story was true, the school cadre ordered him to stop telling it, so as not to destroy the recruits' faith in the Bradley Fighting Vehicle. "They told me that I was never to talk about Desert Storm again."

During this time, Don Chafee also purchased a brand-new white Chevy Beretta. Driving his new car through the gates of Fort Knox, however, he was surprised when the gate guards simply waved him through, without even checking his ID. He soon realized, however, that the Fort Knox MPs drove identical white Berettas as their liaison vehicles—hence, the gate guards thought Chafee was another MP. Don Chafee retired in 1997, completing twenty years of combined service. He currently lives in Vine Grove, Kentucky.

Pat Bledsoe departed Germany in December 1991, with orders to the 5th Infantry Division at Fort Polk, Louisiana. The so-called "Red

Diamond Division," however, had one of the worst reputations of any stateside unit in the Army. Combined with the perennial unpopularity of Fort Polk itself, the unit's morale was understandably low. Still, Bledsoe had the opportunity to make a great impression. "Right when I got there," he said, "they were at gunnery and their lieutenant's gunner went out on emergency leave…so they plugged me in with their lieutenant and I shot a perfect score with him." A few months later, Bledsoe's unit went to NTC where, coincidentally, he ran into Keith Garwick, who was finishing his final assignment as a member of the NTC aggressor unit.

Within a year, however, the 5th Infantry Division had been tapped for deactivation. "I decided to get out of the army," he said. "I knew I wanted to be a firefighter; I was going to try to re-enlist as a firefighter, but I couldn't do that." Leaving the Army in 1993, Pat Bledsoe fulfilled his dream of becoming a professional firefighter, serving as both a fireman and a fire instructor in various organizations around the world—most recently in Djibouti.

Coincidentally, Terry Lorson also became a firefighter. After 73 Easting, he remained in Germany for another ten months before arriving at Fort Carson. He served a brief stint as the battalion commander's Bradley driver before leaving the Army in 1994. He held a variety of jobs before becoming a firefighter in 2002. "I missed the camaraderie that I had in the military," he said, "and I wanted a job with a sense of purpose." Ironically, he signed up to take the Firefighters Exam only weeks before 9/11. He remembered that watching the FDNY in action gave him an even greater appreciation for the perils that firefighters and EMTs face daily. Since 2002, he has been a firefighter for the City of Philadelphia.

APPENDIX A:
PAUL HAINS' LETTER OF MARCH 3, 1991

The following is a transcribed letter written by Paul Hains to his father, Peter C. Hains IV—a Vietnam veteran who had commanded the 1-10 Cavalry Squadron in combat. The letter describes the combat actions of Paul Hains' 3d Platoon in the desert of Southern Iraq.

Dear Dad,

Finally found the will to write—had plenty of time since 1 March. It is amazing the emotional drain one goes through after only 100 hours of operations against the enemy. I feel better now. Smoked your cigar on 27 Feb after a big firefight—it was good! (The cigar I mean)

All told, we spent 100 hours to penetrate over 200 kms into Iraq. In the beginning…we crossed the berm into Iraq; it was easy with little resistance or sign of the enemy. On 24 Feb, we went deeper into Iraq, captured several groups of Iraqi infantry who looked scared to death. On Feb 25, we had a short encounter with dug-in infantry and MTLBs. They quickly gave up after only a few rounds downrange. We captured 8 MTLBs, 3 destroyed, and more than 100 infantry captured. On 26 Feb, we found the folks we were sent to find for VII Corps.

After small, brief encounters with APCs and recon vehicles all morning, we sat on a screen line. At noon, a sandstorm kicked up and around 1400 [*2:00 PM*], visibility was sh*t. We received orders to move to contact another 5 kms. My B section [*a team of two Bradleys, including Rick Michalec's*] on the right made contact—but I was unable to see beyond 200 meters. That section was maintaining contact with our flanking unit, Eagle Troop, as we moved east. B Section…found themselves in a minefield. The troop kept moving until they came in contact with troops and APCs themselves.

I then drove to where I thought my B section was and I found them, out of the minefield and reloading ammunition. I reported the grid of the minefield and escorted B Section back up to the remainder of the troop. The troop was receiving small arms fire from unknown (unseen) infantry positions. The troop then came online because the other scout platoon said he had tanks to our front. [*At around this time, Hains noticed that Ghost Troop had lost contact with Eagle Troop*]. So, I and my wingman drove south to link up with Eagle Troop. As I approached the grid, I heard tank gunfire. I got close enough to the contact point to see muzzle flashes and dark armored vehicles around in the sandstorm. Then I saw what I thought was a T-72 tank. However, I wanted to be certain since firing up a friendly vehicle was easy to do in a sandstorm. My gunner could see lots of "hot" spots, but no positive ID. Suddenly, I saw 600 meters ahead a T-72 showing his right flank to me and firing [*presumably in the direction of Eagle Troop's advance*]. I told the driver to move up behind a mound of dirt and the gunner to prepare to fire.

My gunner still couldn't believe [*that there was a T-72 to their front*]. He was concerned with Eagle Troop in the area, so I told him to go to clear sight channel and take a look. [*To this point, Hains' gunner had been observing the battlefield through his thermal sights. "Clear sight channel" meant switching off the thermal filter and seeing a clear view of the battlespace exactly as it appeared outside.*] Sure enough, he agreed it was a T-72 at less than 600m.

Next, my driver became very excited saying "T-72 Front!" over and over again. I said: "I know; we know." However, he was talking about a T-72 behind the mound of dirt I had decided to pull up behind. I didn't even see it until we had stopped. I dropped the 25mm gun with the commander's override and fired at that thing at 10 meters to our front. [*By now, Hains noticed about eight more T-72s in his sector.*] We shot a TOW missile at the first one, and it went up big time, with debris falling all over the place and on us. We backed up to get out from under the burning fallout. Then I told my gunner to fire the second TOW at one of the others. He traversed to fire and the missile went about 10 meters and dropped to the sand unexploded. Immediately, we switched to 25mm and fired continuously as we backed up. My wingman fired two missiles at two tanks closest to me as we backed up.

After about 15 rounds, the tank we engaged erupted into flame. Not bad for 25mm (right hit/rear side). We reloaded, and as we did, I picked out more tanks to my front, firing to my right with flanks to me [*meaning that these tanks were perpendicular to Hains' position, but had traversed their turrets approximately 90 degrees to engage him*]. T-72s were engaging Eagle Troop, the troop I was attempting to link up with now. In fact, the T-72s were sitting on the contact point grid. My wingman and I continued to engage with 25mm and TOW.

Out of the sandstorm and smoke came a section of Eagle Troop to make contact with us. They approached from the right side with gun tubes on the tanks we were engaging. I got to Eagle Troop, made face-to-face, and began reloading all weapons systems. Darkness fell and the wind died down. Once reloaded, we began to move back towards Ghost Troop. Listening to the troop net I figured we were in heavy contact. My platoon was on the line firing volley after volley under the direction of my platoon sergeant [*Sergeant Woytko; Ghost 34*].

By the time Hawk Company was in place, most of the enemy armor was destroyed out to four kilometers. Our FIST team [*fire support team under Joe Deskevich*] was busy calling fires onto the enemy beyond our weapons range. We broke contact after 2200 hours [*10:00 PM*], passing 3d AD through us.

In all, I feel very lucky and blessed my soldiers performed heroically and after visiting the battlefield a few days later, I am amazed that my platoon lost no soldiers or vehicles. 1st Platoon had one KIA [*Moller*], one WIA [*Lorson*], and one Bradley lost [*Ghost 16*].

Now it's in the politicians' hands. The next two days after the firefight we spent catching prisoners of war. Occasionally, we received small arms fire, but nothing serious. One group of EPWs [*enemy prisoners*] was shot up with 6 seriously wounded. My guys fixed them up with IVs and bandages until we could haul them off in the medic track.

All told, Ghost Troop destroyed close to two battalions of armor with lots of help from the artillery. The troop captured over 250 EPWs.

I love and pray for you,
Paul

APPENDIX B:
WAYLAN LUNDQUIST'S CITATION FOR THE SILVER STAR MEDAL.

The following is a draft citation written by Andy Kilgore to recommend awarding Waylan Lundquist the Silver Star Medal for his actions at 73 Easting.

While performing his duties as PSG [Platoon Sergeant] for 2d PLT, G Troop, SSG Lundquist maneuvered his tank forward while in contact with an unknown number of enemy armored vehicles and troops. With his quick thinking and violent actions, he destroyed three armored vehicles before their crews could even man them. He stayed up in his cupola, exposed to enemy fire, to direct his gunner onto targets and had the presence of mind to engage…an RPG team with the main gun after both the coax and his .50 cal jammed, thus saving his own life along with the lives of his crew.

Later in the same firefight, SSG Lundquist maneuvered his tank section to the northern flank of G Troop where 1st Platoon was in heavy contact with enemy armored vehicles. Along with his wingman, G22, SSG Lundquist quickly took control of the situation and destroyed the armored vehicles. Lundquist repeatedly exposed himself to small arms fire from ground troops surrounding his tank and artillery fire directed at his position.

The courage and valor SSG Lundquist displayed while commanding his tank and leading his tank section in heavy contact with enemy armor and ground troops is a direct credit upon himself, the 2d ACR, and the United States Army.

APPENDIX C:
OFFICIAL RULES OF ENGAGEMENT (ROE) FOR CHECKPOINT DUTY IN AN NASIRIYAH.

The following document outlines the Rules of Engagement (ROE) for the 2d ACR during their checkpoint duties along the UN Demarcation Line near An Nasiriyah. American forces were prohibited from crossing the Demarcation Line or engaging Iraqi forces unless in self-defense. While adhering to this ROE, Ghost Troop witnessed several firefights between Iraqi forces and Shiite rebels in An Nasiriyah. But because the firefights occurred beyond the Demarcation Line, Ghost Troop could not intervene.

A. Iraqi forces on the north side of the Military Demarcation Line (MDL) will not be engaged unless there is clear hostile intent or hostile action. Examples of hostile action or intent include, but are not limited to: enemy weapons tracking friendly forces, or energizing of EW [Electronic Warfare] systems against friendly forces.

B. Iraqi forces on the friendly side of the MDL will be given every opportunity to surrender. A "force" is one or more persons, vehicles, or equipment. All attempts will be made not to provoke an incident. Friendly forces will use the following actions to allow Iraqi forces to surrender. These actions will be done in the sequence they are listed to force the Iraqis to stop.

   1. Attempt to intercept by use of roadblocks, blocking the path of Iraqi forces.
   2. Fire warning shots in front of the Iraqi forces.
   3. Shoot at the Iraqi forces, attempting to make a mobility kill in order to stop the forces.

4. Use of deadly force to kill the Iraqi forces. This will be a last result after fully exhausting the options listed above.

C. Nothing in these instructions denies the soldier the right to self-defense.

D. Iraqi helicopters will be allowed to fly in Iraq only for the purpose of command and control of the Iraqi forces in the field to ensure compliance with the agreements during negotiations at the Safwan airfield. They should avoid Allied positions.

E. No actions will be taken against the Iraqi helicopters unless these aircraft are hostile.

F. No mining, booby-traps, other delayed action devices, or counter-mobility devices are authorized.

G. Unobserved indirect, close air and helo [helicopter] fires are not authorized.

H. Guidance for Control of Civilian Movements in Iraq:
- No Iraqi military vehicles will be allowed to enter the Corps area.
- No commercial vehicles except those carrying humanitarian aid (food, water, medical) will be allowed to enter the Corps area.
- All civilian POVs [personally-owned vehicles] will be stopped and searched.
- No armed civilians will be allowed into the Corps area.

BIBLIOGRAPHY

PRIMARY SOURCES

Interviews:

Interview with Patrick Bledsoe. May 2019.

Interview with Ruben Cardosa. August 2018.

Interview with John Carpenter. April 2019.

Interview with Don Chafee. September 2018.

Interview with Joe Deskevich. November 2016.

Interview with Brian Foley. April 2019.

Interview with Keith Garwick. July 2017.

Interview with Jeff Geoffroy. November 2017.

Interview with Robert Goepp. September 2018.

Interview with Paul Hains. March 2017.

Interview with Tony Harrison. August 2019.

Interview with Andy Kilgore. August 2016

Interview with James Leofsky. March 2021.

Interview with Terry Lorson. April 2019.

Interview with Waylan Lundquist. March 2019.

Interview with John Mecca. April 2017.

Interview with Rick Michalec. February 2019.

Interview with Kenn Parbel. August 2019.

Interview with Tim Tomlinson. July 2017.

Diaries and Personal Papers:

The Personal Papers of Joe Deskevich. Various papers, photographs, and maps containing memories of 73 Easting.

The Personal Papers of Don Chafee. Various papers, photographs, maps, and video footage pertaining to 73 Easting.

The War Diary of Jeff Geoffroy (December 1990 – April 1991).

Archival Material:

Library of Congress – American Folklife Center.

Veterans History Project.

Joseph Deskevich, Jr. Collection (Interview - AFC/2001/001/92568)

Daniel L. Davis Collection (Interview - AFC/2001/001/85953)

Published Works:

Macgregor, Douglas. *Warrior's Rage: The Great Tank Battle of 73 Easting.* Naval Institute Press: Annapolis, 2009.

2d Armored Cavalry, 1989-1991. 2d Armored Cavalry Regiment, 1991. A privately published "yearbook" commissioned by the regiment to celebrate the end of the Cold War and their victory in Desert Storm. Features various photos of the Regiment's duty along the Fulda Gap and in the deserts of Iraq.

SECONDARY SOURCES

Atkinson, Rick. *Crusade: The Untold Story of the Persian Gulf War.* Houghton Mifflin: New York, 1993.

"The Battle of 73 Easting." *Greatest Tank Battles;* Season 1, Episode 1. Breakthrough Films and Television: Toronto, 2010.

Bourque, Stephen A. *Jayhawk! The VII Corps in the Persian Gulf War.* United States Army Center of Military History: Washington DC, 2002.

Clancy, Tom. *Armored Cav: A Guided Tour of an Armored Cavalry Regiment.* Berkely Books: New York, 1994.

Clancy, Tom. *Into the Storm: A Study in Command.* Berkley Books: New York, 1997.

Crawley, Vincent. "Minute By Minute: Death By Death." *Stars & Stripes.* March 9, 1991.

Guardia, Mike. *The Fires of Babylon: Eagle Troop and the Battle of 73 Easting.* Casemate: Havertown, 2015.

Guardia, Mike. *Bradley vs. BMP: Desert Storm 1991.* Osprey: Oxford, 2016.

Kagan, Frederick W. and Christian Kubik. *Leaders in War: West Point Remembers the 1991 Gulf War.* Routledge (Cass Military Studies): New York, 2005.

Lowry, Richard. *The Gulf War Chronicles: A Military History of the First War with Iraq.* iUniverse: Bloomington, 2003.

Summers, Harry. *Desert Storm.* Howell Press: Charlottesville, 1991.

Schubert, Frank N. and Theresa L. Kraus. *The Whirlwind War: The United States Army in Operations Desert Shield and Desert Storm.* Army Center of Military History: Washington DC, 1995.

Stewart, Richard. *War in the Persian Gulf: Operations Desert Shield and Desert Storm, August 1990 – March 1991.* Army Center of Military History: Washington DC, 2010.

Made in the USA
Las Vegas, NV
16 June 2021

24734602R00128